AT THE

POINT

OF A

CUTLASS

GREGORY N.
FLEMMING

At the
Point
of a
Cutlass

THE PIRATE
CAPTURE,
BOLD ESCAPE,
& LONELY
EXILE OF
PHILIP ASHTON

ForeEdge

ForeEdge

An imprint of University Press of New England

www.upne.com

© 2014 Gregory N. Flemming

All rights reserved

Manufactured in the United States of America

Designed by Mindy Basinger Hill

Typeset in Garamond Premier Pro

University Press of New England is a member of the
Green Press Initiative. The paper used in this book meets
their minimum requirement for recycled paper.

For permission to reproduce any of the material in this
book, contact Permissions, University Press of New England,
One Court Street, Suite 250, Lebanon NH 03766; or visit
www.upne.com

Cloth ISBN: 978-1-61168-515-2

Ebook ISBN: 978-1-61168-562-6

Library of Congress Control Number: 2013954865

5 4 3 2 1

And a supplication for our sea-faring people;

that they may more generally turn and live unto

God; that they may not fall into the hands of

pirates; that such as are fallen into their hands,

may not fall into their ways; that the poor captives

may, with cries to God that shall pierce the heavens,

procure His good providence to work for their

deliverance; and, that the pirates now infesting

the seas may have a remarkable blast from

heaven following of them.

COTTON MATHER
Instructions to the Living
from the Condition of the Dead
(1717)

Contents

Illustrations follow page 138.

AT THE

POINT

OF A

CUTLASS

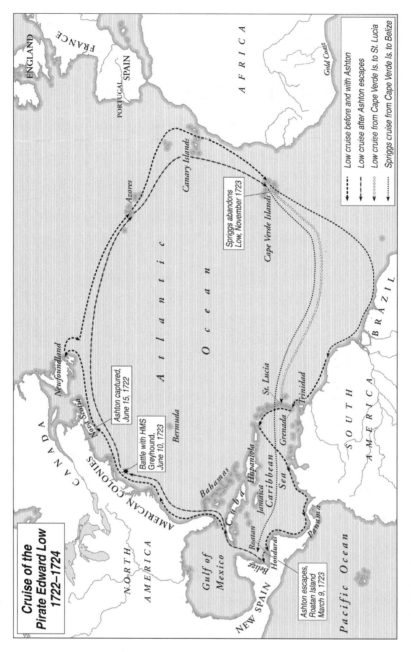

Map by Philip Schwartzberg

Prologue

JULY 19, 1723

Exactly one week before he died, Joseph Libbey stood in court and pleaded his innocence. Libbey had shown the judges a year-old copy of the *Boston News Letter,* from July 1722, that contained depositions by the captains of three fishing vessels. Those statements, sworn under oath, attested that Libbey was a forced man. But over the past thirteen months, Joseph Libbey had made enough mistakes for the witnesses who testified in court to claim he was in fact guilty of being an active member of a pirate crew that had been terrorizing the Atlantic coast. Libbey fired guns during the pirates' attacks on other ships, the witnesses said. He was a "stirring, active man among them" and had been seen going aboard captured vessels in search of plunder.

The gallows was erected on the long, narrow bar of sand and rock that formed Gravelly Point, at the edge of the harbor in Newport, Rhode Island. A large crowd of people had come to watch the condemned men die—not only Libbey, but twenty-five others accused of being pirates. Libbey was one of the youngest of the men, just twenty-one or twenty-two years old that summer. Before his capture he had been a fisherman from the small village of Marblehead, Massachusetts, where he had grown up. Like some of the other men who stood with him at the gallows, Libbey claimed he was the victim of cruel circumstances. He had not chosen to sail with the pirates; he and many of the others had, in one captive's words, gone with "the greatest reluctancy and horror of mind and conscience." In time, however, Joseph Libbey must have given in to the crew's brutality—the threats, whippings, and beatings—and began helping out when the pirates attacked other vessels at sea.

The execution was held shortly after noon on Friday, July 19, 1723. A local minister, Nathaniel Clap, said a final prayer. After that, it was time. Libbey stood on the gallows while a rope was placed around his neck, the thick knot of the noose positioned to the side of his head, under the ear, which was thought to be the most effective placement. When the bodies of the convicted pirates dropped, the ropes snapped tight—but only a few of the twenty-six men died instantly. The rest strangled for a minute or two longer, convulsing and gasping for air as they swung from the ropes. The crowd stood watching the morbid spectacle unfold. The eyes of the men bulged from their heads as they hanged, their lips slowly turning purple. "Oh!" a witness wrote afterwards. "How awful the noise of their dying moans." Finally, the ropes gripping the men's necks cut off the supply of blood to their brains and the flow of air to their lungs, and they died. When the sun set on Newport that day, the spectators had witnessed history, one of the largest mass executions ever held in the nearly two hundred years of the American colonial era.[1]

Two thousand miles away from New England on that summer day, another young man was sitting alone on the ground, surrounded not by a crowd of spectators but by utter solitude. He gazed out at the empty blue sea from a small cay that was no more than a few hundred yards off a remote island at the western edge of the Caribbean. The island had once, long ago, been inhabited by native people, and again later by a small group of British colonists who tried to build a plantation there but failed and left after just a few years. By 1723, the island was wild and desolate, overgrown and uninhabited for the past seventy-five years.

The man who was stranded along its quiet, windswept shore was named Philip Ashton. Four months earlier, Ashton had run for his life into the thick, jungle-like woods of the island when his ship stopped there for repairs and fresh water. Now Ashton was completely alone, and the odds of survival were against him. He had no knife, no gun, and no way to make a fire. He was hungry and growing weaker by the day. He hadn't eaten a cooked meal since he'd escaped on the island and was barely surviving on whatever fruit he could find growing on trees and the raw turtle eggs he could dig out of the sand. "Everything," Ashton later recorded, "looked with a dismal face." Ashton's condition would continue to worsen and within a matter of months, Ashton would be so starved and sick that he would be close to death.

These two men—Joseph Libbey and Philip Ashton—were friends. They had worked together on the same fishing schooner that sailed out of the village of Marblehead in what was then the Massachusetts Bay Colony. Less than a year earlier, Libbey had reached his hand over the side of a boat and saved Ashton from drowning. They had been together on one of the most terrifying nights of their lives, a quiet Friday evening in June 1722, when Ashton and Libbey were attacked and forced to go aboard the pirate ship. They came face-to-face with a raving-mad pirate captain, Edward Low, who captured more ships and killed more people than even Blackbeard—often by hacking the lips or ears off his victims or slaughtering them and roasting their hearts over a fire. It was during their cruise with the pirates across the Atlantic and back that Ashton and Libbey parted ways. By the end of July 1723, Joseph Libbey had been accused of being a member of the vicious pirate crew, and was dead. Philip Ashton was trying to figure out how to survive.

Behind the tragedy of this summer day lies the incredible true story of Philip Ashton—his capture, his escape, his survival, and his rescue. Ashton has been called America's real-life Robinson Crusoe, and in many ways he would go on to become one of history's most noteworthy pirate captives. Today there are no statues of Philip Ashton nor any memorials hidden away in his hometown, the small seaside community of Marblehead, Massachusetts. Ashton does not even have a cemetery headstone, since he more than likely died at sea. No one ever painted a portrait of Ashton, so there is no surviving record of what he looked like. But he did leave an account of his ordeal, and during his lifetime, his incredible story amounted to what in modern times would be termed a bestseller. Ashton's narrative describing his voyage with the pirates and his survival on an uninhabited island is a rare first-person account of a pirate captive and castaway in the early 1720s, when Atlantic piracy was an ever-present threat to men who worked at sea. Copies of the book were published in both America and Europe and may even have been read by the very man who had just written the novel about Robinson Crusoe, Daniel Defoe.

Philip Ashton was taken captive when the golden age of Atlantic piracy was at its peak, and he was thrown into a world overflowing with blood and violence. The pirate captain, Edward Low, was one of the worst of the era. John Hart, governor of the Caribbean Leeward Islands at the time, said of Low that "a greater monster never infested the seas." Ashton sailed with these pirates for nine long months before he marooned himself on the uninhabited island of Roatan, off the coast of Honduras. At first Ashton survived on little more than whatever wild fruit he could find growing on trees, but in time—after he was able to get a knife and build a fire—he figured out a way to catch fish and cook more of his food. He learned to build crude shelters with only his hands and tried designing traps to catch small animals.[2]

Roatan was uninhabited in 1723, but it wasn't far from the epicenter of bloody conflict waged by British merchant vessels, Spanish *guarda costas,* and pirates in the Caribbean. As time passed, Ashton had several unexpected encounters with other men who came out to his island. Some of them tried to help. Others tried to kill him. By the time a small band of woodcutters from the mainland, known as Baymen, came to Roatan and rescued Ashton, his starved body was so thin and frail that one of the men had to pick him up and carry him across the beach. Even then, Ashton was not safe. Nearly two years after his escape, Ashton was almost killed when the very crew of pirates he'd run away from sailed back to the Caribbean and launched a midnight attack on a small island near Roatan where Ashton was living with the Baymen.

Hundreds of working men like Joseph Libbey and Philip Ashton were taken captive by pirates during the early 1700s. Their forced voyages took them across the Atlantic and back, from the sloping hills of the Cape Verde Islands off the coast of Africa to the coastline of Panama and Honduras at the westernmost edge of the Caribbean. In quieter moments, during stops at secluded tropical islands or huddled in the cramped, dark corners of their ship, some captives plotted ways to escape or overthrow the pirates. In the more horrific moments, these men witnessed some of the darkest tortures of the era. Some captives were tied to a mast, many were lashed repeatedly with a whip, sword, or pistol, and others were run in circles below decks while a ring of pirates amused themselves by piercing the men with swords and sharp, nail-tipped poles.

Ashton finally escaped from this terror, but in doing so he fell into a world that was just as dangerous. Ashton is the only American pirate captive who escaped and then lived alone as a castaway on an uninhabited island for more than a year. In retrospect, Ashton's survival seems miraculous, which is precisely how his story was viewed in colonial New England after his return. And yet it was all true. Ashton's narrative is like buried treasure, offering an amazing firsthand account of a harrowing three-year odyssey that touches every corner of the Atlantic.

Ashton's nearly fatal journey began thousands of miles from the Caribbean, and hundreds of miles from the bustle of colonial New England, on a summer day in June 1722. Ashton was one of dozens of New England cod fishermen who were finishing a long week working at sea off the coast of Nova Scotia, three hundred miles northeast of Marblehead. There were a handful of men aboard each of the fishing vessels. Along with his friend Joseph Libbey and four other crewmen, Ashton was sailing a schooner in the direction of the wooded shoreline. By about four o'clock that afternoon, they reached Port Roseway, a quiet natural harbor on the southeastern edge of Nova Scotia. The men prepared to anchor.

Then they saw the large brigantine already sitting in the bay.

CHAPTER I

The Rebecca

The year that forever altered Philip Ashton's life started with a blaze of destruction in Boston Harbor. That first week of January 1722 was bitterly cold in Boston, and just after noon on Monday, January 1, a huge fire tore through a sailmaker's warehouse on Long Wharf, the massive pier at the center of Boston's large inner harbor. The fire completely destroyed at least two of the warehouses that lined one side of Long Wharf and damaged several others nearby. A large quantity of sailcloth that had been in the buildings was burned before the roaring flames could be put out. The fire was initially blamed on the carelessness of some workers feeding a stove in one of the buildings, but a few days later it was discovered that the fire was caused by a chimney in disrepair.

Other than the fire on Long Wharf, most work along what was then America's busiest seaport went on as usual. At least seven merchant vessels finished securing their cargos and organizing their crews in preparation to set sail. The cold snap would have frozen the wet rigging and left dangerous patches of ice on the ships' decks, but even the bitter New England winter could not stop the constant stream of ships from passing in and out of Boston. The vessels that left Boston that week were headed for points scattered throughout the Atlantic coast and the Caribbean, including North Carolina and the islands of Antigua, Saint Kitts, and Jamaica.[1]

One of the merchant vessels that set sail from Boston Harbor that first week of January was a ninety-ton brigantine called the *Rebecca.* The brigantine was probably a little more than fifty feet from bow to stern and had two tall masts fitted out with a patchwork of canvas sails. Trading vessels like the *Rebecca* were distinguished primarily by the types of sails they used and by the way these sails were rigged from variously configured masts. The principal difference among the most common sailing vessels at the time was between square sails and fore-and-aft-rigged sales. On some vessels, large square sails were set more or less perpendicular to the length of a the vessel, hung from a series of long cross-poles extending out from the masts, which were called yards. The term "ship" did not, in the early eighteenth century, refer to any oceangoing vessel but instead specifically defined a large craft with three or more tall masts and a series of square-rigged sails. The workhorses of sea-based commerce in 1722, however, were not ships but smaller vessels like schooners and sloops that carried fore-and-aft-rigged sails. These sails resembled those used on most sailing vessels today and ran, as their name suggests, almost parallel to the side of a ship. Because fore-and-aft-rigged sails could be set at a tighter angle, they allowed a ship to run closer to the wind, giving the crew much more flexibility in setting a course relative to the prevailing winds.

Brigantines like the *Rebecca,* also commonplace in 1722, were fitted out with a unique combination of both sail types. On its foremast, the *Rebecca* flew a series of square-rigged sails, one set above the other and rising high into the air. In contrast, the mainmast positioned at the center of the brigantine flew a large, fore-and-aft-rigged sail. In moderate weather the *Rebecca* would also fly a large billowing jib at its bow, above the bowsprit. Below deck, the hold of the *Rebecca* was likely packed with lumber and shingles, dried fish, and other goods that would be sold in the Caribbean. Just before leaving Boston, the ship would have also taken aboard a supply of fresh water, salted meat, flour or bread, and other provisions necessary to support its crew on the long journey.[2]

The captain of the *Rebecca* was a man named James Flucker. Born in London, Flucker had moved to Boston by 1717, when he was married there. Flucker and his wife, Elizabeth, already had three young children, including his oldest son, Thomas, who would grow up to be the last provincial secretary of the Massachusetts Bay Colony before the Revolutionary War. Captain Flucker had sailed many times between Boston and the Caribbean, and he would continue to lead trading voyages in the years to come. But this trip, his first of the year in 1722, would prove to be unlike any other. The *Rebecca* would reach its destination, the small sugar-producing island of Saint Kitts in the British West Indies, without serious incident. But the journey home would be different. Flucker would be one of only a few members of his crew to return to Boston in the *Rebecca*.[3]

In January of 1722, the *Rebecca's* home port of Boston was, in many ways, still a young city. Massachusetts Bay was a British colony, and the men and women who lived there thought of themselves as British subjects. New England vessels flew the British flag. The colonists' rebellious Boston Tea Party, the first battles of the American Revolution, and the Declaration of Independence were still half a century away. George Washington would not be born for another ten years and Thomas Jefferson for another twenty-one. But in the hundred years since its founding, Boston had also grown into a noteworthy and spreading city. Cramped blocks of brick and wooden houses now lined the streets, home to some twelve thousand people, more than lived in either New York or Philadelphia at the time. Many of the main streets running through the city were paved with cobblestone, though they were often covered with a layer of dirt and dust and, in the springtime, with nearly ankle-deep mud. The streets were crowded from sunup to sundown with horse-drawn carts, peddlers, pedestrians, and stray dogs. Anyone walking along Cornhill, King Street, or Boston's other main roadways would pass dozens of signs advertising the shops, coffee houses, and taverns that sold merchandise, food, and drink.[4]

Boston's size and busy pace of life were due in part to its rank as the largest seaport in colonial America, the center of much of the ceaseless trade of food, building materials, and manufactured goods shipped between America, Europe, and the Caribbean. More than fifty wharves extended into the harbor along the entire length of Boston's winding shoreline. The largest of these was Long Wharf, where the fire had broken out on New Year's Day. That massive wharf reached some 1,600 feet out into the harbor and was lined with a row of warehouses on its northern edge, each facing the water on one side and, on the other, the wharf's thirty-foot-wide roadway that ran directly into King Street. The warehouses along Long Wharf were packed with sails, rope, and a sea of wooden casks filled with merchandise. Carts and wagons rumbled up and down the wharf and onto the cobblestoned way of King Street, which ran directly into the heart of Boston. Fourteen shipyards in Boston produced several hundred new ships every year. At least half a dozen merchant ships arrived or sailed out of Boston every week, and the harbor was crowded with vessels—the "masts of ships here, and at the proper seasons of the year," one observer wrote, "make a kind of wood of trees like that which we see upon the River of Thames."[5]

Sailing out of Boston in the *Rebecca,* the voyage down to Saint Kitts probably took Flucker and his crew six weeks or longer. After reaching Saint Kitts, the crew might have strung a large awning over the ship's deck to shade the men from the hot tropical sun as they set about the weeks of work unloading their cargo from New England and then refilling the ship's hold with sugar or molasses. The *Rebecca* probably finished its work and sailed away from Saint Kitts on its return trip to Boston by the early part of May 1722. On May 28, the *Rebecca* was off the coast of Maryland when the crew spotted a sloop sailing near them, its deck a crowd of faces. They saw "near one hundred men" crammed aboard the sloop, which was bearing down on the *Rebecca.*[6]

⚬⚬⚬⚬

Less than three weeks before the *Rebecca* had left Boston for the Caribbean, another chance turn of events had sealed its fate. That had been in late December 1721, when two mutinous seamen happened to meet near the Cayman Islands and join forces as pirates. One of them was Edward Low, a man who had been born in London but had worked as a rigger for the past decade in a shipyard in Boston. Low had been married in Boston in 1714, but he apparently wasn't destined to be a father or a husband. Low's home life never seemed to be a happy one, and Low apparently didn't take to honest work, either. His first child died shortly after birth. His second child, a daughter, survived—but his wife, Eliza Marble, died at childbirth or soon after.[7]

By the time he was in his early thirties, Low is said to have become difficult at the shipyard where he worked, and he left his job—either by choice or not—sometime in 1721. He then took work aboard a logging sloop bound for the Bay of Honduras, at the western edge of the Caribbean Sea. Work on any trading vessel that crossed huge stretches of open ocean could be brutal, but the logging ships that sailed to the Bay of Honduras were notoriously deadly. The blood-red Central American logwood these ships carried was a highly valued source of clothing dye during the eighteenth century and was a major export out of colonial New England. Yet on every voyage, crews faced the threat of being attacked by Spanish vessels that constantly patrolled the Bay of Honduras and tried to block English logging in the territory. Spanish vessels that caught up with logging crews from England or the colonies would burn the cargoes, destroy the ships, and kill the men aboard. In fact, seamen could sometimes demand higher pay for sailing on logwood ships than on other trading vessels because there was always a chance their ship would be attacked by Spanish vessels. The sloop Low sailed on apparently approached the coast of present-day Belize without serious incident, however, and Low and the other crewmen began to help load the ship with logwood.[8]

One day, as Low and several others returned to the ship with a load of wood, the captain ordered the crew back to shore for another load—without breaking for dinner. The crew protested. An argument flared and Low reportedly fired a musket; according to some accounts, he killed a member of the crew, possibly even the ship's captain. It's impossible to know exactly how the mutiny occurred, but given the path of Low's life over the next few years it's more than likely he was behind the uprising. Low and a dozen other crewmen then abandoned ship, rowing back to shore in the ship's longboat for the night.

Low may have been planning the mutiny for some time, since it's hard to believe he and his conspirators abandoned the ship simply because they were tired and hungry and were told to haul another load of wood. Seamen in the early 1700s were more than used to long hours, poor food in small quantities, and cruel captains with virtually unlimited authority. Perhaps Low had talked about what it was like to live a life of piracy with the band of men who cut the logwood and delivered it to the ship—some of them may have been former pirates themselves. For whatever reason, Low stole away that night as the new leader of a band of lawless sailors.

The men wasted no time becoming pirates. The next day, Low and his companions captured a small ship, which they took as their own, and then set sail in the direction of the Cayman Islands, arriving there in late December 1721. It was there that Low met up with George Lowther, who had become a pirate himself six months earlier after sailing from London in March as the second mate aboard a slaving ship. Lowther, too, had deserted his captain, much like Low had. When Lowther's ship had reached the coast of Africa, there was a delay in taking aboard slaves, so the crew was forced to wait there for weeks while sitting at anchor. Having arrived in "perfect health," many of the crew soon became ill, but they were told they had no choice—they could stay on the coast "till they rotted." Like Low, Lowther helped lead a mutiny against the ship's captain, later claiming the men were being held in "bondage" and subjected to "barbarous and unhumane usage" from their commander. One of the other leaders of the munity, John Massey, was hanged for it, but Lowther went free, deserting with the ship and some of its crew. Like Low, Lowther also started cruising as a pirate. Lowther and his new crew sailed for the Caribbean, capturing and pillaging several ships along the way. When Lowther stopped at the Cayman Islands to get fresh water, he met Low, and the two combined forces. The pirates would sail together through the Caribbean for the next five months.[9]

Low and Lowther were able to pull together a sizeable crew in relatively short order. The two pirates, and the men they recruited, were part of a wave of maritime lawlessness that swept the Atlantic during the early 1700s and created havoc throughout the American colonies. The end of the War of Spanish Succession, a drawn-out conflict that pitted England against France and Spain, had some unexpected consequences for the seafaring world in 1713 and created an inviting climate for new pirates like Lowther and Low. When the war ended, sea-based trade resumed in full force—hundreds of trading vessels began crisscrossing the Atlantic again, packed full of stockpiled goods that had accumulated during the war. Peace also meant an end to the official sanction of privateering by the British and French governments. Hundreds of privateers—crews that had been granted official commissions to attack enemy ships during wartime—chose not to return to work aboard merchant ships but instead to continue to attack and capture ships, but now illegally, as pirates.[10]

Other forces were at work too. Almost certainly fresh in Low's mind were several events that were major catalysts for the new wave of piracy. In late July 1715, a hurricane sank all but one of a fleet of twelve Spanish ships on the reefs off Florida, near modern Cape Canaveral. These ships, too, were packed with goods stockpiled during the war—an amazing treasure of cargo that included chests full of gold and silver coins, pearls and emeralds, and gold bars and jewelry. Since the ships were wrecked in relatively shallow water, the Spanish quickly sought to recover as much as they could. But they were not alone. A number of looters also descended on the shipwrecks when many seamen abandoned their jobs to go searching for Spanish gold. The captain of one British warship said sailors were "all mad to go a wrecking" and "to fish upon the wrecks." Some of these men took away massive hauls of the sunken treasure; one crew is said to have recovered 150,000 Spanish pieces of eight. The Spanish protested loudly, and in fact some of the salvaged treasure may have been stolen from the Spanish camps on shore, not recovered from the ocean floor. Many of the looters, fearing they would be prosecuted as pirates, quickly sailed off for the Bahamas, which was then becoming an established base for piracy.[11]

At almost the same time as the shipwreck of the Spanish fleet, Spain also launched an aggressive campaign to destroy the camps of the English logwood cutters working on the Yucatan Peninsula and to drive them off the land. In early 1716, the Spanish captured more than one hundred of the logwood cutters, known as Baymen, and burned every ship they found. Many of the men who had been living in the area while harvesting logwood soon went to the Bahamas, the new pirate base, and became pirates themselves.

By 1717—just three years after Low had gotten married in Boston— piracy had grown into a widespread and visible threat. Pirate crews were attacking vessels up and down the entire Atlantic coast, reaching as far north as the fishing grounds off Nova Scotia and Newfoundland. Potential captures were everywhere. In the 1720s, the most efficient means of moving raw materials, food, or merchandise any distance was not on land, but by ship over water. Fish, grain, sugar and molasses, lumber, and even horses and other livestock were routinely loaded onto ships for transport, even between Boston and Salem—a short fifteen-mile trip that could easily be made on land in less than an hour today. And shipping by sea was the only means of transportation available when crossing the Atlantic.

Four or five ships—and sometimes more than that—left Boston Harbor every week of the year for ports in Europe, Africa, or the Caribbean. That accounted for only a fraction of the stream of vessels sailing to or from other major ports in England, France, Portugal, Spain, and other American colonies. Trading vessels from the colonies, like the *Rebecca,* carried loads of fish, lumber, and other goods to the Caribbean islands of the British West Indies. They returned with their holds filled with sugar and molasses from the islands' plantations. As a result, most of the ships that pirates captured were not full of treasure, but packed with ordinary trading goods like sugar and molasses, tobacco, and other merchandise. Yet these ships provided pirates with a ready source of food, water, gunpowder, equipment—and new recruits.[12]

❦❦❦❦

By the spring of 1722, Low and Lowther had left the Caribbean sailing in a sloop, a nimble and comparatively small vessel that was widely used for coastal trading in the Caribbean and American colonies. The sloop had a single mast and was easily recognized from a distance by its upwardly sloping gaff that extended from the mast when the large, four-sided, fore-and-aft-rigged mainsail was set. Low had sailed with Lowther for the past five months, with Lowther serving as captain of the crew. While Low and Lowther are nowhere as well-known today as pirates like Blackbeard, they were fast on their way to becoming two of the worst of the pirates to ever sail the Atlantic. Over the next few years, their crews would mark the pinnacle of the golden age of piracy, both in terms of the number of ships plundered and the brutal forms of torture they practiced on the men they captured. The captain of a British warship, Peter Solgard of HMS *Greyhound,* would later call Low "the most noted pirate in America." Like most pirates of the early eighteenth century, Low and Lowther sailed in a small fleet consisting of between one and three vessels at various times, and they attacked any ship, from any country, that they felt they could capture and defeat.[13]

On May 28, 1722, the pirates were heading north, making their way toward New England, when they spotted the *Rebecca,* by then on its return trip to Boston. The pirates' sloop had eight cannon aboard and easily captured the *Rebecca.* The statements from several of the *Rebecca*'s crew members make no mention of a battle or firing of guns, and the pirates probably took the brigantine without firing anything more than a warning shot, since merchant vessels would often refuse to fight pirates because they were known to torture or kill members of crews that had resisted them. The *Rebecca* offered the prospect of much-needed relief to the pirates. With close to a hundred men confined to a single sloop, a vessel that was typically manned by fewer than ten hands, Low and Lowther needed to spread out. They immediately went aboard the *Rebecca* and set about dividing up its contents and their men.

Lowther took several of the cannon, six quarter-casks of gunpowder, and about half of the pirate crew with him. He then sailed off in the pirates' sloop the next day. Low moved onto the *Rebecca* with the rest of the pirates. Most of the crew and passengers aboard the *Rebecca*— including more than a dozen men and five women—were sent off in another vessel, but Low kept Captain Flucker and two other men with him as captives. One of the men was Richard Rich of London, a short man with "flaxen hair," and the other was Joseph Swetser of Boston, a "tall, swarthy man." Both of the sailors were just twenty-two or twenty-three years old.[14]

The rest of the *Rebecca*'s passengers found passage home aboard another ship after Low released them and were back in New England by the first week of June. But by then, so was Low. On Sunday, June 3, 1722, Low's crew struck New England. In that single day the pirates captured three vessels, one after another, as they were sailing near Block Island, just off the coast of Newport, Rhode Island. The captured sloops were robbed and at least two of them were disabled when the pirates stole several sails and masts and vandalized the vessels. One of the victims was a young captain from Rhode Island named James Cahoon, who stood helpless on his wooden deck as the pirates boarded and looted the vessel. The pirates hacked at Cahoon with a sword, leaving him bloodied and badly wounded. They forced Cahoon's crew to disable the vessel by removing the bowsprit and boom and throwing them overboard. Low's crew plundered Cahoon's supply of food and water and took his mainsail back with them to the *Rebecca*.

Another of the sloops taken by the pirates that Sunday was also torn apart and then left stranded at sea about ten miles from Block Island. One of the wealthier passengers aboard the sloop, the adjutant of a militia regiment from New York, was stripped of a sword, a gun, buttons, and a number of articles of fine clothing, including a red Persian silk scarf and a beaver hat with silver lace. The pirates took casks of food, water, and gunpowder from the three vessels they captured that day, but they eventually sailed off to the north without taking any of the vessels or their crews.[15]

Word of the attacks reached Newport the next morning, brought in by a whaleboat that stole away from Block Island that Sunday night. The news of the pirates' captures rocked the seaport community that morning, and a call to arms was sounded—"drums were ordered immediately to be beat about town for volunteers to go in quest of the pirates." By three o'clock that same day, two large sloops with 130 men and fifteen cannon between them had set out from Newport to search for the pirates.

Meanwhile, Low continued on a northeasterly course. The two armed sloops sent out of Newport and a third vessel that sailed from Boston were unable to chase him down. Low and his crew captured several other fishing vessels off the island of Nantucket in the following days, taking as prisoners four or five Native Americans who'd been working on the boats, and then made his way toward present-day Nova Scotia.[16]

CHAPTER 2

The Capture

By the time Low was sailing away from Nantucket, Philip Ashton and a five-man crew of Marblehead fishermen were more than three hundred miles to the north, where they had been working day after day on a small schooner as it tossed on the open ocean. The men had been fishing for cod anywhere from ten to more than thirty miles off Cape Sable, at the southern tip of what is today Nova Scotia. Ashton was a young man, born on August 12, 1702, and in June of 1722, he was just two months away from his twentieth birthday. Little is known about Ashton's youth, but family records suggest he may have grown up in various homes located on what today are Franklin Street and Elm Street in Marblehead, just a short walk from village's rock-lined harbor.[1]

Ashton had been cod fishing for years, and even at the young age of nineteen, he was the captain of the five-man crew aboard the schooner *Milton*. The other fishermen sailing with Ashton were also young men from Marblehead, each of them Ashton's age or younger. They were men Ashton had grown up with and knew well, including one named Joseph Libbey. The men spent most of each day hauling cod out of the sea and onto the deck of their schooner. The vessel reeked of fish, especially below deck in the hold. On days when the sea was rough or foggy, the wooden deck of the schooner could be slippery and the masts and sails dripped with water.[2]

Leaning over the rail at the side of the schooner, the young men caught cod by hand-lining, a tedious method of fishing that was prevalent before the introduction of large nets on offshore trawlers. The men dropped weighted lines into the sea, each of the men typically handling at least two lines at a time. As the fish were hooked, the men hauled the lines back up and lifted the heavy cod over the rails of the schooner and into a box on the deck. Many of the cod Ashton and the other fishermen landed that June were large fish, much longer than the Atlantic cod caught today and twice as heavy. Even a century after Ashton's lifetime, a fisherman off the coast of Massachusetts landed a six-foot cod that weighed 211 pounds. When the pile of fish sitting on the deck of the schooner grew large, it had to be stowed below in the hold. Every few hours some of the crew would break away to clean and pack the cod; with a few rapid slices of a knife, a fisherman would remove the head from each fish and slice its belly almost completely open. The gutted fish were then spread out flat like an open book and packed away in salt below deck.[3]

Cod fishing had put Ashton's hometown, the village of Marblehead, Massachusetts, on the map. Today, salt cod is hardly eaten any more, but in the days before refrigeration, cod was a prized food—high in protein, easy to preserve by drying and salting, and yet still palatable when soaked in water to remove the salt and then cooked. The countless barrels of salted fish hauled in by Marblehead fishermen, dried until it was nearly rock-hard, stood up well over the course of long journeys across the Atlantic. For centuries, ships from as far away as Europe had sailed to the waters off Nova Scotia and Newfoundland in search of Atlantic cod. In Ashton's lifetime, the Massachusetts Bay Colony had taken hold of the fishing industry, and cod shipments to Europe and the Caribbean were a leading export from colonial New England. Three years earlier, the small village of Marblehead—which was then little more than a collection of simple wooden houses built along several narrow dirt roads and the rocky harbor—had landed a massive 8,400 tons of the fish. For most of the year, except during the worst months of the winter, Ashton and his crew would haul the schooner and their gear about a week's sail up to the Canadian coastline, work until their hold was filled with codfish packed in salt, and then sail back to unload their catch in Marblehead harbor.[4]

The pace of the workday at sea depended on the weather and how quickly the fish were coming in. The men spent most of their time out at sea—working, eating, and sleeping aboard a schooner that was no more than fifty feet long, riding low in the water. The schooner was fitted with two masts and a small, cramped cabin. Some days, the men would fish for eighteen hours or more, stopping only for a quick meal or a few hours of sleep. But the men finally got a break on the weekends since, being from Puritan New England, no work was supposed to be done on Sundays. Back home in the Massachusetts Bay Colony, any kind of work—as well as travel, sports, and play—was illegal after sunset on Saturday and all day on Sundays. Innkeepers were not supposed to serve anyone on Sundays except for out-of-town guests staying with them. The Sabbath-day prohibitions were so strict that the governor of the Massachusetts had "argued hard" before the council in 1708 just to get permission for a crew to work on a Sunday to free a ship that had run aground in the harbor. A few years later, America's foremost Puritan minister, Cotton Mather, had warned fishermen to "conscientiously avoid all needless encroachments on the Lord's Day" and promised them that they'd be rewarded with better fishing during the week if they remembered to stop fishing on the Sabbath. So by the time it was Friday afternoon, Ashton and his crew were often sailing back toward the coastline to a quiet cove where they could escape the open sea and rest for the weekend.[5]

Philip Ashton almost certainly had no way of knowing that Low's pirate crew had just ransacked three vessels near Nantucket and was now very close by. In fact, if Ashton was worried about anything as he headed toward shore that Friday evening, it probably wasn't pirates; it was the danger of a run-in with the native Mi'kmaq people who lived on Nova Scotia, the land they called Kmitkinag. Stepping ashore at many points along the Nova Scotia coastline—even to get fresh water—could be perilous for New England fishermen, and that summer would end up being one of the bloodiest seasons in years, marking the start of a violent three-year engagement between the colonies and native people living in Nova Scotia. The entire stretch of the Atlantic that runs from Cape Sable at the southern point of Nova Scotia all the way up to Newfoundland—said at the time to be "the most plentiful fishing in all North America"—was not only the cornerstone of the Massachusetts cod industry. It was also the home of thousands of Mi'kmaq people who lived there and whose distrust of New Englanders had reached a breaking point.[6]

Men from New England had been fishing off Nova Scotia and Newfoundland for close to a century, and for many of those years the occasional contacts between the Mi'kmaq and colonial fishermen were peaceful. Interactions with the Mi'kmaq during Ashton's lifetime mirrored the typical pattern of relations between settlers and native peoples throughout the continent: periods of mutually beneficial trade followed by increasing conflict as a result of the ever-expanding populations of white men, disputes over land use, and cultural misunderstandings. Fishermen would sometimes set up camps along the shore during the fishing season—especially before the widespread use of the larger schooners that allowed crews to stay out at sea for longer stretches of time, as Ashton did, both day and night. These earlier generations of fishermen would haul their catch back to fishing camps each night and dry the split codfish on raised open platforms, or flakes, which were built near their shelters. The fish was often washed in the sea after it was landed and then laid out on the flakes to dry in the sun for about three weeks. During this earlier period, fishermen were frequently on shore and would trade with Mi'kmaq who came to their camps, as well with the Acadians, descendants of the early French settlers of Nova Scotia.

But conflict between fishermen and the Mi'kmaq had become more common in the last part of the seventeenth century, and it had flared up again in the past decade. Relations between New Englanders and the

Mi'kmaq turned ugly as a result of fighting with other Native Americans during King Philip's War (even though the Mi'kmaq were not involved) and after the capture of some Mi'kmaq people by two Boston merchants, William Waldron and Henry Lawton, who sold them into slavery in the Azores. In retaliation, the Mi'kmaq launched raids against New England fishing vessels and attacked fishermen who came ashore for fresh water or to wait out a storm.[7]

These conflicts continued throughout most of the years Ashton had been fishing. The Mi'kmaq, too, depended on fish for their survival and they believed, as they told several fishermen they captured near Cape Sable, that the "lands are theirs and they can make war and peace when they please." During the winter months the Mi'kmaq tended to live in smaller bands inland and away from the coast, but they moved closer to the shore during the spring, summer, and early fall, which was also when the New England fishermen were there.[8]

Ashton and his crew knew they could be ambushed at any time. They had several muskets stowed below deck on their schooner. In fact, just weeks later, at least five other fishing crews would be captured by natives off Cape Sable, the same point where Ashton now was sailing. And another sixteen New England fishing vessels would be captured that month further up the coast, when the Mi'kmaq would set a blockade around a small settlement on the western side of Nova Scotia. Nine of the fishermen taken in July were killed, some were sent away as captives, and some were held and eventually released for ransom.[9]

The newspapers back in Boston were full of reports that summer about captured fishing vessels and the fighting that followed. By July of 1722, concern would be so great that the Massachusetts governor, Samuel Shute, would call for a day of fasting throughout the colony so that people could join their ministers in offering "humble and importunate prayers" to bring an end to these threats—"that the Indians in the eastern parts may be restrained from making further insults on His Majesty's good subjects there, by destroying their substance and carrying them into a cruel captivity." But for Ashton, Shute's proclamation would come too late. In that same proclamation, Governor Shute also pleaded for protection against another major threat to New England fishermen, as well, the "sons of violence" that were terrorizing the Nova Scotia coastline that summer. And those "sons of violence" were already anchored in the very spot where Ashton and his crew were now headed.[10]

It was the third Friday in June, a relatively clear afternoon. Heading to shore for the weekend's rest, Ashton was sailing his schooner toward Port Roseway, a wide natural harbor on the southwestern coast of Nova Scotia. On the sail in, Ashton's crew met up with several other fishing vessels also heading toward shore, including a shallop from Marblehead whose captain was a relative of Ashton's, Nicholas Merritt. The men aboard the ships packed the last of the day's catch in salt and stowed the codfish below deck.

The fishermen approached Port Roseway around four o'clock that afternoon. They could see McNutt's Island, marking the entrance to the harbor, its exposed rocky face sloping sharply down to the crashing Atlantic waves. The rest of the three-mile-long island was blanketed with a thick forest of birch and pine trees that covered everything except the swath of boulders and strewn rocks that formed the shoreline. McNutt's Island sits almost directly in front of the wide entrance to Port Roseway (now called Shelburne Harbor), but because the western channel between the island and the mainland is almost completely closed off by shallows and sandbars, the fishermen had to sail their schooner up and around the island to the east, where there was a deep, open passage. Beyond the island lay the expansive mile-and-a-half-wide mouth of the harbor and, just inside, the calm waters of the protected bay. There were a dozen or so other fishing vessels anchored there by early evening. Easy to sail into and offering good protection during storms, Port Roseway had long been renowned as a resting place for vessels. The weekend break would give the fishermen a chance to relax and visit with each other. They settled in and ate some dinner, most likely a pot of dried beans and salted meat simmered over the fire, or possibly some freshly caught fish.[11]

Near sunset, after the men had been resting in the harbor at Port Roseway for two or three hours, Ashton looked up when he heard the knocking of oars against the wooden hull of a boat moving through the water. Four men from a larger merchant vessel that was also anchored in the harbor were rowing in the direction of Ashton's schooner. The men pulled up to the side of the schooner and climbed aboard, and for a few final moments, Ashton still thought nothing was wrong. Some of the crew from the brigantine, he assumed, men who had been away from their homes in Boston for more than six months, had come over to visit, trade stories, and catch up on local news. Even as the men climbed aboard, there was no cause for alarm. "The men jumped in upon our deck, without our suspecting anything but that they were friends, come on board to visit, or inquire what news," Ashton later recalled.

But something wasn't right. Suddenly the men were moving too quickly, too forcefully. And then panic struck. The men started yelling and cursing, ordering the fishermen around the deck. They had been hiding pistols and cutlasses under their baggy clothing when they climbed aboard, and they instantly drew them out. The blade of a cutlass whipped past Ashton's face. The four attackers were pirates, men from Low's crew, and they quickly took stock of Ashton's crew. They barked threats and insults across the deck and demanded that the fishermen surrender and give up their schooner.

The fishermen had several muskets below deck, but Ashton realized it was impossible to even think about going to find them now that the pirates had come aboard and were holding them at gunpoint. "It was too late for us to rectify our mistake, and think of freeing ourselves from their power," Ashton wrote. "They drew their cutlasses and pistols from under their clothes, and cocked the one and brandished the other, and began to curse and swear at us and demanded a surrender of ourselves and our vessel."[12]

The pirates took Ashton and another member of his crew, Joseph Libbey, as captives and forced the two of them into their boat. They left four others—three men and a teenage boy—on the schooner. As the pirates pulled away from the fishing boat and rowed back toward the brigantine, Ashton and Libbey could only have been filled with dread. On what had started out as a quiet summer evening, the start to a weekend ashore, Ashton and Libbey now found themselves moments away from being forced to climb up onto a pirate ship. Sitting in the small boat as the pirates rowed back toward their vessel, the two fishermen got a closer look at the brigantine, its wooden hull darkened and stained from repeated trips back and forth between Boston and the Caribbean. The ship was the *Rebecca,* now under the command of Edward Low.

The *Rebecca* was armed with two carriage guns—cannon on simple wooden wheeled platforms—and another four swivel guns mounted on the decks. The ship's deck was packed with a raucous crowd of men. There were close to forty pirates on board, not including any of the seven or eight other captives taken that evening, some of whom may have been brought to the ship before Ashton. The pirates standing around the deck might have taunted and shouted at the fishermen as the captives were hauled aboard. "You may easily imagine how I looked and felt, when too late to prevent it, I found myself fallen into the hands of such a mad, roaring, mischievous crew," Ashton wrote.[13]

Ashton and Libbey were told to wait on the deck. Whenever pirates captured a vessel, they rowed a boat over and climbed aboard, or brought members of the crew from the captured vessel over to the pirate ship. Forcing the crew to line up on the deck at gunpoint, the pirates tore through captured vessels in search of anything of value—not just gold or silver, but weapons, ammunition, clothing, sails, food, water, brandy, rum, and wine. They took everything they thought they could possibly use, and sometimes they destroyed the rest or dumped it overboard. But most worrisome of all for the men like Ashton and Libbey who worked aboard captured ships, the pirates often took several members of a crew along with them as captives.

Pirate ships during this era each carried a written list of articles that outlined the fundamental rules of behavior, punishments, and the system for distributing spoils among the crew. The articles on Low's ship specified the allocation of shares when valuables were taken off a captured ship; the captain would get two shares, the quartermaster would get one and a half, the gunner, boatswain, and other officers would get one and a quarter, and the rest of the crew members would get one share each. Low's articles also outlined a number of rules prohibiting activities that could be either dangerous or detrimental to morale at sea, including cowardice or drunkenness during battle, gaming or cheating other members of the crew, and snapping of guns in the hold below deck. When new recruits joined the crew, they marked their agreement by signing their names to the ship's articles. Pirates used a mix of enticements and threats—and sometime outright violence—in order to win the consent of the young men they wanted to join their crew. Sometimes the pirates would try to lure the seamen by describing the freedoms that their lifestyle offered and how rich they could become from plundering captured ships. But this gentler approach could quickly turn to violence if a captive refused to sign the articles. It was not just willing recruits who signed. Since the pirates always needed more men, many captives were also forced—at gunpoint—to sign the articles.[14]

A short time after being brought aboard, Ashton was sent to the captain's quarters in the cabin of the brigantine. Low asked Ashton to join the pirate crew. Ashton said he wouldn't. "I told him, *No;* I could by no means consent to go with them.... For indeed my dislike of their company and actions, my concern for my parents, and my fears of being found in such bad company made me dread the thoughts of being carried away by them, so that I had not the least inclination to continue with them," Ashton wrote.

Instead, Ashton told Low he would leave peacefully and without trouble if Low would only set him free on any of the fishing boats in the harbor, or even stranded on shore. But Low refused. He needed more young men like Ashton for his crew. Since separating from Lowther, Low now had just forty men on his crew, and he needed to increase the size of his force in order to be able to easily overpower the crews of other ships. Low planned to accomplish that before leaving Port Roseway that weekend, and the fishermen were ideal choices. All the prisoners Low and his crew selected that weekend would be young men, none of them older than twenty-one, who were miles from home, unattached, strong, healthy, and knew their way around ships and the sea.

When Ashton refused to join the crew, Low had him forced below deck into the hold. Low's crew finished searching the rest of the fishing vessels in the harbor, taking a number of other young men they thought might make good captives or recruits. Ashton spent all of that first night in the hold of the brigantine along with the other captured men, including his cousin Nicholas Merritt, Joseph Libbey, and another Marblehead fisherman, Lawrence Fabins. Ashton says nothing of how they passed the time that first night. The cramped space in the hold would have been dark and rancid, lit only by one or two candle-lanterns, if at all, and reeking with the foul smell of stale bilge water, rotten food, and the fishy odor of work and seawater that was soaked into the fishermen's clothes. The men might have spoken quietly among themselves, or they might have leaned their heads back against a post or the ship's wall and closed their eyes while listening to the muffled sounds of laughter and drunken shouts coming from the pirate crew on the deck above them.

The next morning, Ashton and many of the other fishermen who were at Port Roseway—between thirty and forty captives in all—were moved over to another of the fishing schooners in the harbor. Like Ashton's, it was a schooner from Marblehead that the pirates now turned into "a sort of a prison." The men were held on the schooner under the watch of armed pirates for all of that Saturday, day and night. Meanwhile, Low's crew continued to search the fishing vessels being held in the harbor. The pirates took food and clothing from a number of the vessels. They also looked over the schooners in search of a newer, faster ship, which they planned to take as well. Finally, at about noon on Sunday, the quartermaster from Low's crew came back for them. All but six of the fishermen who had been held aboard the schooner were going to be released and would be on their way home in two days. But Ashton and five others—including Libbey and Merritt—were taken back to the brigantine to see Low.

They had been chosen.

⚜⚜⚜⚜

Ashton and Libbey must have had some idea of what was coming. Back home in Marblehead, they had almost certainly heard stories about pirate captures. Five years earlier, in 1717, Ashton was just fourteen years old when a massive crew of nearly 150 pirates had crept up the New England coast. Those pirates were under the command of Samuel "Black Sam" Bellamy, who was sailing two vessels, a large ship called the *Whydah* and a snow, a large merchant vessel similar to a brigantine but rigged with a third, angled mast. Bellamy was capturing vessels as he headed north toward New England. Not far from Cape Cod, the pirates captured a pink that had just set sail from Nantucket. Bellamy sent seven of his men aboard with orders to follow him. But those pirates quickly found their way into the stores of wine aboard the pink, got drunk, and fell fast asleep. That night, the captain of the captured pink took control of his vessel and sailed back to the shore of Cape Cod, where the seven drunken pirates were arrested and thrown into jail.[15]

The rest of Bellamy's crew did not do any better. That same night, a huge storm hit the area and Bellamy's large ship ran aground on the sandy shallows just off Cape Cod, sinking on April 26, 1717. All but two of the men aboard the *Whydah* drowned, and dozens of bodies washed up on the shoreline in the following days. Another eighteen pirates in Bellamy's crew were aboard the snow that had been anchored nearby. They were able to survive the storm and sailed north toward the Maine coast the next morning.[16]

Nine of the pirates—the seven who had been arrested after passing out drunk on the captured pink and the two who'd survived the shipwreck—were all brought to Boston on horseback and put into jail there on Saturday, May 4. Six of them were convicted at their trial. The pirates were hanged at Boston Harbor, where one of the leaders of Boston's

Puritan church, Cotton Mather, used their public execution to deliver a thunderous warning against the dangers of the lawless and evil lifestyle that pirates led. Mather had met with the pirates on several occasions to offer his counsel and pray with them, and he later published a narrative about their demise. Mather optimistically gave his narrative the subtitle "The End of Piracy"—but in fact the end was nowhere in sight.[17]

It was less than two weeks after the shipwreck off Cape Cod when a shallop sailed back to Ashton's hometown of Marblehead. Shallops were slightly smaller than schooners, also with a fore-and-aft-rigged mainsail, and were widely used as coastal vessels by New England fishermen during the early 1700s. The crew of this shallop had been captured and held for several days by the few members of Bellamy's crew who had survived the storm near Cape Cod and fled to the north. The pirates had been looking for a new vessel and overtook the shallop near Monhegan Island off the coast of Maine. The pirates held the fishermen captive on Monhegan for a day or two but ended up taking another vessel instead. The pirates then let the fishermen go, sending them back to Marblehead with at least two other captives. The fishermen's brush with the pirates was the talk of Marblehead for days after their return in early May of that year.[18]

❦❦❦❦❦

When Ashton, Libbey, and a handful of other fishermen were brought back onto the *Rebecca* on Sunday afternoon, June 17, Low was waiting for them on the quarterdeck with a pistol in his hand. Low was, as Ashton was about to learn, an awful man. He may have been a short or "little" man, though there is no surviving record of exactly what he looked like. One of the few portraits of Low is an engraving of him standing on a rocky shoreline during a storm. Low is shown with a plump, almost boyish face, his overcoat fastened at the top but blowing open around his waist in the wind. Low is clutching a tricornered hat on his head as if to secure it against the storm. He has two pistols and a sword hanging from his waist. Whether or not the engraving accurately captures Low's true appearance remains unknown, but even if he was small in stature, his temper was without bounds. Low was a violent and explosive man.[19]

The reports from dozens of crews attacked by Low over the next few years paint a picture of someone who was either a natural-born killer or a raving-mad psychopath. Low tortured prisoners by slicing off their ears or lips and then roasting them over a fire, sometimes while his victims watched. Before the weekend was over, Low would beat and then hang two of the Native Americans he'd just captured off Nantucket. In time, Low's own crew would desert him because of the sick cruelty he unleashed on captives. But for now, Low was in charge.[20]

Standing before Low on the quarterdeck, Ashton and the others likely expected Low to force them at gunpoint to sign the ship's articles. But he didn't. Holding a pistol in his hand, Low barked a different question at them, loudly demanding to know whether any of the fishermen were married. The question caught Ashton completely off guard, and he stood terrified at "the fierceness of the man." Why was Low asking him that, and what should he say—that he *was* married, or that he was not? "This short and unexpected question, and the sight of the pistol, struck us all dumb, and not a man of us dared to speak a word for fear there should have been a design in it which we were not able to see through," Ashton wrote. Confused and panicked, the men kept silent.

That sent Low into a rage. The sight of the fishermen standing in front of him and refusing to answer, Ashton recalled, "kindled our new master into a flame," infuriated by the fact that "so many beardless boys should deny him an answer to so plain a question." Low walked over to Ashton, glaring at him. He cocked his pistol and pressed it to Ashton's head. "You dog!" Low shouted. "Why don't you answer me?" Low threatened to shoot Ashton that instant if he did not answer. So Ashton and the other captives did, each saying in turn that they were not married. At this, Low lowered the pistol and turned away, apparently calmed for the moment.

As it turned out, lying and saying they *were* married might have been the better answer. Low's obsession with his captives' marital status seems to have stemmed from his wife's death and pangs of regret or longing—"an uneasiness in the sentiments of his mind"—related to his young daughter back in Boston. Ashton came to this conclusion much later, after spending many months aboard Low's ship. "Upon every lucid interval from reveling and drink he would express a great tenderness for [his daughter], insomuch that I have seen him sit down and weep plentifully upon the mentioning of it," Ashton wrote. This apparently made Low decide to recruit only unmarried men: "And then I concluded that probably the reason of his taking none but the single men was that he might have none with him under the influence of such powerful attractions as a wife and children, lest they should grow uneasy in his service and have an inclination to desert him, and return home for the sake of their families."

A little while later, Low came back to the group of captives waiting on the deck. He asked them again if they would sign the ship's articles and join the crew. The men still refused. Low started working over the captives one at a time. He grew angrier, sharply insisting to Ashton that he join the crew. "But within a little while we were called to him singly, and then it was demanded of me with sternness and threats, whether I would join with them?" Ashton wrote. But he continued to refuse Low's demands. "I still persisted in the denial, which through the assistance of Heaven I was resolved to do."

More time passed and some members of Low's crew tried a softer approach. Ashton was led below deck to the cramped quarters in the steerage, near the stern of the brigantine. Some of the pirates were resting and relaxing there in the dimly lit, stuffy space. The men were laughing and drinking, and they greeted Ashton warmly. "A number of them got around me, and instead of hissing, shook their rattles, and treated me with an abundance of respect and kindness in their way." The pirates repeatedly prodded him to join them in having a drink. Ashton had nothing to worry about, the pirates told him. In fact, sailing with them would be profitable and fun, much better than life as a poor fisherman. "They did all they could to sooth my sorrows, and set before me the strong allurement of the vast riches they should gain, and what mighty men they designed to be," Ashton wrote. But Ashton refused both the drinks and the pirates' offer; their "fair and plausible carriage, their proffered kindness, and airy notions of riches" had no effect on him, he said.[21]

A little while later Ashton was brought back up onto the deck. Low stepped up to him again, still holding a pistol in his hand. Low might have had a few drinks himself by then, and he was enraged by Ashton's repeated refusals. Low's voice carried across the deck as he continued to bark a steady stream of threats at the men, punctuated by "flashes of swearing and cursing." Low called Ashton an "impudent dog." He took another step toward Ashton and jabbed a pistol against his head. "You dog, you!" he shouted. "If you will not sign our articles and go along with me, I'll shoot you through the head!" Ashton begged and pleaded for mercy. "I told him that I was in his hands, and he might do with me what he pleased, but I would not be willing to go with him." It didn't matter, Low said, because Ashton and the other captured fishermen would sail away with the pirates in two days anyway, willing or not.

Low's other worry that weekend was finding a better ship. Low was already frustrated with the brigantine *Rebecca,* which he considered a "dull sailer." A slow ship was a curse for a pirate. Success and survival both depended on being faster than other vessels, whether it was to overtake a prize or to evade a pursuer. So in addition to food, water, and new recruits, Low continued to search for a better vessel, and he chose another Marblehead fishing schooner from among those that had anchored in Port Roseway for the weekend. The one Low selected, called the *Mary,* was relatively new, clean, and a good sailing ship. It was a Marblehead fishing schooner much like the one Ashton had been working in only days before, though this ship was newer and perhaps larger, about fifty feet long and sixteen feet abreast. It was a sleek, nimble vessel, able to navigate shallows and small harbors, yet heavy enough to hold a sizeable crew and withstand longer, deep-water voyages. The schooner had two masts, both fitted with large fore-and-aft-rigged sails, though in fair weather the crew would raise other sails, including a jib, to catch every possible wisp of wind. The new schooner was smaller than the brigantine—about fifty tons compared to the ninety-ton *Rebecca*—but its fore-and-aft-rigged sails allowed Low to haul closer to the wind than in the brigantine. Low renamed the schooner *Fancy* and moved his entire crew and the captives over to her.[22]

Bringing the *Rebecca* and the schooner *Fancy* alongside each other, the pirates spent hours working creaky block-and-tackle pulleys to move the heavy cannon from the deck of the brigantine over to the schooner. The men also moved casks of food, water, and other supplies the pirates had taken from the fishing boats they captured and stowed them aboard their new schooner. Low ordered Flucker, the captain of the *Rebecca,* to take his brigantine back to Boston with the remaining fishermen and their vessels. When Ashton saw that most of the fishermen were being released, he went with one of the other captives, his cousin Nicholas Merritt, and again tried to convince Low to let them go. But Low refused and told the men he would shoot them on the spot if they tried to get away. So the *Rebecca* headed back to Boston without them. Ironically, on the sail back home Flucker met up with a vessel, the *Flying Horse,* that had been sent from Boston to find Low. The captain of the *Flying Horse,* forty-one-year-old Peter Papillon, decided to escort the *Rebecca* back to Boston, where they arrived less than ten days later, on June 27. A number of the items the pirates left aboard the *Rebecca* were auctioned off after its return to Boston, including turtle net, a scarlet jacket, a small still, a jack and pendant, some cable and canvas, and a small boat. Meanwhile, Papillon was ordered to set sail on another search for Low's crew less than a week later.[23]

Back at Port Roseway, Low's crew prepared to set out in the *Fancy.* But just before the schooner left the harbor, there was a brief instant when Ashton thought he would be able to escape. Several members of the pirate crew had taken the ship's boat ashore to collect fresh water for the next leg of their voyage. The pirates had at least one dog aboard with them, and the men who went ashore for water brought a dog in the boat with them. By the time they returned to the schooner and were hauling the heavy wooden casks of water aboard, they realized they'd forgotten to bring the dog back, and it was now barking and howling from the shoreline. Low demanded that a few men quickly row back to shore to get the dog.

Immediately, two other captured fishermen—John Holman and Benjamin Ashton (who may have been a cousin of Philip Ashton's)—jumped into the boat to go back. Seeing his chance, Ashton also stepped toward the rail and started climbing over the side into the boat with them. But Low's quartermaster, John Russel, grabbed Ashton by his shoulder and pulled him back onto the schooner. There were enough men going back for the dog already, Russel said. So Ashton—who suspected what the other fishermen had in mind—was forced to watch from the deck while the men scrambled onto the shore and ran free. He couldn't even try jumping overboard and swimming to shore, since Ashton—despite spending most of the year at sea—could barely swim.

Once Russel realized two fishermen on shore had run off, he turned on Ashton, cursing at the top of his lungs and accusing him of being in on the plan. Ashton insisted he did not know they were going to run off. In fact, since the opportunity to take the boat back to shore had come up so suddenly, the men hadn't even had a moment to talk about escaping. But Ashton's denials only fueled the quartermaster's anger.

Russel pulled his pistol, pressed it against Ashton's head, and fired. There was a snap, but no explosion. The pistol had misfired. Ashton stood terrified before the quartermaster. Again Russel cocked his pistol and fired at Ashton. Another misfire. And then a third time, again with no result. The enraged quartermaster then aimed the pistol over the side of the schooner, pointed it at the sea, and fired again. This time a spark ignited the powder and the gun fired. Ashton barely had time to catch his breath. Russel raised his cutlass and charged at Ashton. "The quartermaster upon this, in the utmost fury, drew his cutlass and fell upon me with it, but I leapt down into the hold and got among a crowd that was there, and so escaped the further effects of his madness and rage," Ashton wrote.

The fishermen who were left onboard, including Ashton, Libbey, and Merritt, were now "forced" members of the crew, men who were compelled against their will to sail with the pirates. Standing on the deck of the schooner, the reality of Ashton's situation sunk in. "All hopes of obtaining deliverance were now past and gone," Ashton wrote. "The brigantine and fishing vessels were upon their way homeward, the boat was ashore, and not likely to come off again. I could see no possible way of escape; and who can express the concern and agony I was in?"

Captives who escaped or were released after attacks often went before a justice of the peace when they returned home to sign sworn statements on behalf of their fellow crewmen who were forced onto the pirate ship. Copies of these statements were published in newspapers, and captured sailors would rely on these published statements as proof of their innocence if they were ever brought to trial for piracy. Three men from other fishing vessels that were in Port Roseway that weekend—including the captain of the schooner *Mary* that Low had taken as his new vessel—signed a statement on behalf of Ashton, Libbey, Merritt, and the fourth fishermen from Marblehead, Lawrence Fabins, when they returned to Massachusetts. The statement on behalf of the fishermen attested that the "pirates kept them by force and would not let them go though they pleaded as much as they dared to." It was published three weeks later, in the July 9, 1722, edition of the *Boston News Letter.*[24]

The extent to which these "forced" captives took to life as pirates would vary from one man to the next over the coming weeks and months, even within the handful of Marblehead fishermen taken at Port Roseway. But for now, the fishermen's names were apparently listed in Low's book as having signed the ship's articles. "So I found all my cries and entreaties were in vain and there was no help for it—go with them I must," Ashton wrote, "and as I understood they set mine and my townsmen's names down in their book, though against our consent."

Ashton could only try to stay out of the way in a corner of the ship while the pirates prepared to set out to sea again.

CHAPTER 3

To the Azores

By late afternoon on that Tuesday, four days after the captures at Port Roseway, the normally quiet harbor was bustling with activity and noise as Low's crew prepared to set sail. Near evening, Low or his quartermaster gave the order to raise the anchor and to unfurl the sails. The schooner slowly got underway.

As the crew sailed out of the harbor and approached the outer edge of McNutt's Island, the seas picked up. The ship started to roll and bob as its bow broke against the higher swells of the open seas, the waves no longer held back by the protective patches of land that sheltered the harbor. Ashton instinctively pushed his feet against the deck to steady himself against the rolling motion of the ship. The dark rocky edges of McNutt's Island, visible off to the starboard side of the schooner, were slipping away. It was one of the last known landmarks Ashton would see for nearly three years.

As Ashton looked around the schooner, much of it seemed familiar to him. Below deck, the hold still carried the odor of salt cod, though the pirates had likely thrown most of the fresh catch overboard. The newly refitted *Fancy* was no longer a fishing boat, however. Low's crew had spent much of the weekend turning it into a battle-ready pirate ship. They had moved their heavy weaponry—two cannon and four mounted swivel guns—onto the schooner, as well as casks of food, gunpowder, gunshot, and the entire assembly of crew and prisoners along with their trunks and bedding.

Low's new vessel was a stark contrast to the fishing schooner Ashton was used to. Ashton's schooner had held a six-man crew—five men and a teenage boy. Packed with fish, rope, and supplies, there was barely a quiet corner where a man could rest for a moment on his own. But the *Fancy* was now a bustling, frenetic world of its own. There were about fifty men crowded above and below the decks of the schooner. All of these men—the crew and the captives—had to live and work together in the cramped confines of their stinking, overcrowded schooner.

It was a loud, drunken, and boisterous atmosphere, particularly for fishermen who were accustomed to long hours of quiet work, with long stretches of the day filled only by the sounds of wind on the sails or stays, gulls feeding, and water lapping against the wooden hull of the ship. Ashton found himself surrounded by a noisy crew of pirates, happy and drunk after a successful run up the Atlantic coast. "I soon found that any death was preferable to being linked with such a vile crew of miscreants, to whom it was a sport to do mischief, where prodigious drinking, monstrous cursing and swearing, hideous blasphemies, and open defiance of heaven, and contempt of hell itself, was the constant employment, unless when sleep something abated the noise and reveling," he wrote.

As the ship sailed up past the eastern coast of Newfoundland, the pirates' revelry only heightened when they spotted what could be their biggest prize yet. Approaching Saint John's harbor in a thick fog, they made out what appeared to be a large trading vessel resting at anchor, perhaps on its way from Massachusetts to England and well-laden with supplies in anticipation of its long voyage. "This they looked upon as a boon prize for them, and thought they should be wonderfully well accommodated with a good ship under foot, and if she proved but a good sailor, would greatly further their roving designs and render them a match for almost anything they could meet with," Ashton wrote.

Low silenced his crew. He ordered all but a half-dozen of his men to go below decks, creating the appearance of a harmless fishing boat sailing into the harbor. The pirates then headed for the larger ship—"great was their joy at the distant prospect how cleverly they should catch her." Low planned to come alongside and then launch a surprise attack.

Before reaching the ship, however, Low met up with a smaller fishing boat coming out of the harbor and learned that the larger vessel was a British warship. It was either the *Solebay* or the *Panther,* two frigates that had arrived from England just two weeks earlier to protect the harbor and fishing grounds off Newfoundland from pirates. Low immediately altered his course and fled into a small bay on the northern tip of Newfoundland, stopping at a town called Carbonear. The close call should have been a lesson for Low, but apparently it was not. It wouldn't be the last time he got himself into trouble by chasing after a warship.[1]

Low was not destined to sail across the Atlantic in the single schooner, however. After stopping in Carbonear—where Ashton remained aboard, but the pirates went ashore, looted the town, and destroyed several houses—Low sailed out to the Grand Banks, the rich fishing grounds a little more than a hundred miles off the Newfoundland coast. There was a crowd of vessels working the waters there and Low successfully took and plundered at least seven of them, including a large 350-ton French fishing vessel called a "banker" because it was fitted out for extended offshore fishing trips to the Grand Banks. Low kept the banker, establishing a fleet of two ships and dividing his crew between the schooner and the newly captured French banker.

Low was already proving himself to be a fearless captain. He had taken nearly twenty-five ships in the month since he'd separated from Lowther and set out with his own crew up the Atlantic coast. He bore down on any vessel he encountered even though, as had happened near Saint John's, the prey would sometimes prove to be a heavily armed Royal Navy frigate. In fact, Low boldly led his crew to loot a small Newfoundland town and then to take seven or eight more fishing vessels on the Grand Banks despite his discovery of a warship in the area.

Leaving the Grand Banks, Low planned to head back to the Caribbean, but his best route there was an indirect one, a course determined by the trade winds. In the Atlantic regions just to the north and south of the equator, the prevailing winds blow from east to west, and are known as the northeast and southeast trade winds. Much further north, above 30 degrees latitude, the prevailing winds blow from the west, and these "westerlies" provide sailing ships a generally reliable west-to-east route. For centuries spanning the age of sail, ships bound from New England to South America—or even further west to the Pacific—would set out in the opposite direction, first heading east toward Europe. Stopping to resupply at several clusters of islands off Europe and Africa, vessels would then slowly arc south and then finally turn westward toward South America.[2]

Low's course across the Atlantic not only took advantage of the prevailing wind patterns, but it also followed the sea routes established by well-known natural landmarks that offered the surest way to navigate on the open ocean. Sailing a ship across the Atlantic in 1722 still required a tricky mix of mathematical calculations and guesswork. Once out of sight of any point of land on the Canadian coastline, especially on a crossing that would take weeks, the pirates wouldn't know for certain exactly where they were each day. They could estimate their latitude—how far north they were from the equator—by measuring the angle of the sun and the horizon at midday and then calculating the ship's location by comparing the measurement to a set of declination tables. But a reliable method for determining a ship's longitude—or how far to the east or west a ship was on the map—would not be developed for at least another decade. So in Low's day, the pirates had to sail from one point of land to another, trying their best to follow a straight line along the compass heading that would lead them to their next landmark. Low planned to sail the two ships almost due east from Nova Scotia toward the Azores Islands, nearly two thousand miles across the Atlantic. He could then sail in a southeasterly direction until coming in sight of the Canary Islands, off the coast of Africa, and then due south until reaching the Cape Verde Islands.[3]

<hr />

This course across the Atlantic took the pirate crew out onto open water, day after day, hundreds of miles from any shore. With the crew divided between the Marblehead schooner and the French banker, the men spent their time on the voyage to the Azores tending the sails and lines, repairing the vessels, cleaning their guns, and sharpening knives and cutlasses. The days at sea could seem endless. "Day after day, this view continues the same," one sailor wrote of the long crossing. "The ocean, the clouds, the breeze, even the very fish that gambol about the bows seem to be the same, and one could easily fancy the vessel to be set here in mid-ocean, like one of those little miniature ships we see on old-fashioned clocks, rolling and pitching all day, but making no headway."[4]

The crossing gave Ashton a chance to learn more about the other men he was trapped with aboard Low's ships. Most of them were in their twenties. Some were, like Ashton, from the New England colonies, others from England or Ireland, and a few others were Africans or Native Americans. Many of the men had come aboard—either willingly or by force—when the vessel they were working on was captured by the pirate crew, but had decided to join up with the pirates and sign the ship's articles. Charles Harris, one of the shorter men aboard, had been born in London and was the second mate of the Boston logging ship *Greyhound* when it was captured by Lowther and Low off the coast of Honduras in early January, shortly after the two pirates had joined forces. When Low and Lowther separated five months later after capturing the *Rebecca,* Harris stayed with Low. Harris and Low had similar backgrounds: both were Boston-based mariners born in London, and both had most recently been employed on logwood ships. The two might even have known each other back in Boston. Harris, who was about twenty-five years old, would soon become a quartermaster under Low and before long would go on to command his own sloop in Low's fleet. Things would not end well for Harris, however. It would be his sloop that was captured by the British warship near Newport less than a year later, and Harris would be one of the twenty-six pirates hanged there as a result.[5]

Other captives were also won over by the pirates during the cruise across the Atlantic, either unable to face the whippings and beatings they were continually subjected to or giving in to the temptations of the easier lifestyle they could enjoy aboard ship as a signed member of the crew.

There was a twenty-one-year-old sailor from Wethersfield, Connecticut, Thomas Powell, who had been captured by Low and Lowther while the two pirates were sailing together in the Caribbean. Powell said he was taken by force, but over time he too became an active member of Low's crew and became the gunner aboard the pirate ship. John Brown, a twenty-nine-year-old sailor from County Durham in northern England, said Low beat him "black and blue" to force him to sign the pirates' articles, but before long Brown seemed to have reconciled to life as a pirate as well. He would rather, Brown told a shipmate, "be in a tight vessel than a leaky one" and claimed he was not a "forced man." Even Ashton's former crewmate on his fishing boat, Joseph Libbey, seemed to have succumbed. In time, Libbey started taking a more active role in manning weapons on deck during attacks and boarding ships once they were captured.[6]

Ashton was determined to resist joining the pirates, but it was painful. Along with a handful of other captives like him, Ashton did whatever tasks he was assigned—manning lines and sails, cleaning or caulking the ship—but otherwise secluded himself away and tried to avoid the threats and whippings of Low and his quartermaster. Even after setting sail from North America, the pirates would come after Ashton and several other captives, whipping them or waving a sword and demanding yet again that they sign the ship's articles. "They used once a week, or fortnight, as the evil spirit moved them, to bring me under examination, and anew demand my signing their Articles, and joining with them," Ashton wrote. Each time he refused and then tried to dash away from them and hide. Often his only choice was to scramble below deck. "I had no way to avoid" the pirates, he said, "but by jumping down into the hold where for a while I was safe."

Captives like Ashton—"forced" men, as they were known—were commonplace among pirate crews in the early 1700s. Pirates have long been portrayed as ferocious, rum-drinking, and cutlass-waving rovers who wore red kerchiefs tied around their heads, black pointed hats, and the occasional eye patch or peg leg. Much of this was true about the men who sailed with Low and other pirate captains during the 1720s.

But pirate crews were not just made up of pirates. They were also made up of captives, hundreds of men who were taken by pirates and forced to sail with them during the surge of piracy that swept through the Atlantic in the first few decades of the eighteenth century. Most of these captives were working aboard a fishing boat or merchant vessel when the pirates captured it, and they'd been one of the unlucky ones forced to sail away with the crew. Today there is no line of work—outside of the armed services, perhaps—where men and women, in broad daylight, are captured at gunpoint while doing their jobs and forced away from their homes and families for months on end. But in the early 1720s, pirates were taking trading ships and fishing vessels at a rate of one a week or more. The possibility of capture was a fact of life.

The captives were indispensible to the pirate crew. The pirates needed these men to help run the ship, which is why they were captured and forced aboard in the first place. The captives had to live, sleep, eat, and work alongside the pirates. They cooked for the crew, cleaned and repaired the vessels, and helped man the sails. There were jobs aboard a sailing ship that required many hands, especially during the capture of another vessel. There were also cold, nighttime watches to cover and chores the pirates themselves did not want to do. The pirates often forced captives to go with them to help move goods and merchandise off other vessels, particularly when there was a sizeable haul or large weapons. Low's crew often took cannon and guns from vessels, and captives were sometimes forced to help move the heavy iron cannon along with casks of gunpowder and shot over to the pirates' ship. On some pirate vessels, especially those with small crews, captives were given significant responsibilities, including being put in charge of steering the vessel or helping to sail a second ship when it was taken.[7]

Ashton and other captives were subjected to an endless array of threats, beatings, and torture from Low and other pirates who tried to force them to sign their names as members of the crew. If, like Ashton, they were determined not to join the pirates, they had to walk a very fine line. They had to avoid helping out in even the smallest way when the pirates attacked and plundered ships, since doing so—even once—could result in their being convicted if they were ever caught and brought to trial. But at the same time, the captives also had no choice but to live with the pirates. They needed to cooperate just enough to be tolerated aboard ship and allowed to live, since captives who crossed their captain one too many times were, on some crews, shot in cold blood. And the pirates almost always had the upper hand. They kept a pistol, cutlass, or any number of other weapons within their reach day and night. "This deters the forced men from seeming inclinable to leave them," wrote one man who was captured by some pirates from Low's crew. "And though there may be a greater number of forced men than pirates, it is not likely they should attempt to rise against them."[8]

Another of the captives taken by Low was Thomas Mumford, one of five Native Americans who had been fishing near the island of Nantucket when Low spotted them on his way up toward Nova Scotia. Two of the other men captured with Mumford were hanged by Low's crew during the weekend stop at Port Roseway, but Mumford had been spared. Mumford spoke almost no English and was treated as a servant aboard ship, often doing much of the cooking for the crew.[9]

Ashton himself tried to keep a low profile aboard ship. He spent hours at a time down in the dark hold, staying out of the way of Low and the more violent of the other pirates. When Ashton continued to resist the pirates' demands that he join their crew—or when a pirate in a foul mood decided to take out his anger on Ashton—they would occasionally chase him down with swords or sticks. "The best course I could take was to keep out of the way, down in the hold, or wherever I could be most free from their perpetual din," Ashton wrote. He never knew when Low approached him if his continued resistance would push the captain too far and result in Ashton also being shot or hanged. "I looked upon myself, for a long while, but as a dead man among them, and expected every day of examination would prove the last of my life."

Ashton was not Low's only target. There was another melancholy young sailor from Boston aboard named Joseph Swetser, who also repeatedly refused to join up with the pirates. About twenty-four years old, Swetser had been working on the crew of the *Rebecca* when Low captured the brigantine at the end of May. Forced to sail with the pirates, Swetser tried to keep to himself, doing routine shipboard jobs and sometimes helping Mumford with the cooking. Like Ashton, Swetser repeatedly asked Low if he could be released from the ship, and he did not participate in attacks on captured vessels. One day Low had Swetser dragged up from the hold where he was hiding out below decks, tied him to the mast, and threatened to whip him for his refusal to cooperate. Despite their steadfast resistance and pleadings to be set free, however, the captives like Ashton and Swetser were needed hands aboard the ship, and Low refused to release them. "Low had often told me (upon my asking him to send me away in some of the vessels which he dismissed after he had taken them) that I should go home when he did, and not before, and swore that I should never set foot on shore till he did," Ashton wrote.[10]

∾∾∾∾∾

By July, Low's fleet approached the island of Saint Michael in the Azores, a cluster of Portuguese islands nearly a thousand miles from Lisbon. Pirates survived by capturing ships and their cargo; on occasion it also made them rich. The men on Low's crew were ordered to be on constant lookout for a passing vessel, particularly when nearing any coastline. Sighting a vessel at sea can be difficult, particularly when the skies are less than clear. Against a cloudy, gray sky and the churning green-gray sea, a passing ship can be barely visible, often appearing as little more than two or three twig-sized masts set against the distant horizon. As an incentive for lookouts to stay alert, Low's articles guaranteed the man who first spotted a new prize his choice of the best pistol or small arms from the collection of all the weapons the pirates took from a captured vessel.

As they sailed closer to Saint Michael, the pirates spotted a pink, a large vessel with two or three masts and a distinctive narrow, rounded stern. The pink was flying a Portuguese flag and Low's crew set out after it. Whenever a target was sighted, the pirates would set a course to cut off the other vessel, but depending on the distance they had to sail to close the gap and the direction and speed of the wind, the chase could go on for hours. With both vessels under sail and working with the same winds (though in light winds oars were sometimes used as well), it could take an entire day or longer for a pirate ship to close the gap and come close enough to their prey to even consider firing upon it. Some survivors of attacks reported being chased for up to twelve hours until the pirates drew within three hundred feet or so, the relatively short distance required for cannon or musket shot to cause any damage. When Low's crew first spotted the Portuguese pink, there was some distance between the pirates' two vessels, the Marblehead schooner and the French banker. As the *Fancy* and the French banker headed toward the pink, the Portuguese crew veered toward the schooner, apparently attempting to stay clear of the larger banker. Before long, however, the pink was cornered by the two pirates, their decks crowded full of men waving their muskets and standing at the ready by the heavy guns.

Low's ship was fitted out with at least two cannon and four swivel guns, and the French banker he captured at the Grand Banks had two more cannon. But the pink turned out to be even more heavily armed, with fourteen guns aboard. It might easily have overpowered any one of the pirate vessels, but caught between the two approaching vessels the Portuguese captain apparently surrendered without a fight. It was another lucky break for Low's crew.

Not long after the pink surrendered, its captain might have been ordered over to Low's ship for questioning, and a band of pirates would have rowed over to board the captured pink to search its cargo. Armed with pistols, cutlasses, and axes, the pirates climbed aboard the vessel and launched a roughshod hunt for anything of value. They searched the men working aboard the captured ship, tore open chests, and broke into the holds to get below decks. "The first thing the pirates did was to strip both passengers and seamen of all their money and clothes which they had on board, with a loaded pistol to everyone's breast ready to shoot him down who did not immediately give an account of both and resign them up," the survivor of one pirate capture recounted. "The next thing they did was, with madness and rage, to tear up the hatches, enter the hold like a parcel of furies, where with axes, cutlasses, etc. they cut, tore, and broke open trunks, boxes, cases, and bales, and when any of the goods came upon deck which they did not like to carry with them aboard their ship, instead of tossing them into the hold again they threw them overboard into the sea."[11]

The most valuable goods Low's crew found aboard the pink—gunpowder, arms, rope, flour or bread, molasses, sugar, water, and, of course, any gold or silver—would be brought back to the pirates' vessels for use while under sail or, in the case of money and other valuables, for eventual distribution among the officers and crew in "shares" determined by rank, as specified in the ship's articles. The pirates who went aboard the pink were required to turn over to the captain or quartermaster any gold, silver, or jewels they found aboard a captured vessel. But the men were also looking for small items that they could keep for themselves—clothing, blankets, or anything else that caught their eye.[12]

Low's crew would paw through the chests and storage areas on a ship and snatch up anything that struck them as useful. The pirates took clothing off many of the vessels they captured, including several of the fishing schooners taken back at Port Roseway. The assortment of weapons and personal effects taken from a sloop the crew had captured near Block Island included everything from a gun, a sword with a red velvet belt, knives, and scissors to a military uniform, a gray broadcloth coat, nine bags of coat and jacket buttons, shoe buckles, a Persian silk scarf, paper money, a quantity of silk and mohair, and a beaver hat with silver lace.[13]

The looting could make for a wild, celebratory scene. "After this the quarter master of the pirate and several others went on board [the] ship, broke open the hatches, hoisted out and took 40 hogsheads of rum, one hogshead and several barrels of sugar, some money, watches, a negro man, one of the pumps, all things that was valuable both of linens, woolens, and bedding, and sundry stores," reported the survivor of another pirate attack.[14] Rum, beer, and wine were among the most popular types of plunder. Finding a supply of liquor in the holds would fuel the pirates' rampage. "The pirates made themselves very merry aboard of Captain Carry's ship with some hampers of fine wines that were either presents, or sent to some gentlemen in Boston," noted the report from a pirate capture near the Grand Banks. "It seems they would not wait to untie them and pull out the corks with screws, but each man took his bottle and with his cutlass cut off the neck and put it to their mouths and drank it out."[15]

When Low's crew began searching the Portuguese pink, however, they discovered the cargo wasn't nearly as exciting—the pink was loaded almost entirely with wheat. But the pink itself was worth keeping, since Low was already frustrated by the speed of the French banker he'd taken at the Grand Banks which "went heavily." Low had watched the pink as it sailed during the brief chase. Sensing that it was "a much better sailer" than the banker, he decided to change vessels again. The pirates were ordered to dump almost all the cargo of wheat overboard, cask by cask, though they kept some of the grain stowed below decks as ballast. Then they moved their guns, food and water, and personal belongings over to the heavily armed pink. The pirates sent most of the Portuguese crew away in a launch, keeping only a few aboard as captives. Then they then set fire to the abandoned French banker.

꧁꧂

Low left the Azores with a larger and faster vessel, the Portuguese pink he called the *Rose,* but that capture would come back to haunt another of the fishermen taken captive, Ashton's cousin Nicholas Merritt. At the time, the thought never occurred to Merritt, who didn't expect he would soon be back to the Azores and, like Ashton, was trying his best to keep out of the way of the pirates. At some point Merritt had gotten on the wrong side of an older, temperamental pirate called Jacob and had become the target of frequent beatings. Merritt hid from Jacob as much as he could, but there was little else he could do. Meanwhile, the pirates continued on their circular route across the Atlantic. Leaving the Azores, the crew sailed in a southeasterly direction for the Canary

Islands, which lie just over a hundred miles off the northern edge of Africa. Since they were now running low on water, the pirates sailed into the channel between Tenerife and Grand Canary, where they met up with a fishing boat and forced it to lead them into a port on Tenerife where they could resupply with water. By the first of September 1722, the fleet had sailed still further south and was approaching the Cape Verde Islands, a cluster of ten islands situated three to four hundred miles off the western coast of Africa. But the old pirate Jacob continued to whip Merritt aboard the schooner. The young fisherman desperately wanted to get off the vessel. One day when several other crewmen were going over to the pink, Merritt pleaded with them to tell Low about how much he was "beat and abused" by the old pirate Jacob.[16]

About this same time, the pirates were near at the Isle of Maio, one of the southernmost of the Cape Verde Islands, when they encountered and captured the sloop *Thomas and James,* from Bristol, under the command of James Peare. Low kept the sloop, increasing the size of his fleet to three vessels. Apparently sympathetic to Merritt's complaints about his treatment by Jacob, Low moved Merritt over to the newly captured sloop along with nine other men. Most of the other men Low put on the sloop with Merritt were also forced captives, including a Portuguese sailor who had been taken in the capture of the pink at the Azores. Through brief, hushed conversations, Merritt soon learned a number of the other captives aboard the sloop also wanted to escape. The men quickly put a plan in place.

The chance came in the early hours, "a little after break of day," on Thursday, September 5. The three vessels in Low's fleet were sailing in a northerly direction, heading from Maio toward another of the Cape Verde Islands, Boa Vista. The distance between the schooner, the pink, and the sloop gave the men aboard the sloop the chance they were looking for. Three of the captives positioned themselves at the bow of the *Thomas and James* and another three near the stern. The leader of the plot, a large man named John Rhodes, stepped into the cabin, grabbed several pistols, and stood in the cabin door and told the other four men on the sloop about their plan to desert the pirates. They were going to sail the sloop away from Low's ships that day. Anyone who wanted to join them was welcome, Rhodes told the group, "but if any man attempted to make resistance, he swore he would shoot down the first man that stirred." Nobody spoke out against the plan. "There being five of us that wanted to gain our liberty, he was sure of us; and as for the other four they saw plainly it was in vain for them to attempt to oppose us," Merritt recalled.

Setting a course away from the pink and the schooner—Merritt said "we hailed close upon a wind and stood away"—the men aboard the sloop were able to slip away, and the pirates either did not notice or chose not to come after them. Out on their own now, the captives initially planned to set out for England, a trip of some 2,500 miles to the north, but the men had barely enough water to survive for more than a few weeks, and what little water they did have aboard was barely drinkable, "very muddy and foul." They had a sufficient supply of bread on board, but only two or three pieces of meat to share among the ten men. The scarcity of water forced the men to ration themselves to a single cup a day for several weeks. Given their short supply of food and water, the men decided that instead of heading for England they should sail back to the Azores, unaware of the dangers awaiting them there.

Relations between the Portuguese on the Azores and the English— particularly any Englishmen believed to be associated with pirates—were tense at best, and often outright hostile. When New England sea captain Richard Tillinghast arrived at the Azores in 1723, he was immediately suspected of being a pirate—and his vessel was fired upon several times as it came into the harbor. Tillinghast was forced to lower his sails and row ashore with several other men. There, he was questioned by Portuguese authorities and put into jail while his vessel was searched. The captain's chest of papers was hauled ashore and its contents inspected, and the letters he had on board were torn open. Finally, the Portuguese determined that Tillinghast was not a pirate and they let him go free.[17]

Much of Tillinghast's misfortune was caused by the pirate Low himself, who would soon return to the Azores and capture more ships, including one shortly before Tillinghast arrived. Low viciously beat some of the men aboard the Portuguese vessels he captured at the Azores, cutting the ears off of several of them. "The Portuguese were greatly enraged against the pirates for abusing their people and taking their vessels," Tillinghast reported after his visit.

So, although Merritt and the other captives probably did not have much choice, the Azores were not the best place for them to land. On September 26, they arrived at Saint Michael, a "rugged and mountainous" island, a long, bow-shaped strip of hilly land that stretches for about forty miles end to end. At many points along the island's shore, the steep hills rise directly from the water's edge. It had been twenty-one days since Merritt and the others had escaped from Low, and only a month or two after Low's first stop and capture of the pink at the Azores. At first there was no sign of trouble. Several of the men went ashore and met up with a consul, a magistrate, and several other officers, who returned to the sloop to inspect the vessel and listen to the crew's story. The captives were told they would be welcomed and safe on Saint Michael. "The consul told us there should not a hair of our heads be hurt," Merritt recalled. Going ashore, the crew was questioned by a Portuguese officer, the governor. Through an interpreter, the men made their case and apparently were cleared of any suspicion. But a more senior Portuguese officer, a "*crusidore*" who apparently had jurisdiction over all of the Azores islands, refused to clear the men and instead ordered Merritt and the others into jail.[18]

The next day, the argument between the governor and the *crusidore* over the fate of the nine sailors continued. The *crusidore* brought forth several of the Portuguese men who had been aboard the pink when Low captured it and who may have been anxious to take revenge on Merritt and his companions—though Merritt suggests the Portuguese did not go so far as to testify that the men actively participated in the attacks. "They brought several witnesses Portuguese against us, as that we had taken them and had personally been active in the capture and abuse of them, which yet they agreed not in; and only they generally agreed that they heard some of us curse the Virgin Mary, upon which the *crusidore* would have condemned us all for pirates," Merritt wrote.

In the captives' defense, the governor argued that the fact that the men had risked their lives by sneaking away from Low, despite having little food and water aboard, was proof that they were not pirates and should be freed. But those arguments did not help. It seemed to Merritt that the Portuguese sailor who had been aboard the sloop with them had inflamed the official's anger and that there was to be no forgiveness. The men were put in jail, and Merritt worried for days that he would be hanged as a pirate. Barely a month after successfully escaping from Low, Merritt and his companions were now captives again, passing day after day in a cramped and dirty prison cell on a Portuguese island in the middle of the Atlantic.

Merritt spent four months in a stone cell in what he calls the "castle" on Saint Michael, his condition gradually worsening. At first the prisoners had a "tolerable allowance, of such as it was, for our subsistence," but after three months their rations were cut back to a single bowl of cabbage and bread soup each day. Merritt still had occasional contact with the governor who had come to his defense, and the officer continued to urge the *crusidore* to release the men. Eventually, Merritt and three others were moved to another prison on Saint Michael, joining the rest of their former shipmates.

As the days passed, Merritt's condition grew worse. Sometime after he was moved to the new prison, in late March or early April, he contracted smallpox, which at the time was widespread and often fatal. Merritt was forced to spend day and night in his prison cell, battling a high fever with his skin broken out in small red bumps. The conditions in prison were hardly suitable for recovery, and what little food and water he had available to him could not have helped. "In about five or six days the pock began to turn on me and then it made me very sick, and at times I was something out of my head; and having no tender or watcher, I got up in the night to the pail of water to drink, which at another time, and in another place, would have been thought fatal to me," Merritt wrote.

The consul who had befriended Merritt and his companions when they had first arrived at Saint Michael sent him several bundles of straw to use as a bed, so that he didn't have to lie on the hard prison floor. Even the Portuguese who were guarding Merritt took pity on him. "I could see," he recalled, "how they stared upon me, looked sad, and shook their heads, which told me their apprehensions, that I was a dead man." His guards gave him some brandy and wine, believing the alcohol might help drive out the smallpox.

Merritt survived his battle with smallpox, however, and eventually recovered. He spent several more months in jail until the Portuguese released him in June 1723, a year after he was taken captive by Low off Nova Scotia. The friendly consul took Merritt into his house and provided him with his first decent room and board in many months. Several weeks later, near the end of June, Merritt secured passage with an Irish captain, John Welch, who was bound for Lisbon. When the ship arrived in Portugal three weeks later, Welch initially threatened not to release Merritt until he earned enough money to pay for his passage over, but Merritt was able to earn his freedom by working for several months unloading cargo from Welch's ship.

Merritt finally secured work aboard another ship from Lisbon bound for Boston. The vessel arrived in Boston on September 25 and Merritt arrived safely back home in Marblehead three days later. His homecoming was a tremendous relief, ending what was almost certainly the most tumultuous year of his life. Yet standing at the doorstep of his father's home and looking out toward the familiar water of Marblehead harbor, Merritt could never have guessed the fate of his cousin, Philip Ashton.

CHAPTER 4

Dangerous
Waters

It was the second week of October, 1722. Edward Low and his crew of pirates were near Boa Vista, one of the largest of the Cape Verde Islands, about three hundred miles off the coast of Africa. By now, Ashton had been held by the pirates for almost four months. It was just over a month since Merritt and the other captives had separated from Low's crew and set sail for the Azores. The pirates had spent the month since Merritt escaped at the Cape Verde Islands, repairing their two vessels and making a number of captures that allowed them to stock up on provisions for the long voyage back across the Atlantic.

As a wooden ship sailed through the ocean, especially in warmer climates, a thick layer of barnacles and seaweed accumulated on the hull of the vessel. This growth dragged the ship down, significantly slowing the rate at which the hull moved through the water. A ship's hull could also be weakened by hole-boring worms that found their way into the wooden planks. Copper sheathing, which was used in the latter part of the eighteenth century to protect the wooden hulls of ships from these very problems, was still decades away from gaining widespread use; the Royal Navy's first test of copper sheathing would not occur until 1761. For Low, like any pirate, the condition of his vessels and the speeds they could sail were a constant worry. After more than three months of nearly continuous sailing, both the Marblehead schooner and the Portuguese pink needed repairs and to have their hulls scraped clean.[1]

Arriving at Boa Vista shortly after losing the sloop, the pirates found a secluded harbor that offered shelter from the winds and a relatively shallow approach. The crew brought the schooner *Fancy* aground as close to shore as possible. After unloading loose equipment and securing anything left aboard, the crew fastened a number of ropes to the schooner and its masts. A crowd of men standing on the shore slowly pulled the ropes down toward them until the vessel was turned partly onto its side, exposing much of the hull. The crew then spent days scraping the hull clean and repairing any holes or damaged sections of the schooner.[2]

After careening the schooner, the crew then pulled the pink *Rose* to shore and cleaned and repaired it as well. Throughout much of the four to five weeks that Low's crew spent at Boa Vista, the pirates remained on the hunt for merchant vessels passing through the area and made several more captures. On Tuesday, October 9, they captured a slave ship called the *Liverpool Merchant*. Low took six captives from the slave ship and brutally beat at least one of the men to try and force him to sign the ship's articles. The pirates also ransacked the well-stocked ship, taking three hundred gallons of brandy, two large deck guns on carriages, a mast, rope, and "a considerable quantity of provisions and dry goods." Another vessel captured during the pirates' stay at Boa Vista was the *Sycamore Galley*. Low and his men took at least three captives from the *Sycamore Galley,* including the ship's doctor, John Kencate, and boy named John Fletcher, who was taken "because he could play upon the violin."[3]

After careening the two vessels, the pirates sailed to another of the Cape Verde Islands, Saint Nicholas, still searching for fresh drinking water, also a constant worry for the pirates. Low had many more men to feed aboard his vessels than on the typical merchant or fishing vessel, but as a pirate he did not have the luxury of being able to stop at ports to get water or buy food. The pirates had to find or steal everything they used—the vessels they sailed, the guns they fired, and the food they ate. Low's crew was constantly on the hunt for food and water and took casks full of these provisions, in addition to guns, rigging, and sails, from just about every vessel that was captured. The water used for drinking and cooking at sea consisted of whatever could be taken from a captured ship or any available river or spring on land where the pirates stopped. It was stored in wooden casks, the barrels often coated with mildew from repeated use, and the drinking water was often murky or muddy. When water supplies ran low it had to be rationed, and water sources on remote islands and harbors could be seasonal and unreliable. Low was sometimes forced to spend days sailing from one island to the next until he found fresh water.

The food aboard the ship was spotty as well, and the portions doled out to the captives like Ashton were probably small. On most days, meals aboard the vessels consisted of salted—and sometimes rancid—beef or pork, perhaps boiled with beans or peas, and rock hard crackerlike bread or biscuit. The hardtack was often moldy and infested with maggots. "Thus, with salt water, moldy biscuits, a small portion of rice, and beef, we lingered out a long passage for thirty days," one sailor wrote. Ashton also soon found that Low's crew of pirates drank freely—most likely beer, cider, rum, and wine, depending on what they had taken from their latest captures—and given the poor quality of drinking water aboard ship, liquor was generally a more palatable and reliable beverage for most sailors during this era anyway, not just for pirates.[4]

Low lost more men while stopping for water at Saint Nicholas in the Cape Verde Islands. Seven or eight captives, including another of the Marblehead fishermen, Lawrence Fabins, went ashore to hunt for fowl and never returned. Presumably they ran off. Ashton, meanwhile, was still stuck aboard with the pirates, and the vessels set off again, this time away from the Cape Verde Islands and in search of the southeast trade winds that would push them westward toward the coast of Brazil.

The crossing took about eleven weeks. Once back in the Americas, however, Low's luck took a turn for the worse. The pirates were nearing the northern coast of Brazil when they were caught up in a fierce tropical storm. It was now hurricane season, and the vessels were slammed by torrential winds that blew them hundreds of miles closer to the coast of Brazil than they had planned. As the storm struck, it brought shrieking winds and huge, swelling seas that tossed the schooner and the pink like tiny twigs in a rolling tub of water. When hit by a storm at sea, sailing ships have two choices. They can set their sails and point away from the wind, letting the storm push the ship along with it, and simply do whatever they can to keep the vessel from twisting too far in one direction or the other so that it does not take a broadside hit from a wave and get knocked down. But being so close to the coast of Brazil, this was not an option for Low's crew, which was in danger of running aground and smashing against rocks or shoals in the area. Their only other option was to take in the sails, turn directly into the oncoming winds, and ride out the storm. This is most likely what the pirates did.[5]

There are few experiences more terrifying than clinging to the deck of a sailing ship, looking out at the huge, hurricane-force waves that can reach heights of forty feet or more, dwarfing the ship. For five days the crew held onto anything they could reach and waited for the sudden crack or jolt that would indicate the ship's hull had smashed against rock. The vessels tipped sharply as they climbed one tall wave after another. After cresting atop a wave, the vessels rushed precipitously down the other side into a deep trench of the sea. "The uproar which was set up at this time from the howling of the wind, the beating and dashing of the waves, the working of the ship, and creaking of the masts and clashing of the backstays, intermixed with the hoarse calling of the sailors made 'night hideous,' and rendered the scene altogether indescribable," wrote one seaman who survived a similar hurricane on a sailing ship. "That was a dreadful night to me, and to all on board; we met each other with melancholy looks, at the same time clinging to anything which was within reach, to prevent ourselves from being thrown down."[6]

Ashton felt the panic aboard Low's vessel. Although he had experienced bad weather at sea before, Ashton had never seen anything like this. And at night, when it was dark, Ashton could not even make out the tall, cliff-like waves until the moment they appeared towering directly in front of the ship. The crew spent hour after hour in helpless terror, worried at any moment they would be "swallowed up by the violence of the wind and sea." Men worked frantically to keep the wooden ship pointed into the wind, to secure the crates and tools that were crashing into each other on the deck, and to grab hold of anything they could as the ship listed and rocked in the foaming, surging seas. Even the most ruthless of the pirates were scared. "Such mighty hectors as they were in a clear sky and a fair gale, yet a fierce wind and a boisterous sea sunk their spirits to a cowardly dejection," Ashton wrote, "and they evidently feared the Almighty, whom before they defied, lest He was come to torment them before their expected time."

At the height of the storm, the thrashing of the seas was terrifying. Wave after wave jolted the vessel, and it seemed to Ashton and the others like the hurricane would never end. "You might plainly see the inward horror and anguish of their minds," Ashton wrote. "Like men amazed or starting out of sleep in a fright, I could hear them every now and then cry out, *Oh! I wish I were at home.*"

When the hurricane passed, Low sailed in a northeasterly direction up the coast of South America. The pirates made for several islands near Guiana. This cluster of three islands, arranged roughly in the shape of a triangle, includes Devil's Island, which many years later would become an infamous French prison best known from the book and movie *Papillon*. Either at Devil's Island or one of the other Triangle Islands, the schooner *Fancy* anchored offshore while the Portuguese pink *Rose*—with Low and Ashton aboard—was taken ashore for another cleaning.[7]

Once again, the crew spent hour after hour in the hot sun clearing everything possible off the deck, removing the guns, securing the ship, and fastening long ropes to the masts. When the pink was ready, some of the men went ashore and stood ready to haul down on the lines. Others, including Ashton, were sent far up the masts and out onto the yards, the long spars extending from the tops of the masts from which sails were set. There, they sat perched on the yards and helped secure the lines as the pink was pulled down onto its side. The men were also adding more weight to the masts so that the heavy vessel would roll more easily.

The command was given, and the pirates on shore began pulling with all their might. But then something went wrong. Suddenly the vessel had tipped too far over into the water. One side of the pink's cabin slipped underwater, and a rush of seawater started pouring into the vessel through the open portholes. Weighted down by water, the pink started rolling even further over onto its side. Low, who was still aboard the ship and inside the cabin, was able to escape immediately. But the ship's doctor, John Kencate, was also in the cabin at the time and was trapped. By now the water "rushed so violently" through the portholes that Kencate was unable to climb out. Seeing this, Low turned back and, reaching through one of the stern-facing portholes of the cabin, was able to grab the doctor by his shoulder and pull him free.

At this point Ashton was still clutching one of the yards furthest up on the pink's tall center mast, which by now had practically dropped into the water. Ashton dashed back across the nearly horizontal mast toward the deck, holding on with all the strength he could muster. He barely knew how to swim. Falling into the water, which was still deep below the ship, might well have meant drowning. The pink's masts soon sunk below the surface of the water, with the vessel almost completely overturned and a large part of its keel exposed above the water. Ashton and several other crew members quickly scrambled up onto the pink's exposed hull and clung to the wet, slippery planks.

Meanwhile, water continued to pour into the overturned vessel. The weight of the water caused the pink's hull to sink back down below the waterline, and eventually it turned back toward an upright position again. Ashton and the others, who had been perched on the hull while it was exposed above the water, moved back onto the masts and clung to them. Some of the pirates launched a small boat and started circling the now sinking vessel, picking up survivors. But the pirates refused to take Ashton. With no other choice, Ashton dropped into the water and made his way to the ship's buoy—probably a buoy set atop the anchor line to mark its position—and clung to it, desperately trying to keep his head above water as he floated in the sea. The small boat passed by once again, now packed full of rescued pirates and riding low in the water, but again the men on board refused to pick up Ashton. "Then I called to them to take me in, but they being full of men still refused me, and I did not know but they meant to leave me to perish there," Ashton wrote.

It was Ashton's former crewmate, Joseph Libbey, who saved his life. Libbey had been allowed in the boat, and he yelled to Ashton to swim over. "But the boat making way ahead very slowly because of her deep load, and Joseph Libbey calling to me to put off the buoy and swim to them, I even ventured it," Ashton wrote, "and he took me by the hand and drew me in board."

Ashton was lucky to have survived. At least two other men had drowned during the mishap. And the disastrous careening meant Low had lost the pink, his flagship. All the remaining pirates crowded back onto a single vessel, the schooner *Fancy*. The pirates headed out to sea again, leaving the Triangle Islands behind them and setting a northerly course for the Caribbean. But now the crew was running out of food and water. The pirates had just made a 2,600-mile journey across the open Atlantic, and much of the food and water they still had when they stopped to careen was lost when the pink sunk. Low and his men couldn't sail into port, the way a merchant vessel could, to get fresh provisions since in 1722 most of the islands in the Caribbean were held by England or France, and officials from either country were more than willing to hang anyone suspected of being a pirate.[8]

With nearly ninety men now crammed aboard, the ship was soon almost entirely out of drinking water. Ashton and most of the other men were rationed to a single cup of water a day for more than two weeks. They sailed 650 miles up the coast to the island of Tobago, but the strong currents near the island, combined with light winds, made it impossible to bring the schooner close enough to go ashore. By the time they reached the island of Grenada, a French colony, Low was so desperate that he decided to risk a landing. Low sent all but a dozen or so men below decks so the schooner would appear as though it was a trading vessel. The French came aboard Low's schooner when it arrived in the harbor, but he told them he had come from Barbados, an island about 150 miles to the northeast, and had lost all of his water. Apparently seeing no reason for concern, the French allowed Low's men to come to shore to refill their water casks.

But something about the encounter with the pirates raised suspicions among the French. The next day, they sent out a seventy-ton sloop, much larger than the schooner *Fancy*. The sloop had four guns and about thirty men aboard and approached Low's schooner to take a closer look as it sat anchored in the harbor. As the French sloop drew alongside the schooner, Low grew suspicious. Low quickly called the rest of his men from below decks. With close to ninety men aboard and twice as many guns, Low easily overpowered the French crew and took the sloop as his own.

Leaving Grenada, the pirates sailed in a northerly direction along the chain of Caribbean islands that make up the West Indies. The ports and islands throughout the Caribbean were a major destination for trading ships packed with everything from grain, lumber, and merchandise to sugar, logwood, and slaves. The pirates sighted a number of vessels in the area and captured close to a dozen more, mainly sloops, while sailing toward Saint Croix, just sixty-five miles off the coast of what is today Puerto Rico. The crew then anchored just off Saint Croix.

It's possible that some of the men on Low's crew were now sick or injured. There was a doctor aboard the pirate ship, John Kencate, who had nearly drowned during the failed careening just a few weeks earlier. Kencate had been taken captive in September near Boa Vista, off the coast of Africa. Before Kencate came aboard, however, Low's crew had sailed for at least six months without a doctor, and the men were probably suffering as a result; work aboard a sailing ship was hazardous, and most large merchant vessels and naval ships at the time carried a doctor as a member of their crew.

A ship's doctor was forced to deal with a seemingly endless variety of injuries, illnesses, and complaints. Falls, bruises, and broken bones were common among mariners, who regularly had to climb tall masts on pitching seas and who could be crushed between two vessels when they were brought alongside each other. On one voyage, a sailor fell twenty feet or more from a mast and smashed his head on the deck. He not only suffered a large bump on his forehead, but his left eye swelled up so much he could not open it, and a few days later he died. A man who was working on one of the masts when Low and Lowther captured the *Rebecca* in May 1722 had fallen to the deck and broken his arm, but Lowther had kept him as a captive nonetheless. Men aboard a sailing ship also suffered from chaffing, burns, boils, insect bites, and cuts. Meals at sea could be unhealthy as well; the meat and bread stored below decks in wooden casks and crates was often wormy and practically rotten, and drinking water was taken from any available spring or stream, all of which made diarrhea and dysentery common complaints aboard a ship.[9]

Kencate could have insisted to Low that he couldn't treat the injured and suffering men because he had no equipment or medicines. For whatever reason, Low suddenly decided while anchored off Saint Croix that he wanted to get a doctor's chest, a wooden chest several feet wide with a dozen or more small drawers and compartments that held an assortment of medicines, herbs, and metal tools. The chest Low wanted would, in most cases, contain any number of powders, oils, and extracts believed to heal the body or cure illnesses. In the early eighteenth century, many of these medicines were herbal, often including rosemary, rhubarb root, mint, absinthe, and horseradish. A medicine chest would likely also contain sulfur, lead powders, and potentially one or more opium-based concoctions. The treatments and concoctions could at times be quite strange. Powered lead monoxide, for example, was often boiled with pork lard and olive oil and then formed into a plaster that was applied to the skin to cure corns and calluses, or even to close up small cuts. Deeper lacerations were stitched up with painfully large sail needles and waxed twine, without the benefit of any anesthesia other than a possible swig of rum or brandy. A doctor's chest would also contain various instruments, including dental forceps for removing teeth, razors, knives and lances, enema syringes, and one or more frightening-looking saws for amputating arms or legs.[10]

Low gave some money to several Frenchmen he had just captured and sent them off in a sloop to Saint Thomas, just forty miles to the north, to buy a doctor's chest. Low told the men if they were able to buy a doctor's chest with the money he'd given them, they would be given the sloop and set free, but if they failed he would kill all of their men and burn their vessels. Fortunately for the captives, they were successful, returning little more than twenty-four hours later. The chest they brought back was short on its supply of medicines, and the instruments were not very good, but it gave Kencate something to work with.[11]

✦✦✦✦✦

Leaving Saint Croix, Low's crew then headed in a southwesterly direction toward the northern part of Colombia. They planned to cruise to the far western edge of the Caribbean, which is bordered by Panama and present-day Nicaragua and Honduras, but they made sure to take a southerly route that looped them well below the island of Jamaica. Jamaica's main seaport, Port Royal, lay on a curved finger of land jutting out into the sea on the southern side of the island. Conveniently located near the center of the Caribbean, Port Royal was a popular stopover for merchant vessels that needed to restock their holds with food, water, and supplies. But of more concern to Low, the strip of land that formed Port Royal's protected harbor was then the principal base for the British warships sent to the Caribbean to hunt for pirates.

That fall, Port Royal was still reeling from a devastating hurricane that had slammed into the island on August 28, 1722. The storm poured massive waves over the town, crashing onto roads and houses that in some cases were only feet above sea level. The swelling seas dumped tons of large stones and rocks onto the town and flooded it with about five feet of water during the height of the storm. Some vessels that were anchored at Port Royal during the hurricane were wrecked when they crashed against the shoreline, and others were washed up onto the land. Houses, wharves, and a church were washed away and destroyed. Close to four hundred people were killed.[12]

It was less than two months later, on the afternoon of October 13, that the Royal Navy frigate HMS *Mermaid* had sailed into the devastated Port Royal harbor. Signs of the destruction were everywhere. The ship's captain noted in his logbook on the day he arrived that they "saw the hulks of several merchant ships lost 28th August in the hurricane." The *Mermaid* had come to the Caribbean to help in the hunt for pirates. In fact, the very day after the warship anchored in Port Royal, a merchant vessel arrived in the harbor and reported that it had just been captured and plundered by two pirate ships off Cartagena, on the coast of Colombia. The pirates who attacked the merchant vessel were not Low and his crew, since they had been making their way toward Brazil at that time. But word of the attacks would send the *Mermaid* out looking for pirates in that same area of the Caribbean, and when it did, Low's crew would be there too.[13]

Despite the fresh reports of pirate attacks in the area, the *Mermaid* could not set sail right away. The ship badly needed repairs; in fact, it was in worse condition than even its captain or crew realized when they came to rest in the harbor. Many of the men aboard the *Mermaid* were very sick, and several of them would die over the next several months. The sickest of the crewmen were sent ashore to recover, and a number of workers from Port Royal were brought aboard to help with the cleaning and repairs. Given the delays, several weeks after arriving in Port Royal the captain of the *Mermaid* sent about twenty of his men in a sloop to accompany another warship, the *Lancaster,* which was going to hunt for pirates near the Cayman Islands, about 250 miles to the northwest of Jamaica. Meanwhile, the rest of the men on the *Mermaid* set about repairing the ship. On the morning of November 10 the *Mermaid* moved to an area just off the tip of Port Royal called Coconut Hole so it could start to repair and careen the warship. The crew set about corking the ship's hull and overhauling its rigging. The work continued throughout the month of November, and by the first week of December the crew fastened lines to the masts and hauled the ship over onto its side so they could scrape the keel and bottom of the hull.

As soon as the underside of the ship was exposed, the men realized how badly off they were. Parts of the ship's hull and keel were damaged beyond repair. The crew had no choice but to remove these sections and replace them. The men also soon discovered that a section of the mainmast was cracked. These repairs resulted in more than an additional month's delay, so it was not until the end of January 1723 that casks of fresh food, water, and gunpowder could be loaded back onto the ship and the crew could prepare to set sail. On Saturday, January 26, the *Mermaid* finally left Port Royal harbor.[14]

The warship was heading for Portobelo, an old seaport on the northern tip of the curve of Panama. But it would be anything but a successful voyage for the *Mermaid*. Its run of bad luck continued only a few hundred miles from Jamaica when the crew was trying to hoist its boat up onto the ship during rough weather. Standing on the pitching deck, clusters of men pulled with all their might on two ropes, each looped through a block and tackle hoist and then reaching down to the heavy longboat that was heaving in the sea below. As the men pulled on the ropes to raise the boat, one of the ringbolts fastened to the longboat snapped off. At the same time, a hard squall struck the ship, making it impossible for the men to haul the longboat up in the pitching seas. They were forced to cut the remaining line and let their boat blow away. Sailing off, the *Mermaid* reached Portobelo by the first of February and anchored at a cay just off the town. Even more repairs had to be made to the damaged ship now, and two more members of the crew died during the stop at Portobelo. To make matters worse, at some point on the journey between Jamaica and Panama, the *Mermaid* sighted Low's crew in the *Fancy* and the French sloop and gave chase but was unable to close in on and capture the pirates.

Low had been making his way toward Panama at the same time as the *Mermaid*. On January 25, 1723, the day before the *Mermaid* set sail from Port Royal, Low's crew captured two more trading vessels from New York as they were within sight of their destination, the island of Curacao. The pirates took four men from one of the ships as captives, whipping one of them repeatedly because he had previously served on a British warship. Low kept one of the vessels captured near Curacao, a snow called the *Unity*. A snow was a large merchant vessel similar to a brigantine, but distinguished by a third mast, a "trysail mast," that angled up from the mainmast. Low was now sailing in the French sloop he captured at Grenada. Ashton was still aboard the schooner *Fancy*, which Low put under the command of a quartermaster, Francis (or Farrington) Spriggs.[15]

Spriggs had been a shipmate of Low's former partner, George Lowther, aboard a slaving ship from England and had turned pirate when Lowther did. But Spriggs had stayed with Low when Lowther and Low split up in May. For Ashton, sailing with Spriggs was no better than with Low. As Ashton was about to learn, Spriggs' short temper and violent flare-ups could be just as bad.

The pirates were about 9 degrees north latitude, somewhere between Cartagena, Colombia, and the northernmost tip of the coastline of Panama, when they spotted the sails of two more ships. The pirates set off after them. Drawing closer, they could see that one of them appeared to be a slaving ship, but on the other ship the pirates soon began to make out the "range of teeth"—the rows of portholes that cannon were fired through—dotting the side of the large ship. It was the *Mermaid*. As soon as they realized they were chasing a naval warship, the pirates backed off. They put a number of captives on the snow *Unity* they'd captured near Curacao and set it free. In the two remaining pirate vessels, Low and Spriggs immediately changed their course and fled. But the *Mermaid* set out after them and quickly closed the distance. As the warship gained on them, the possibility of capture created a panic on deck. Even Ashton was terrified, and if he had been asked to help man a line or a sail as the crew rushed to get away, he would have done everything he possibly could. If the *Mermaid* captured the pirates, Ashton almost certainly would have been assumed to be a pirate himself and imprisoned, if not hanged. Even the testimony of shipmates might not be enough to convince British officials in Jamaica, where pirates were tried and hanged, that he was an innocent captive. "And now I confess I was in as great terror as ever I had been yet," Ashton wrote, "for I concluded we should be taken and I could expect no other but to die for company's sake."

The *Mermaid* closed in, gaining on the pirates under full sail. It set its course for Low's sloop, the larger of the pirates' two vessels. The warship was now within gunshot range, trailing by only several hundred yards. But one of the men aboard Low's sloop knew the area where they were being chased and told Low about a patch of shallow shoals nearby. Based on that advice, Low steered his sloop into the area. Low, in his sloop, was able to pass through the shoals safely, but the *Mermaid*—either because of its larger size or because the men at its helm were unfamiliar with the hazard—ran aground. Low escaped once again. But the attack separated him from his quartermaster, Spriggs, in the *Fancy.* Spriggs had veered away from Low during the chase and sailed the schooner down to the South American coastline. Heading toward Colombia, Spriggs hid out in a bay near San Bernardo.[16]

Nobody aboard the *Fancy* knew where Low and the rest of the crew had gone. On his own now, Spriggs—with Ashton aboard—soon set sail again in a northwesterly direction toward the Bay of Honduras, the western edge of the Caribbean Sea that is bordered by the coastlines of Honduras and Belize. Spriggs had only twenty-two men aboard the schooner *Fancy,* and many of them were as unhappy as Ashton was. Ashton's conversations with other captives aboard Spriggs' ship started as little more than a knowing glance or a quiet whisper of commiseration: "we hardly daring to trust one another and mentioning it always with utmost privacy, and not plainly but in distant hints." But through these hushed conversations Ashton learned that seven other men aboard the *Fancy*—one-third of the small crew—were also prepared to risk an escape.

Spriggs stopped at the island of Utila, about twenty miles off the coast of Honduras, to careen the schooner. He then planned to leave the Caribbean and sail back up to New England to increase the size of his crew and to stock up on food and supplies. The stop at Utila gave the captives time to form a plan. When they got to New England and were near a seaport, the men would wait for the pirates to drink themselves to sleep, lock them below deck, and then take control of the ship. They would bring the schooner into the port and plead their case to the authorities, hoping that turning over some fourteen pirates, including Spriggs, would be proof of their innocence.

It was near the beginning of March, five weeks since separating from Low, when the day to set sail for New England finally arrived. Ashton was buoyed by the prospect of heading toward home. But as the crew sailed away from Utila, the men saw a large sloop bearing down on them. Short-handed, Spriggs put up as much sail as he could and tried to get away. But it was no use. The approaching sloop quickly came within range of the *Fancy* and they were again under attack. Spriggs was heavily outnumbered—there appeared to be close to a hundred men aboard the approaching sloop. The sloop fired one of its cannon, hitting the schooner on the very first shot. But Spriggs refused to give up. He continued sailing, trying to outrun the sloop.

Finally the sloop raised a dark flag with a familiar pattern on it, revealing not only that it was a pirate, but that it was Low himself. Recognizing Low's flag, the pirates aboard with Spriggs shouted in celebration. Seeing that the *Fancy* was still under the control of Spriggs and had not been captured by the *Mermaid* or another frigate, Low's crew joined in. "Hideous was the noisy joy among the piratical crew, on all sides, accompanied by firing and carousing, at the finding their old master and companions," Ashton recalled.

But as it turned out, Spriggs had heard about the captives' plans to escape when they reached New England and he accused Ashton of being a leader of the plot. Spriggs went aboard Low's sloop to complain, angrily demanding that those in on the plan should be shot. Low seemed unconcerned, however. Perhaps he was emboldened by his steady run of luck (he'd just captured the sloop he was sailing in, as well as more men, near the mainland) or was simply feeling carefree in the aftermath of his reunion with the rest of the crew. Either way, Low laughed off Spriggs' complaints, saying that he would have done the same himself if he had been in the captives' situation.

When Spriggs came back to the schooner, he was drunk and furious. He berated Ashton and the other conspirators for plotting in secret. "Upon this he comes on board the schooner again, heated with drink, but more chased in his own mind that he could not have his will of us, and swore and tore like a mad man, crying out that four of us ought to go forward and be shot," Ashton wrote, "and to me in particular he said, 'You Dog, Ashton, deserve to be hanged up at the yards-arm for designing to cut us off.'" Spriggs continued to shout at the men for several hours, creating a racket aboard ship. But given Low's complacency, Spriggs could do nothing more.

Ashton came to realize that he was safer among the pirates than he first thought when he was taken captive almost nine months before. Low's brutality would reach new heights within a matter of weeks, but there is no evidence he ever killed a forced captive like Ashton. Both Low and Spriggs could be viciously cruel. They beat forced men to make them sign the ship's articles and tortured other sailors who refused to give up valuables hidden away on their vessels. Low had hanged two Native Americans the weekend Ashton was captured, and before the month was over, his crew would slaughter a ship full of Spanish sailors near the coast of Belize. But most of the men that the pirates killed were sea captains.

Low and most of the members of his crew had all previously worked aboard merchant vessels and they felt an allegiance toward other men who worked at sea. In fact, pirates would purposely abuse and kill a captain to punish him for treating his crew harshly. Virginia governor Alexander Spotswood, who had helped bring in the pirate Edward Teach, known as Blackbeard, called pirates "barbarous wretches" who would "cut off the nose and ears of a master but for correcting his own sailors." Despite his brutal treatment of captains, however, Low never seems to have killed any of the captives he forced aboard over the course of several years, even those like Ashton who resisted joining the pirates.[17]

One of Low's articles specifically stated that "good quarters to be given when craved," which meant the pirates would offer a place on board to any man who was willing to join them. In time, after talking to others on the crew he sailed with, Ashton concluded this meant the pirates did not plan to kill him. "I learned from some of them that it was one of their Articles not to draw blood or take away the life of any man after they had given him quarter, unless he was to be punished as a criminal; and this emboldened me afterwards so that I was not so much afraid to deny them, feeling my life was given me for a prey."

❧

As the celebration of the pirates' reunion died down, they set about finding a spot to clean Low's ships again. The pirates sailed to a secluded string of islands about forty miles off the coast of Honduras, which, with Utila, are known today as the Bay Islands. The two largest of these islands, Roatan and Guanaja, are surrounded by miles of reef and dozens of small islands and cays. The large reef that encircles the islands closes them off at many points to ships, which cannot cross over the rocky barrier that lies only feet below the waterline as far as several hundred yards offshore. On the southern side of the islands, however, facing the mainland of Honduras, there were several well-known harbors and coves that were accessible to ships. Low's crew made its way to one of the most protected harbors in all of the islands, also called Port Royal, near the southeastern end of Roatan.

Port Royal is a deep, three-mile-wide harbor that is almost completely closed off by the reef, several long stretches of sandbars, and half a dozen small islands and cays. Combined with the reef, these smaller islands create a barrier that makes the harbor a secluded hideaway. At some points along the outer perimeter of the harbor, even as far as a half-mile offshore, the shallows are only knee-deep where the wall of the reef peaks. Dark rocks stick out of the water on top of the sandy shallows like the sharp teeth of a saw blade. There are only three narrow channels leading through this barricade of sand and coral that are deep enough for a vessel of any size to pass over and enter Port Royal harbor. Low's crew carefully slipped their vessels through one of these channels and past the reef, edging between several islands, and then into the deeper harbor. They anchored the vessels near one of the islands less than a mile from the shoreline.[18]

The pirates would spend about a week at Port Royal. Nobody knows why the area was named Port Royal, although Roatan had been used by generations of pirates as a resting area and secluded hideout well before Low and Spriggs stopped there, and the name may have been drawn from the more famous Port Royal in Jamaica, which was many years before the home base for the pirate Henry Morgan. In fact, even Morgan, one of the most successful English privateers of the past century, had stopped at Roatan at least once to rest and take on water, and some believe he buried gold and silver treasure on the remote island. That had been during Morgan's first campaign as a privateer, a two-year voyage from 1663 to 1665 that included a number of attacks against Spanish ships and villages at several points throughout present-day Mexico and Nicaragua. Though his methods of attack were largely the same, Morgan—unlike Low and Spriggs—was plundering legally as a privateer. He had a commission from Lord Windsor that authorized him to attack the ships and villages of nations at war with England, and he was obligated under his commission to turn over a percentage of his spoils to the government.

Morgan had a crew of more than one hundred men on that first voyage. Before stopping at Roatan, he headed north past the Yucatan Peninsula and then sailed to the southernmost edge of the Bay of Campeche at the mouth of the Tabasco River. Guided by some natives, Morgan's men made their way hundreds of miles up the Tabasco River and over the swampy lands to reach the village of Villahermosa. The men plundered the village, taking whatever gold, silver, and any other valuables they could find, as well as a number of prisoners. Morgan's crew then slogged back to the Gulf of Mexico to sail away, but when they got there, they found their ships had been captured by a Spanish band of about three hundred men. The Spaniards attacked the privateers, but eventually Morgan's crew fought them off, although the Spaniards left in Morgan's ships. Stranded on the shore, the privateers soon captured two barks and four large canoes called *piraguas*. *Piraguas* were popular vessels in the western Caribbean, small enough to navigate among the many cays and sandbars that bordered the coast, but still large enough to carry dozens of men. Many *piraguas* were fitted out with a sail to help with larger open-water crossings, and some also mounted one or more swivel guns.[19]

Morgan's men plundered at least one more village as they made their way south toward the Bay of Honduras, and they eventually sailed to the island of Roatan to rest and find fresh water. After stopping there, Morgan's men sailed back across the bay to the coast of Honduras, where they navigated up a river that carried them across the mainland to the old Spanish town of Granada on the shores of Lake Nicaragua. The sixteen-hour sack of Granada was brutal. Morgan's men fired a huge volley of gunfire on the town, overturned eighteen large cannon that had been set up to protect the town, and sunk a number of vessels. Morgan and his men then made their way back to the Caribbean, where they hit several other towns and islands before returning to Jamaica by September 1665.

For Low and Spriggs, as for Morgan, the harbor of Port Royal on Roatan proved to be a safe place for the pirates to unload and clean their ships, to get fresh drinking water, and to rest. Because the harbor is almost entirely closed off by two long points of land at either side, in addition to the islands, cays, and reef that form its outer edge, Port Royal provided them with good protection from any bad weather. It had several sources of fresh water and offered a nearly constant and refreshing gusty sea breeze. At that time of year, the tropical climate—particularly on the breezy islands just offshore—was pleasant. And yet Roatan itself was uninhabited, and the cays just offshore gave the pirates a good vantage point to watch for approaching ships, including any other British warships or Spanish privateers. It was a relaxing stop and was probably the most carefree time in Low's five years as a pirate.

The next chapter of Low's life would be bloodier than ever. Within just four months he would lose half his crew after being pounded in a day-long battle with another warship. Low's treatment of his captives would turn particularly ugly, and even his own crew would eventually desert him. Spriggs, too, was in for a rough couple of years. But for now, the pirates were on top of the world. Because cleaning the ships required a stay of nearly a week, Low and some of his officers set up a small camp on another of the islands in the harbor so they could relax while their men worked. Safely within the remote harbor, the pirates lowered their guard. While most of the crew worked on unloading the ship and pulling it onto its side for cleaning and repairs, Low and his companions built simple shelters on their small island and spent the days eating, drinking, firing their guns, and celebrating.

Ashton, meanwhile, was forced to stay with the schooner—at least for a few more days.

CHAPTER 5

Roatan

On Saturday, March 9, Ashton was on the deck of the schooner when he saw a longboat from another of Low's vessels approaching with seven men aboard. The men were rowing in the direction of the main island of Roatan to fill the ship's casks with fresh water. Ashton called out to the ship's cooper in the longboat, asking if they were going ashore. Yes, the cooper answered, they were. Ashton asked if he could go with them. The cooper hesitated, so Ashton pressed him a little harder: "I urged that I had never been on shore yet, since I first came on board, and I thought it very hard that I should be so closely confined, when everyone else had the liberty of going ashore."

So the cooper agreed to take him, "imagining, I suppose," Ashton later recalled, "that there would be no danger of my running away in so desolate uninhabited a place as that was." Ashton quickly climbed down and into the longboat. Ashton took nothing with him when he climbed into the boat, not even a pair of shoes. "Had I been aware of such an opportunity but one quarter of an hour before, I could have provided myself something better," Ashton wrote. But by the time he spotted the approaching longboat, it was too late. This, Ashton thought, was the chance he had been waiting for, and he did not want to miss it or to give the cooper any reason to suspect what he had in mind.

The men continued to row the boat in toward the shore. The long island of Roatan is made up of a series of tall, mountainous hills, and the peaks towered above the men as they made their way to land. At many points along the shoreline of Port Royal harbor the land rose sharply from the water, forming steep, rocky walls. Thick patches of bush and trees clung to the tops of these walls and blanketed the hills as they reached to the sky. But at a few points along the shore, the valleys between the tall hills gave way to some small patches of flatter ground, and at several of these spots Ashton could make out some narrow strips of beach scattered along a roughly half-mile curve in the middle of Port Royal harbor. The cooper and his men rowed their boat up to one of these beaches where, hidden behind the slight rise of the sand, was the mouth of a freshwater creek, a small run no more than ten feet wide and almost completely concealed by the thick woods, where the water ran gently down from springs high in the hills. The men beached the boat and climbed ashore.

Getting out of the boat, Ashton's bare feet touched the sandy ground. The beach was narrow and coarse, a slight rise of brown sand, pebbles, and shells that was just four or five feet wide between the water line and the beginning of the thick growth of grass and weeds. The beach ran along the water for close to a hundred yards. Just over the slight hump of the beach, not even two paces from the harbor's edge, was the mouth of the creek, slowly running under a thick, green canopy of leaning palm trees and large bushes. Ashton helped the men drag the heavy wooden casks onto shore and rolled them over the beach and to the edge of the creek. The creek was shallow, just one or two feet deep in most places, with gently sloping edges. Ashton lay down by the trunks of some palms and mangroves lining the edge of the creek and lowered his head, taking a long drink of the cool, fresh water.

Filling the casks took some time. As the men worked, Ashton stepped back out onto the beach and started walking slowly along the sand, stopping occasionally to casually pick up a stone or shell as he moved away from the men. As the distance between Ashton and the men grew, Ashton edged slightly closer to the woods that bordered the beach. The cooper looked up and called out to him—where did he think he was going? Ashton said he was going to look for coconuts, since some coconut trees were growing near the beach. That seemed to satisfy the pirates for the moment. Ashton kept walking.

In an instant, Ashton turned away from the water and into the woods. The woods along the beach were so thick that within a dozen steps, he was completely hidden by the dense overgrowth. As quietly as he could, Ashton stepped over the roots, sticks, fallen palm branches, and dry leaves carpeting the ground. He tried to run more quickly, but the sharp broken sticks lying on the ground pierced his bare feet, and the crisscrossing web of bushes and vines made it impossible to move in a straight line. At points the overgrowth formed a barrier so thick he had to crawl on his hands and knees to get past. "I betook myself to my heels, and ran as fast as the thickness of the bushes and my naked feet would let me," Ashton wrote.

Ashton decided the safest course would be to keep the men within earshot, rather than running as far away from them as he could. Instead of heading directly away from the beach, he worked his way up the sloping hill and then curved back so he was above where the men were filling the water casks. This kept Ashton out of their sight, but just within earshot, allowing him to hear bits and pieces of their conversation. He lay down in the thick brush to wait.

Eventually the men finished filling each of the casks and called out to Ashton to tell him they were leaving. Ashton heard them but didn't answer. The men started shouting for him. Between their calls, Ashton picked up bits of their conversation: "the dog is lost in the woods and can't find his way out," said one. Before long they realized Ashton planned to stay hidden. "He is run away and won't come again," a voice said. The cooper told the others he would never have brought Ashton along with them if he'd known the fisherman would run off like this. But the pirates wanted to get back to their ship and eventually they gave up waiting. "They plainly saw it would be in vain to seek for me in such hideous woods and thick bushes," Ashton wrote.

By now the cooper realized Ashton had planned to escape. Rather than getting angry, he shouted a final warning: "the cooper at last, to show his good will to me (I can't but love and thank him for his kindness) called out to me, 'If you don't come away presently I'll go off and leave you alone.'" That, however, was "the very thing" Ashton wanted, to "be rid of them and all that belonged to them."

Even after Ashton could no longer hear any conversation, he waited a while until he was sure the men had left. Then he carefully made his way back down to the beach, but stayed some distance from the creek where they had landed to get water. He could still see the vessels in the harbor. The sight of the pirates, even at a distance, was unnerving. Just days before, Spriggs had threatened to hang Ashton from the mast for conspiring to escape with several other captives on the schooner; Spriggs was only kept from killing Ashton by Low's refusal to agree to it. Now Ashton worried that Spriggs would send an armed search party back to the island to hunt him down. So he sat in a secluded spot hidden in the thick bush and waited. Within a day, the ships set sail and then they were gone. Finally, he was free.

When he was sure the pirates were out of sight, Ashton walked down to the beach and looked around. The island he was on was wild and desolate. To the south, facing the harbor where the ships had been anchored, he saw the scattering of islands and, just beyond, a long white line of surf where the waves broke continuously over the reef. Beyond that, there was only the deep blue water of the sea. Roatan is a long, bean-shaped island, about thirty miles long but just two or three miles across, forming a slightly curved strip of land. The shore of the closest mainland, present-day Honduras, is about forty miles due south of Roatan.

When Ashton turned inland, he saw a heavy forest that blanketed the steep hills where he had been hiding. An endless series of rounded, tree-lined peaks dotted the entire length of the island for as far as he could see. Along the shore, the island winds were almost constant, strong, steady gusts that blew from the east across the harbor, creating a noisy rustle in the leaves of the palms, oaks, and other trees. Every now and then the gusts would stop for a moment—a minute, maybe two—and then start back up, slamming in again from the eastern horizon. Ashton could hear an assortment of birds calling from the trees, some sounding a rapid series of high-pitched chirps, others an occasional short whistle.

These two sounds, the gusting winds and the birds, were the only noises he heard.

The reality of Ashton's situation was that he was not only alone, but that he had marooned himself with practically nothing. "I was upon an island from whence I could not get off," Ashton wrote. "I knew of no humane creature within many scores of miles of me; I had but a scanty clothing, and no possibility of getting more; I was destitute of all provision for my support, and knew not how I should come at any; everything looked with a dismal face."

Ashton started exploring the area near where the men had come ashore for water. He could walk along the beach only a short distance before it ended, replaced by a barricade of thick, curving mangrove roots that grew in large, twisting masses from the soil and shallow water along the shoreline. At other points, there was no beach at all, and the water washed directly against steep walls of rock and sand. The brown and gray rocks along these exposed edges were splashed with patches of clay, giving the walls a reddish hue in many areas. To pass by the patches of mangrove or the steep, rocky walls, Ashton had to step out into the knee-deep water and slosh his way along the shore, but some of these areas stretched for hundreds of yards at a time.

Ashton decided to head back into the woods to see what he could find there. The shoreline was quickly overtaken by the brush and woods, and as Ashton started walking inland the seaside environment seemed to disappear. There was almost no breeze now, and he found himself standing in a thick and humid tropical forest. Walking was hard and slow. Trees, saplings, and vines grew everywhere, tangled over and around each other to create a thick web that was sometimes impossible to get through. Ashton had nothing with him—no knife or machete to hack away at the overgrowth—and he constantly had to push the vines and leafy branches out of his way as he passed. Every few minutes he came face to face with a larger fallen branch or tree trunk or a tightly woven bunch of vines that was so thick he had to climb over or under it, or walk around. Much of the jungle-like terrain was growing on steep hills that ran sharply up the side of the island, which made passing even harder.

Ashton had only the clothes he was wearing when he left the schooner: pants and a long frock, both made of coarse linen, and a wool cap on his head. He had no shirt. And worse, he had no shoes. His hands and bare feet quickly became scratched, cut, and bruised from walking across the broken sticks and shards of bark that covered the ground.

The first thing Ashton had to do was find food. Fortunately, there were many types of fruit and nut trees growing on the island, and Ashton had landed there at a time of year when some of them were in season. The most obvious were coconuts. Ashton saw hundreds of coconuts growing in the palm trees, but he had no way to break open their hard outer or inner shells to get to the rich white coconut. Ashton did not recognize the many other types of tropical fruits growing on the trees and vines, yet he had no choice but to try to eat some of them anyway. Walking through the woods, he came across some trees with small dark fruit hanging in bunches from their branches, each round fruit about the size of a large grape or small fig. These were coco plums, and in time he would find both black and white varieties of the plums. Ashton also found grapes growing on vines, and he ate many of these grapes and plums during his first days on the island. He soon discovered another variety of plum, called hog plums, and ate those as well.

But because Ashton did not recognize many of the types of wild fruit he saw, he was nervous about trying them. There were mangoes growing on the island, but Ashton does not talk about eating them and, months later, may have been led to believe they were poisonous. He says he found a "noxious fruit" called the "*Mangeneil Apple,*" which he "often took up in my hands, and looked upon, but had not the power to eat." This may have been mango fruit, and since the skin of the mango can be an irritant if eaten, it's possible that Ashton later heard from other men he encountered in the area that mango was poison.

Ashton came across another strange fruit lying on the ground where it fell from tall trees in the wood. This fruit had a brown, fuzzy skin and was about the size of a pear. It had a thick outer skin, but broke open easily when struck against a rock or tree trunk or sometimes when it fell from the tree and hit the ground. The inside of the fruit was mushy, like a banana, with a bright pinkish-orange color. Ashton didn't dare eat these at first. But before long, he saw wild hogs eating the fruit where it had fallen to the ground, and he decided it probably wasn't poisonous. So he tried one. The soft inner fruit had a custardy taste similar to watermelon. This turned out to be the sapote fruit, although the name Ashton uses, which he learned later on, is "*Mammees saporters*" (islanders today still call it the mamey apple). Ashton ate many of the sapote, describing it as a "very delicious sort of fruit."

But whatever fresh fruit Ashton could find growing on trees and vines was the only food he had to eat. Since he hadn't had the time to bring anything with him when he jumped in the longboat to go ashore, he had no tools of any kind—no knife, no gun, no way to start a fire. Ashton could already see that there was plenty of wildlife on the island, but without even a knife he would only be able to eat or use what he could pick, catch, or break with his bare hands or teeth. Early Spanish explorers had left hogs on the island in the early 1500s, and there were now wild hogs running in the woods. Ashton also saw deer, sea turtles, and an abundance of birds—ducks, pelicans, galdings, parrots, and many others. But since he didn't have a gun, he had no way to kill them.

After a few days of wandering, Ashton decided to make a trap by digging a large pit and then laying branches and palm leaves over the top to hide the hole from passing animals. Ashton started digging, but it was slow work. He soon realized that working with only his bare hands he couldn't possibly dig a pit deep enough to trap or hold an animal of any size. So he gave up. Besides, even if he had been able to capture a small animal or bird, he had no knife to skin and clean his catch, nor any way of making a fire to cook it.

When he wasn't looking for food, Ashton continued to wander the island. He discovered several rocky, dried-up gullies that made it a little easier to walk through the woods and up into the hills. The largest of these gullies were nearly as wide as a single-lane road and at some points were sunk into a crevice as much as three or four feet below the ground. Every now and then a small tributary gully, each about a yard wide, would branch off to the left or right and shoot almost directly up one of the steep hills. These dried up creek beds made getting around the island a little easier, though Ashton still had to walk in bare feet over a scramble of large and small rocks and dried leaves. Ashton was able to make it up to the tops of some of the higher hills on the east end of Roatan, which tower eight hundred feet or more above the water. But there were few fruit trees higher up in the hills, which were densely covered with pine trees and bush. "The mountains are covered over with a sort of shrubby black pine, and are almost inaccessible," Ashton wrote. "The valleys abound with fruit trees, and are so prodigiously thick with an under-brush that it is difficult passing."

⚬⚬⚬⚬⚬

Within days, Ashton sensed he was completely alone on Roatan. It's unlikely that he walked the entire length of the island, but it was clear that there were no signs of human life or even abandoned settlements anywhere near the eastern end of the island where he escaped. "Thus I was left upon a desolate island destitute of all help, and much out of the way of travelers," Ashton wrote. He saw no footsteps other than his own, and except for a few lime trees and some pieces of broken pottery, he found no signs of civilization. The pottery shards were remnants of native tribes indigenous to the Bay Islands that had lived on Roatan centuries before. Columbus had provided the first recorded sighting of the Bay Islands on his fourth visit to the New World in 1502, when he encountered natives living on Guanaja, an island just fifteen miles east of Roatan. Most of the Bay Islands, including Roatan, had originally been populated by these native tribes. In the coming months, Ashton would find more broken shards of pottery that were the only evidence of Roatan's original inhabitants.

By the 1600s, Europeans had started coming to Roatan. Demand for dye-rich Honduran logwood drew European crews to the region by the shipload, and the ensuing territorial conflict between the English and the Spanish at times spilled over to the Bay Islands. English logging crews would hide out on the islands or use them as launching points for attacks against the Spanish. There were also several English attempts to establish more permanent settlements on Roatan during the mid-1600s, most likely clustered around the eastern end of the island where Ashton was. The first of these settlements was a short-lived colony established by William Claiborne of Virginia in 1638. Claiborne's charter was through the Providence Company, which had been organized by the Puritan Party in England and spent a decade attempting to establish colonies on several small islands in the Caribbean. But Claiborne's colony on Roatan survived for just four years before the colonists were removed by the Spanish by the end of 1642, and nearly a century later, Ashton would see no evidence of the settlement. A few logwood cutters had continued to use Roatan as a base for launching attacks against the Spanish, but Spanish forces retaliated over time and by 1650 were successful in removing the rest of the British, as well as the few remaining natives. Except for the occasional visit by pirates or other ships seeking fresh water or a resting place, Roatan had been uninhabited for almost seventy-five years, until the day Ashton set foot on the island in 1723.[1]

Ashton believed he was better off than as a captive of Low's pirate crew. "This wilderness," he wrote, "I looked upon as hospitable, and this loneliness as good company, compared with the state and society I was now happily delivered from." His situation on Roatan was far from ideal, however. Most frustrating of all, Ashton was unable to take advantage of so much of what the island did offer: the wild hog and deer, the birds, even the abundant coconuts that were encased in impenetrable, rock-hard outer shells. "But of all this store of beast and fowl, I could make no use to supply my necessities, though my mouth often watered for a bit of them," Ashton wrote. "Yet I was forced to go without it for I had no knife or other instrument of iron with me by which to cut up a tortoise when I had turned it, or to make snares or pits with which to entrap, or bows and arrows with which to kill any bird or beast withal." He also had no way to cook any food, "nor could I by any possible means that I knew of come at fire to dress any if I had taken them, though I doubt not but some would have gone down raw if I could have come at it."

As the spring nesting season arrived, Ashton saw a number of sea turtles coming onto the sandy beaches scattered along the island. He had heard that the turtles lay their eggs in the sand, so he started searching the beach one day with a long stick, poking it into the sand as he walked along to see if he could find a nest. Sea turtles bury their eggs in a deep hole and then smooth out the sand over the nest, leaving no mound or other markings. Eventually, Ashton's stick-poking technique worked. The point of his stick came out of the sand with pieces of broken egg clinging to it. Dropping to his knees, Ashton dug into the sand and found a large nest filled with more than a hundred small round white eggs, each about the size of a walnut. The eggs looked like they were still fresh enough to eat. He took a small, tentative taste. The raw egg was barely palatable, but it did provide him with something besides fruit to eat. He also spread some of the raw egg on strips of palm leaves and hung it in the sun to dry for several days. The eggs then became "thickened and somewhat hard, as if they had been boiled," and slightly easier to eat. "But after all, they are not very good at the best," Ashton notes, "yet what is not good to him that has nothing to live upon but what falls from the trees?"[2]

Ashton started spending much of his days near the water, where the wind cooled the air and he could be on the lookout for any passing ships. The gusty breezes also helped keep the vicious mosquitoes and sand flies away from Ashton. The island was thick with the insects, and Ashton's feet and legs were soon covered with swollen red bite marks. Ashton found a flat area near the water and started to build a type of lean-to out of fallen branches and palm leaves. He gathered a number of branches and leaned them against a sturdy limb extending from a tree that was standing not far from the beach. He then tied these poles to the tree branch using strips of palm leaves and covered the frame with more palm leaves to serve as a roof. This shelter, and others he built around the island over time, provided some relief from the heat of the tropical sun and the cool dew of the night.

Ashton's only encounters as he rambled back and forth each day were with the wildlife living on the island. The birds were a constant presence, sometimes flying out of the trees squawking in alarm when his footsteps broke the silence of the woods as he was walking through the brush. Occasionally as he walked through the woods or along a rocky gully, Ashton would stop suddenly at the sight of a snake in his path. Most snakes on the island were relatively small and harmless, and Ashton was never bitten by a snake when he was living there. Some snakes were very long and thin, with copper-colored skin. There were also venomous coral snakes, which were mostly nocturnal and had black and red stripes. Ashton also saw several boa constrictors during his time on the island. The huge boa, its light brown skin dotted with darker brown and black markings, could be all but hidden in the thick forest; they were usually coiled, but when extended they looked to Ashton like "old fallen stocks of trees covered over with a short moss." Walking through the woods, Ashton didn't even know he was steps away from the huge snake. "The first I saw of these greatly surprised me, for I was very near to it before I discovered it to be a living creature, and it opened its mouth wide enough to have thrown a hat into it, and blew out its breath at me," Ashton recalled.[3]

The wild boars that roamed the island could be more of a problem. Sometimes the boars could be aggressive, and one came charging through the woods at Ashton one day. Ashton stood watching the boar charge at him, completely defenseless. Then, at the last moment, he reached for a tree branch. "So as he drew nearer to me I caught hold of the limb of a tree which was close by me and drew my body up by it from the ground as well as I could," Ashton wrote. "While I was in this hanging posture the boar came and struck me, but his tusks only took hold on my shattered trousers and tore a piece out, and then he went his way."

In time, Ashton came to know every detail of the Port Royal harbor: the location of several fresh runs of water, including the spot where he had escaped from the pirates, the areas where various plum, sapote, and other fruit trees grew, the best routes for passing from one hill over to the next, and the secluded beaches that were tucked away in coves along the shoreline. Looking toward the sea, he could always tell where he was from the line of distinctive islands and cays that stretched across the wide harbor. Closest to shore—less than two hundred yards away—were two forbidding rocky pieces of land jutting up from the water. The larger of these was called the Cow and the smaller the Calf. The Calf lay in front of the Cow, closest to shore, and was barely more than a large boulder, its top no wider across than the length of a man. It was formed of dark gray jagged-edge coral limestone that rose straight out of the water. Its walls were so steep and the pointed edges of the rock so sharp that Ashton would have found it practically impossible to climb onto, even if he'd had a way to get out to it. Besides, the formation was almost entirely rock—except for a few scrubby shrubs clinging to the rock, there was almost nothing growing on the mass of stone, and there would have been no reason to try to get onto it.

Just beyond the Calf, separated by a narrow channel of waist-deep water, was the other island, the Cow. That island was larger, maybe a hundred yards from one end to the other, and from land it looked like a giant prehistoric turtle floating in the water. The main section of the Cow formed the rounded shell of the turtle's body, a curved hump of the dark limestone covered by a dense morass of thorny bushes and windswept trees. To the east and almost separated from the main section were two tall columns of bare rock that formed the turtle's neck and head. The largest of these columns was the tallest point on the island. Long, snake-like vines of thick, prickly cactus ran all over the island, clutching to the rocks above the water.

On either side of the Cow and Calf, separated by less than a mile, were the two largest islands in the harbor. These islands were flatter, sandier, and much more inviting. Low's crew had almost certainly anchored near one of these two islands to careen their ships. To the west was a patch of land that several decades later would be named Captain Cusack's Island after James Cusack, one of the British commanders who led an expedition to Roatan to secure Port Royal for England in 1742. Today, the island is known as Lime Cay. To the east is the largest of the islands in the harbor, which has been known over the years as Fort George,

George Cay, Fort Morgan, or Fort Cay. Ashton could make out the outlines of a curved fort wall and a small stone guardhouse that were built on the island more than a half-century earlier, in the mid-1600s.[4]

Ashton looked out to each of the islands with longing. He wished he could find a way to get off of Roatan, if only for a few hours, to escape the nearly constant assault of the mosquitoes and sand flies. There was almost no relief from the insects. Unlike the mosquitoes, the tiny sand flies were barely visible and made no sound, but their bites could be just as painful, as Ashton soon learned. "The islands are also greatly infested with vexatious insects, especially the mosquito and a sort of small black fly, something like a gnat, more troublesome than the mosquito," Ashton wrote.

At each end of Port Royal, about three miles apart, the shoreline curved outward in two rounded points that formed the edges of the harbor. From these points, several smaller cays were much closer to shore than the larger islands. At the eastern end was a small cay known at the time as Careening Cay. At the opposite end, at the western edge of the harbor, were several even smaller cays that are little more than sandbars with a clump of bushes and a few small trees. After weeks of being bitten by mosquitoes and sand flies every day, Ashton was desperate enough to try to get himself out to one of these small cays. "This led me to think of getting over to some of the adjacent cays that I might have some rest from the disturbance of these busy companions," Ashton wrote.

Getting out to the cay seemed impossible, however. Although the two cays at the western end were little more than two hundred yards from shore, Ashton could barely swim. He could walk out from the shoreline for some distance until the water was so deep that it reached his shoulders. And the water surrounding the cay was also a lighter shade of turquoise, which indicated that there was another fifty-foot patch of water that was shallow enough for him to walk the rest of the way to the little island. But that still left a deep channel that Ashton had to get across. "My greatest difficulty lay in getting over to any other island, for I was but a very poor swimmer; and I had no canoe, nor any means of making one," Ashton wrote.

Ashton found a long, hollow bamboo pole and decided to try using it as a float. He stepped into the water, waded out until he was up to his chest, and then placed his arms over the pole and kicked his way through the water. Seeing that the pole supported him, he turned and kicked his way out to the small cay. When he got there, he found the cay was just a small patch of land, little more than a heap of sand, shells, and dried pieces of broken coral. A few bushes and one or two solitary trees were rooted in the soil. There was very little sand on the ground; instead it was strewn with larger rocks, shells, and pieces of driftwood that washed up from the sea. There was no food, water, or shelter on the cay, but it sat facing the open sea and there was a constant and strong breeze, which meant there were no mosquitoes or flies.

Ashton started spending more of his days sitting on the small cay, sleeping or staring out at the sea. He would spend his nights on Roatan, where he had food and his shelter, but then he would tie his clothes to the top of his head and swim out to what he called his "day island" where he passed the time. The cay was set right against the shallows on top of the reef that formed the curved outer border of the harbor. The water for at least twenty feet in front of the cay was barely knee-deep and scattered with small rocks that rose out of the shallow sea. The approaching waves broke over the reef, creating a line of white foamy surf, and washed over the rocks and sand to the foot of the cay. Looking out, Ashton could see only the dark blue water of the Bay of Honduras and, on clear days, the peaks of the Central American mainland in the distant horizon. Day after day, he sat and stared for hours at a time. "Sometimes," Ashton wrote, "I have sat leaning my back against a tree, with my face to the sea, to look out for the passing of a vessel for a whole day together."

Even using his bamboo pole as a float, crossing between Roatan and the small cay could be dangerous. The currents could be strong, especially for a weak swimmer like Ashton. Swimming back to the island one day, he lost hold of his bamboo pole. Due to the strong winds blowing from the east, the waves washed over Ashton as he was trying to swim to shore and pushed him further and further out, toward the open sea.

He finally managed to claw his way back to land. Another day, as he was just approaching the shallow water near his small day island, he felt something ram hard into his thigh—a sharp blow "just as I set my foot to ground." He looked down and saw that he'd been hit by a hammerhead shark. Hammerheads grow to between five and fifteen feet long and occasionally come close to shore to cruise along reefs, walls, and shallows. Some species, like the great hammerhead, can be bold and aggressive. Ashton rushed up onto the shore before the shark could turn and come at him again—"I escaped falling a prey to his devouring teeth"—but he "felt the blow he gave me some hours after" the encounter. Over time, Ashton became stronger and more confident as a swimmer and eventually came to explore some of the other nearby cays as well.[5]

Roatan's plentiful supply of fruit, along with the occasional turtle egg during the nesting season, made it possible for Ashton to survive. But it offered little else. "This was the place I was confined to, this my society and fellowship, and this my state and condition of life," Ashton wrote. Other than looking for food, he found very little to do. Every day was the same—what he ate, what he did, what he saw. Ashton's diet of wild fruit, and little else, was far from balanced. He'd had no contact with another person for months. He'd sometimes spend almost an entire day just staring out at the empty horizon of the blue sea. "Here I lingered out one day after another," he wrote, "I knew not how, without business or diversion; unless gathering up my food, rambling from hill to hill, from island to island, gazing upon the water, and staring upon the face of the sky may be called so."

Around October, after Ashton had been alone on the island for about seven months, the blistering heat of the tropical summer gave way to the cooler rainy season. More than half of Roatan's annual rainfall comes in the four months between October and January, soaking the island almost constantly. Heavy sheets of rain fell for hours, day after day, and the temperature dropped by about twenty degrees. It was impossible for Ashton to stay dry. With only the palm branches that formed the roof of his lean-to for protection, Ashton was now wet much of the time and his body was chilled from the dampness clinging to his clothes and skin and from the hard north winds that slammed "raw cold" air into the harbor. "Under all this dreadful distress, I had no healing balsams to apply to my feet, no cordials to revive my fainting spirits, hardly able now and then to get me some figs or grapes to eat, nor any possible way of coming at a fire which the cool winds and great rains beginning to come on, now called for," he wrote.

To make matters worse, Ashton's feet had deteriorated to the point where even walking a few hundred yards became excruciatingly painful. Having landed on the island with bare feet, his daily treks to find food meant walking over thick forest floors littered with brush, pointed sticks, and rough rocks, as well as over the beaches covered with sharp broken shells. Before long, his feet were constantly bruised, cut, and sore. His feet, ankles, and legs were also dotted with red bumps from countless mosquito and sand fly bites. As the condition of his battered feet worsened, he could only walk short distances across the rocky shore or through the rough woods. "Very often as I was treading with all the tenderness I could, a sharp stone or shell on the beach, or pointed stick in the woods, would run into the old wounds, and the anguish of it would strike me down as suddenly as if I had been shot through," Ashton wrote.

Soon after the rainy season arrived, Ashton became sick. His situation went from uncomfortable to dangerous. With no dry clothing, no fire, and only the barest of shelter, Ashton could find no relief from the downpours and cooler winds. He was too weak to move around, so he just lay on the ground shivering until he fell into a deep sleep. Ashton was, he recalled, "lonely, melancholy, wounded."

The passing days turned into weeks and months. It's not clear how long Ashton was sick. He later guessed it might have been about a month during September or October 1723 that he spent lying on the ground, barely strong enough to get a few bites of fruit from time to time. He became so weak and frail that he could barely move around. "As my weakness increased upon me, I should often fall down as though struck with a dead sleep, and many a time as I was thus falling, and sometimes when I laid myself down to sleep, I never expected to wake or rise more," Ashton wrote. "I often laid myself down as upon my last bed and concluded I should certainly die alone and nobody knew what was become of me."

Ashton barely resembled the person he once was. His malnourished body was thin and frail, his hair long and scraggly, and his feet covered with cuts and sores. At some points Ashton was so sick that he was not entirely lucid, slumped on the ground in a weak, feverish fog. "In the midst of this, my great soreness and feebleness, I lost the days of the week, and how long I had lain in some of my numb sleepy fits I knew not," he recalled. Given his condition, limited diet, and exposure to the elements, it is almost certain that Ashton's health deteriorated to a dangerous point. He described himself as "very weak and faint." As "almost dead." But his luck had not run out.

⦅⦆⦅⦆⦅

Help came in November. One day Ashton suddenly spotted a lone man paddling toward him in a canoe. In the nine months Ashton had spent on the island, he had never seen anyone. With little else to do, he had continued to spend many days sitting at the edge of the beach, leaning against a tree and gazing out to the sea. Half-wondering if he was seeing things, Ashton watched the man approach in his canoe or *piragua,* almost as if he had appeared out of nowhere. The man had a dog with him in his boat, but was otherwise alone. Ashton stayed where he was. "A friend I could not hope for, and I could not resist or hardly get out of the way of an enemy; nor need I fear one," he wrote. Eventually, the man paddling toward the shore spotted Ashton sitting on the beach and, clearly surprised, called out to him.

Ashton answered, telling the man that he was alone and that it was safe to come ashore. The man was surprised to find anyone living on the island, and he was even more shocked by Ashton's tattered clothing and ragged appearance. He paddled up to the beach and stepped out of his canoe. "As he came up to me, he stared and looked well with surprise; my garb and countenance astonished him; he knew not what to make of me," Ashton wrote. The man stepped back a little, letting the sight of Ashton sink in, and then finally approached and shook Ashton's hand.

The stranger was much older than Ashton, originally from Scotland, and he didn't say much; he was quiet and serious, with "a grave and venerable aspect." Ashton learned little about him—not even his name—except that after working on the mainland that are now Honduras and Belize for several decades, he'd fled to Roatan, believing his life was in danger. "He acquainted me that he had lived with the Spaniards twenty-two years, and now they threatened to burn him; I knew not for what crime," Ashton wrote. In addition to his dog, the man brought a gun with him and planned to feed himself by hunting on the islands. He had also brought several pounds of smoked or salted pork in his canoe. Seeing how thin and weak Ashton was, the old man immediately gave him some of the meat.

But the man did not stay long. He was anxious to go out hunting, and after just two nights on the island, the man suggested taking the canoe to a nearby island to hunt for deer and wild hog. Ashton still felt too weak to go, however, and his bare feet were too sore for him to be able to keep up with the man as he hiked through the brush and woods. So the man set off alone, promising to be back before long.

He never came back. About an hour after he'd set out, another heavy storm broke, bringing "most violent gusts of wind and rain." The weather was so rough that Ashton assumed the man's canoe probably capsized, and he never saw the man again. It was a tragic turn of events for Ashton, who for a few short days believed his solitude was over. "I began to experience the advantage of a companion, and find that two is better than one," he recalled. But as soon as the Scotsman left in his canoe to go hunting, Ashton was left again in his "lonely condition." "I no sooner saw the dawnings of light after so long obscurity," he wrote, "but the clouds returned after the rain upon me."

But the Scottish stranger had left behind many of his supplies, far more than Ashton could have dreamed of even a week earlier. He now had about five pounds of pork, a knife, a bottle of gunpowder, small metal tobacco tongs, and a flint he could use to strike a fire. Given Ashton's deteriorating health over the past several months, this may have saved his life. "For now I could have a fire, which was very needful for me, the rainy months of the winter," he wrote. Having a knife and fire also meant he could clean wild game and cook it. "I could cut up some tortoise when I had turned them, and have a delicate broiled meal of it," Ashton wrote.

Having a fire meant Ashton could catch and eat lobster as well. He found he could catch them by wading out into the harbor, about waist deep. In one hand he held a small bundle of sticks from a tree, like a pine tree, which grew branches that were sticky with pitch. Ashton lit the sticks on fire, creating a crude type of a torch that he held just above the water as he waded out. The light from his torch caused the lobster, which were attracted to the dim light, to scurry toward Ashton along the ocean floor. Holding a forked stick in the other hand, he poked at the lobster as they came near to him and tossed them back onto the beach. "In this manner I supplied myself with a mess of shell-fish, which when roasted is very good eating," he wrote.

But while he now had the food and tools the Scotsman left behind, Ashton was alone again. And he had only more solitude to look forward to, month after month of seclusion on the island. Only when the fighting near the logwood camps in nearby Belize spilled over to the islands would Ashton's solitude be broken again.

CHAPTER 6

The Baymen

On March 10, 1723, the day after Ashton ran away from the pirates on Roatan, four sloops from New England were anchored a little more than one hundred miles to the west, just off the shore of what now forms the mainland of Belize. Like the vessel Low had sailed on from Boston nearly two years before, these sloops were filling their holds with huge stacks of the prized Central American trees known as logwood and would soon set sail back to New England. Suddenly the men working on the sloops spotted a sight that was every bit as frightening to them as a pirate: a vessel flying a Spanish flag. Spain had been trying to block English and colonial logging along the Central American coast for decades, waging a constant battle to drive the woodcutters and logging ships out of the area, both through diplomatic channels in Europe and through patrols and stealth attacks throughout the Bay of Honduras.

The New England sloops that sat anchored in the shallow bay as they were being loaded with logwood were an easy target for the approaching Spanish vessel, which had ten large guns and close to sixty men aboard. The Spanish ship quickly captured three of the sloops, all from Newport, Rhode Island. The fourth, from Boston and under the command of a man named Edward Loyd, stole away as quickly as it could. Loyd's crew cut their cables and set sail immediately. The Spanish ship followed Loyd for a short time but couldn't catch up and eventually returned to the other captured sloops.

But barely three or four hours later that same day, the pirate crews of Low and Spriggs, which had just left Roatan, sailed into the bay. Low's former partner, George Lowther, was with them. With a complement of three vessels and more than one hundred men, most of them either manning heavy guns or armed on deck with muskets and pistols, the pirates outnumbered the Spanish crew and immediately captured the ship, as well as the three New England sloops. The pirates' capture quickly turned into a horrifically bloody massacre. Low's crew killed as many as fifty of the Spanish seamen, butchering some of the men and hacking their bodies into pieces, according to the report from one sea captain who witnessed the attack. Seven of the Spanish sailors survived when they jumped overboard and frantically swam ashore.[1]

Tragically, the captures and killings that day were not at all unusual for the Bay of Honduras, an area extending from the curved coastline of Belize and Honduras out to the islands of Roatan and Guanaja. The bay was one of the most dangerous and deadly arenas of sea-based conflict in the early eighteenth century, all because of a rare tree growing in the swamps and marshes of the Central American coastline. By the peak of Atlantic piracy in the 1720s, the unquenchable British thirst for the logwood tree was fueling decades of violence and warfare between merchant ships, pirates, woodcutters, and the Spanish.

The miles of wet, tropical land fed by a vast web of rivers and swamps that ran through coastal Belize created a fertile ground for logwood (*Haematoxylum campechianum*). What made logwood so valuable was its dark inner wood, so rich in color that when a piece of the wood is placed in a pail of water, the water turns blood red. The purplish-red heartwood of the logwood tree was used for centuries throughout Europe as a dye for clothing and fabric, and most of the popular dyewoods, including logwood and other species like *braziletto,* were found only in the region of the Yucatan Peninsula and present-day Belize.

Some logwood was shipped to Europe through Jamaica, but by the 1720s a large share of the wood was hauled back to New England and re-exported from there. The high price paid for logwood meant that it was one of the most valuable exports from all of the American colonies during this period, second only to tobacco. Logwood exports out of Boston were a major source of profits, and many of the men engaged in the logwood trade had strong ties to Boston. In fact, within a matter of years, a group of traders would donate several loads of logwood to pay for the construction of a steeple for Boston's new Anglican church, Christ Church, now known as Old North Church, the very steeple that fifty years later would be lighted by two lanterns on the evening of Paul Revere's infamous midnight ride at the start of the American Revolution. In appreciation for the donation that helped fund the steeple, the church dedicated a large, plush pew, which still stands today near the front of the Old North Church, to the "Gentlemen of the Bay of Honduras."[2]

The men who were rugged enough—and brave enough—to live in the crude, semipermanent camps throughout the wet woods of Belize, where they harvested logwood, were known as Baymen. These men were willing to risk their days cutting and hauling the hard logwood trees, working and camping out in a wild, swampy world, its rivers infested by crocodiles and the forests thick with mosquitoes. Baymen were forced to watch constantly for any sign of Spanish attackers. Some people claimed the rugged Baymen were themselves only a step removed from pirates. The British government suspected that Baymen helped out pirate crews sailing in the Caribbean by providing them with vessels, weapons, gunpowder, and shot. That may have been true, since some Baymen were former pirates and some pirates were former Baymen. In fact, each time the Spanish launched a successful attack on the Baymen's camps, they not only drove the woodcutters off the mainland, but also inflamed their anger against the attackers. Within a year's time, the governor or Bermuda, John Hope, would blame the surge in Atlantic piracy on Spanish efforts to clear out the Baymen. "Revenge very soon enters an injured mind," Hope wrote in August 1724. "[I]t is no great wonder if they embrace the only thing left them to do. . . . This, my lords, is the reason and source of piracy."[3]

Spain had tried for decades throughout the seventeenth and eighteenth centuries to stop the widespread British and colonial logging on Central American soil that was, in Spain's eyes, a critical piece of its global empire. The battle against logwood cutters was first concentrated on the western edge of the Yucatan Peninsula, in modern Mexico, and later moved south to the area that today forms Belize. By 1713, England believed its vessels had a legal right to take logwood from the region, based on its interpretation of the Treaty of Utrecht that was signed at the end of the War of Spanish Succession. But Spain didn't see it that way. Spanish patrols known as *guarda costas* launched aggressive and sustained attacks, capturing English and American logging ships and cutting off supply routes near the Bay of Campeche. Spanish crews could be ruthless when they captured a foreign ship.[4]

The Baymen living and working there responded by attacking Campeche Town, on the northwestern side of the Yucatan Peninsula, but by early 1716 the Spanish captured more than one hundred Baymen and burned every ship they found. The captain of a logwood ship who returned to New England the first week of May that year brought word of the sweeping Spanish attack. "Nine weeks ago the Spaniards from Tabasco had entirely cut off the western lagoon and Island of Trieste, and captivated 150 men, whites and blacks, burnt all the logwood, destroyed the craft, took a pink and a sloop which they carried away, burnt the hulks and a snow," read the report in the May 7, 1716, edition of the *Boston News Letter.* "They took also a vessel of marooners that belonged to the Bay and carried to Campeche Town, where they erected a mighty gallows and threaten to hang them all." By 1717, Spain had successfully cleared the Baymen out of the Bay of Campeche in western Yucatan, and the Spanish ambassador to the Court of St. James in England filed a strongly worded memorial to the British government warning that any logwood cutters remaining in the area near the Isle of Trieste would be treated as pirates.[5]

But England continued to reject Spain's arguments about logwood cutting in the region and before long the Baymen simply moved their operations to the other side of the peninsula to the coast of present-day Belize along the Bay of Honduras, where there were acres more of rivers, swamps, and logwood trees. By the 1720s, the tremendous demand for logwood meant it sold for high prices, profitable work for captains and their crews who were willing to risk a voyage to the Bay of Honduras. Each year, hundreds of vessels from England and New England headed there to fill their holds with stacks of the wood. At times there could be two dozen sloops and other vessels anchored just off the coast, loading logwood. Arriving merchant vessels would typically meet up with crews of Baymen and try to win their favor with a "frolick," a seaside party that revolved around bowls of rum punch and gifts of more rum. Some woodcutters would sell poor quality wood or hollowed-out logs to captains who cheated them out of rum. "The wood-cutters are generally a rude, drunken crew, some of which have been pirates, and most of them sailors," wrote one sea captain who'd spent time with the Baymen a few years earlier. "Their chief delight is in drinking; and when they broach a quarter cask or hogshead of wine, they seldom flit from it while there is a drop left."[6]

The steady stream of ships sailing into the region, typically well-stocked for their long journeys, did not only attract Spanish vessels. The Bay of Honduras—and its secluded islands of Roatan and Guanaja—were popular with pirates as well, particularly Low and Spriggs, who would spend more time cruising or hiding out in the Bay of Honduras than anywhere else in the Atlantic. In fact, English pirates were just as serious a threat to the logwood traders as the Spanish were. Just three years before Low and Spriggs had arrived, in early April 1720, the crew of another trading vessel from Boston was nearly done loading a cargo of logwood when a large ship and four sloops bore down on them. The captain of the merchant ship, William Wyer, knew almost instantly from the black and red flags flying on the approaching ships that they were pirates and he had little doubt it was a pirate named Edward Teach, the infamous Blackbeard. Teach became known as Blackbeard because, according to one of his captives, he had a "very black beard which he wore very long." Teach had followed Wyer into the bay, stung by Wyer's refusal to surrender to some of the pirate's crew just eleven days earlier. That first encounter had been off the coast of Roatan, when a pirate sloop that was part of Teach's fleet came alongside Wyer's ship at about nine o'clock on the night of March 28. There were about fifty men aboard and at least ten guns mounted on the sloop. When the pirates came within range, they launched an initial blast of two cannon shots and a volley of musket fire. Wyer's crew fired back at the pirates several times. The men from Teach's crew then shouted over that if Wyer's men fired another shot, they would kill everyone aboard. But Wyer and his men kept firing and the battle continued for several more hours, until about midnight.[7]

Finally, Wyer was able to slip away, and he continued to make his way toward the coast of Belize. Teach was enraged that Wyer had gotten away without surrendering, and he was now determined to destroy his ship. With all five of the vessels in his fleet, Blackbeard followed Wyer into the bay. He told another ship captain he captured in the area that he refused to let Wyer go free and "brag when he went to New England that he had beat a pirate."[8] But Wyer's men were not ready to stand up to the full force of Teach and the hundreds of men on his crew. As the pirates bore down on Wyer's vessel anchored in the bay, Wyer called his crew onto the deck and asked them if they would defend their ship. The men said that if the attackers were Spanish they would fight back, but if they were pirates they would not. Wyer sent a few men in a pinnace over to the approaching vessels. The men came back with word that the five ships, including the sloop that had attacked Wyer near Roatan, were all pirates. Wyer's crew quickly abandoned ship; "all declared they would not fight and quitted the ship, believing they would be murdered by the sloop's company, and so all went on shore."[9]

Three days later, Teach sent word ashore for Wyer to come aboard his ship. Wyer agreed to go, and Teach told the captain that he would let him go free, but he would burn his ship because it was from Boston, where six pirates had been hanged three years before. The next day, the pirates boarded Wyer's ship, still packed full of logwood ready to be shipped back to Boston, and set fire to it. The blazing ship sank into the sea. Teach then let Wyer sail home with another captured sea captain, and the men arrived back in Boston at the end of May.

Wyer's ship was just one of dozens of logwood vessels that were captured by pirates during the early 1720s, many of them taken over by the crews or burned. The pirates would also chase down and attack

Spanish ships they encountered, just as Low had when he sailed to the coastline shortly after leaving Roatan. The area was so dangerous that within a year or two, a British warship would be sent to patrol the bay on a nearly continuous basis, hunting down both pirates and Spanish vessels and escorting convoys of logwood ships on their sail between the coast and Jamaica.

⊷ͼϿϾϿ·

In January of 1724, the conflict from the Bay of Honduras spilled over into Ashton's quiet, solitary world on Roatan. Wandering along the beach one day, he stopped suddenly when he spotted a small *piragua,* a canoe-like wooden craft constructed from a hollowed log, that had washed up on the shore. At first Ashton thought it might have been the craft belonging to the old Scotsman who'd spent a few days with him on Roatan, but as he got closer he realized it wasn't. The *piragua* had simply been lost and washed ashore. Ashton took the abandoned vessel as his own. It probably had a small mast and sail, and it gave him far greater access to the water and surrounding islands than he'd ever had before. He could now use the canoe-like vessel to paddle back and forth to his small island, where he still spent many of his days, and to explore other islands and cays around Port Royal. The *piragua* was a nice diversion for Ashton. "When I had got this little vessel in possession, I began to think myself admiral of the neighboring seas, as well as sole possessor and chief commander upon the islands," he wrote.

Feeling confident in his new craft, a few weeks later Ashton decided to try making a longer trip to the largest of several nearby islands, Guanaja. This island, historically known as Bonacca, lies about twenty miles to the east of Roatan and is about ten miles long, roughly one-third the size of Roatan. The trip would require navigating the *piragua* a long distance across the open water and, even with the sail rigged, would take the better part of a day. Ashton packed a supply of food—figs, grapes, and some tortoise meat—and set off.

As he drew closer to Guanaja, Ashton noticed a sloop at anchor in a bay at the island. He decided to change his course, heading away from the ship and instead approaching the island from its other side. Continuing on a course toward the sloop would have required paddling further out to sea to avoid a rocky point extending out from the island, which would have both exposed Ashton to rougher water and revealed himself to a potentially hostile crew while he was still a significant ways offshore. That was something he couldn't risk. "For in the midst of my most deplorable circumstances, I could never entertain the thoughts of returning on board any pirate, if I should have the opportunity, but had rather live and die as I was," Ashton wrote.

Ashton paddled toward shore and secured the boat on the beach. He then set out through the woods in the direction of the bay where he'd spotted the ship. But the jungle-like forest on Guanaja was as thick and impassible as on Roatan, and Ashton was still barefoot. At some points he had to crawl on his hands and knees under the overgrowth for long stretches at a time. While Guanaja is smaller than Roatan, it is just as mountainous and its tallest hills are even higher. Crossing the island took Ashton two days of climbing and crawling through the thick brush, walking late into the night.

Nearing the opposite coastline where he thought he'd seen the sloop, Ashton made his way down to the shore. But when the bay came into view, he saw nothing but the sea. There was no sign of the sloop, nor any men. He walked down onto the beach, but still saw no signs of any activity. Exhausted from the brutal hike across the island, Ashton sat down, leaned back against a tree at the edge of the empty beach, and fell asleep almost immediately.

It seemed like only moments later when Ashton was awakened by the sharp crack of gunfire. Looking across the beach, Ashton saw nine *piraguas* in the water, bearing toward shore with their guns aimed squarely at him. Ashton instantly jumped up and fled back into the woods. "I soon turned about and ran as fast as my sore feet would let me into the bushes, and the men which were Spaniards cried after me, 'Oh Englishman, we'll give you good quarter,'" Ashton wrote. Later on, Ashton would wonder if he should have risked going with the men, since that would have gotten him off the island and, at the very least, kept him from falling back into the hands of pirates. "But such was the surprise I had taken, by being awakened out of sleep in such a manner, that I had no command of myself to hearken to their offers of quarter, which it may be at another time under cooler thoughts I might have done," Ashton wrote.

So Ashton kept running—and the Spaniards kept firing. The volley of bullets missed him, but just barely. He could hear the musket shot flying past his head and snapping off small branches from the trees near him as he fled. When he got deeper into the woods Ashton hid himself in a large thicket and waited for several hours. Eventually he heard the knocking of the Spaniard's paddles as they headed away, and he carefully made his way back down to the shore. It had been a narrow escape. When Ashton returned to the beach and looked at the tree he'd been sleeping against, he found six or seven bullets lodged in the bark, within a foot of where his head had been resting.

Hidden on the beach, Ashton now saw a sloop sailing away, the *piraguas* in tow. The sloop was flying an English flag. From this, Ashton concluded it had been captured by the Spaniards in the bay. But even with the Spaniards now gone, Ashton found Guanaja had little to offer. Foraging for food proved more difficult than on Roatan, and after he had eaten what he'd brought with him, he had little to sustain him. The mosquitoes and flies were also even worse than on Roatan. "The difficulties I met with here made me lay aside all thoughts of tarrying any time to search the island," Ashton wrote. The hike back to his *piragua* took another three days, the thick brush again battering his sore feet. When he finally reached his boat, he set out at once and arrived back at Roatan well after dark.

More months passed. March of 1724 marked the first anniversary of Ashton's solitary life on Roatan. His only contact with other people during the past year had been limited to the three days he'd spent with the quiet Scotsman who'd come briefly ashore and his recent encounter with the Spanish on Guanaja. For the remaining 361 days of the past year he'd been alone, with only the sounds of birds, the wind in the trees, and rain pattering on the leaves above his head. When he was not looking for food, Ashton spent most of his time sitting with his back against a tree at the edge of the beach, staring out to the sea, or paddling out to his small cay where he could sit or sleep as the hours passed.

Though he was no longer sick, Ashton's health continued to deteriorate. He'd lost considerable weight. The stoic Ashton doesn't record what he thought about as he passed day after day, and he barely hints at his condition. "Here I lived (if it may be called living) alone for about seven months more, from the time of losing my North British companion; and spent my time after my usual manner in hunting for my food, and ranging the islands," Ashton wrote.

One day in June 1724, Ashton was sitting on his small day island. It had been four or five months since his trip to Guanaja. Suddenly he spied two large *piraguas* making their way through the water. As the men in the *piraguas* drew closer, they must have noticed smoke from a fire Ashton had built back on Roatan, and they stopped paddling. Ashton jumped into his own boat and quickly paddled back to the island, which offered more protection than his small cay. Seeing him, the men continued paddling toward the shore, but now moved more slowly through the water. Seeing how cautious the men were as they approached, Ashton decided they probably were not pirates and, once back on the island, stepped out onto the beach facing them. Ashton was about to call out to them, but before he could, the men stopped paddling and shouted across the water at him, asking him who we was and where he was from.

Ashton told them he was English and had escaped from pirates. Hearing this, the men paddled a little closer and then asked if anyone else was on the island with him. Ashton said there wasn't. He then asked the men who they were. They said they were Baymen and had come over from the mainland. Ashton invited them to come ashore. Still worried about falling into a trap, the men paddled the rest of the way to the shore but landed a little ways away from where Ashton stood. They sent a single member of their party onto the island. Ashton walked over to him. "When the man came up to me he started back, frightened to see such a poor, ragged, lean, wan, forlorn, wild, miserable object so near to him: but upon recovering himself, he came and took me by the hand," Ashton wrote.

Seeing how weak Ashton was, the man then picked him up and carried him in his arms down to where the rest of the men had beached the two *piraguas*. Ashton told them in more detail the story of how he had escaped from the pirates and survived alone on the island for more than a year. "I gave them a short history how I had escaped from Low and had lived here alone for sixteen months (saving three days), what hardship I had met with, and what danger I had run through," Ashton wrote. The other men were just as shocked by Ashton's appearance. "They stood amazed!" Ashton wrote. "They wondered I was alive!"

The men then offered him a few sips of rum to revive his "fainting spirits." But the strong rum proved too powerful for him. "This small quantity, through my long disuse of any liquor higher spirited than water, and my present weakness, threw my animal spirits into such a violent agitation as to obstruct their motion, and produced a kind of stupor," Ashton wrote.

Finally, Ashton revived. In all, there were eighteen Baymen and their cook—an "Indian woman"—in the party that came to the islands. The two leaders of the group were John Hope, whom the men called "Father Hope," and another man called John Ford. As Baymen, they'd had a number of run-ins with the Spanish over the years, and on a previous occasion Hope and Ford had sought refuge on the nearby island of Barbareta, which lies less than two miles from the eastern tip of Roatan between Roatan and Guanaja. The Baymen had lived there for four years. Now they were back again because they had heard new rumors on the mainland that the Spanish were planning an attack on their logging camp. So the crew had loaded up supplies—including two barrels of flour, guns, ammunition, nets for catching tortoise, and their hunting dogs—and made their way out to the islands.

This time, the Baymen decided not to go back to Barbareta. Less than two miles from the southern shore of the island, there are two flat, sandy cays. Like the smaller islands that Ashton used off Roatan, these cays are continuously swept by the sea breeze, which keeps them free of mosquitoes and sand flies. Rather than setting up camp on Barbareta, the Baymen most likely made their way out to one of these two cays, the largest of them a strip of land just over three hundred feet long with a small patch of bushes, trees, and palms growing in the middle and a white, sandy beach around its edge. Today these cays are known as the Pigeon Cays. Ashton went with the Baymen over to the new island, where they established their base camp, collecting wood from several of the larger islands and building two shelters. The men lived on the smaller island but went out often to the other islands to hunt for deer, hogs, and tortoise and to collect drinking water.[10]

Ashton may not have been strong enough at first to help gather wood or build the shelters, but he continued to live with the Baymen for some time. The men treated him well. They gave him several articles of clothing, including a robe or blanket—a "wrapping gown"—to sleep in, the first additions to Ashton's wardrobe since he'd set foot on Roatan wearing only his pants and a frock. He was now also eating better with the Baymen. As he regained his strength, he went hunting with the men on the nearby islands. When they shot a wild hog, the men would frequently dry it the same way as the buccaneers that had been working the Caribbean waters for the past century had done, cutting long strips of meat from the hog and smoking them. The Baymen also killed plenty of deer and tortoise. What the men did not eat fresh they smoked and saved, and they always had a ready supply of meat. The Baymen fed Ashton well, and his spirits were lifted by being in the company of other people on a daily basis. He undoubtedly felt better than he had since he was captured by Low's crew two years earlier. "And now I seemed to be in a far more likely way to live pretty tolerably than in the sixteen months past," Ashton recalled, "for besides having company, they treated me with a great deal of civility, in their way."

But the Baymen were also a rugged group, used to the hard and dangerous work in the swampy logging camps on the mainland, and it showed in their coarse language and habits. "But after all they were bad company, and there was but little difference between them and the pirates as to their common conversation," Ashton wrote, "only I thought they were not now engaged in any such bad design as rendered it unlawful to join with them, nor dangerous to be found in their company."

Even so, Ashton was not as safe as he thought. His troubles were far from over.

<hr />

While Ashton had spent the better part of two years living on the islands, most of that time alone, the pirate crew of Low and Spriggs had followed the winds and the major trading routes in another loop up and across the Atlantic, leaving a trail of carnage in their wake. Low's crew captured nearly twenty more vessels in the first three months after Ashton escaped on Roatan in March of 1723. The first of these captures had come within a day or two after the pirates sailed away from Roatan, when Low had avenged the Spanish attack on three New England logging sloops near Belize, butchering almost all the Spanish sailors he found there. Low's fleet then sailed north for several weeks, heading past the westernmost tip of Cuba. Low was in the *Fortune,* a sloop with ten guns and about seventy men aboard. Spriggs had come back aboard Low's sloop. A new quartermaster, Charles Harris, was now in command of the second sloop, the *Ranger,* with eight cannon and just under fifty men. One of the pirates' two vessels was probably the French sloop taken at Grenada, and the other sloop was taken from some Baymen near the mainland of Honduras or Belize. Low had given those Baymen his Marblehead fishing schooner, the *Fancy,* in return.

On May 8, 1723, Low's crew captured at least six vessels off Cabo de San Antonio, at the western tip of Cuba. The captain of one of the captured vessels, John Welland of Boston, was taken with four of his men over to Harris' sloop and questioned about the gold and silver he had on board, which the pirates then took from him. Several hours later, Welland was moved over to Low's sloop, where he was hacked repeatedly with a cutlass; one of the strokes sliced off his right ear. Welland was then forced below decks, where he lay for two or three hours while his wounded head continued to drip blood onto the wooden floor. Eventually Welland asked another captive for some help. The man brought Welland some water and then went to get Kencate, the ship's doctor. Meanwhile, up on the deck, the pirates tortured other captives by burning them "with matches between their fingers," according to one survivor, searing their flesh to the bone "to make them confess where their money was." They cut and whipped a number of the other captives, and sank one of the ships.[11]

Low planned to force another member of Welland's crew, twenty-two-year old Henry Barnes, who was from Barbados. The next day, Low captured another ship and decided to release Welland and some of the other sailors, letting them go free in the newly captured vessel. Hearing this, Barnes tried to hide on the ship until it sailed away, but the pirates realized he was missing. When Low threatened to burn the entire ship, Barnes came out of hiding and went aboard one of the pirates' sloops.

Allowing many of the men from captured ships to go free could be risky, however, and would nearly prove to be fatal to Low in the weeks ahead. Even so, there was no practical incentive for Low to massacre an entire crew (although the pirates had killed almost every member of the Spanish crew they captured in the Bay of Honduras in March). After capturing vessels from England or the American colonies, Low eventually allowed most of the crew to go free rather than kill them or take them aboard. The pirates captured ships to take any valuables, food, or supplies that might be on board or, in some cases, to gain an additional vessel or a replacement for one of their older or slower ships. Accounts of Low's captures over the course of his career as a pirate include frequent mentions of taking or forcing one or two recruits from any given prize, but most of the men aboard captured vessels were eventually freed. The crew and passengers aboard the brigantine *Rebecca,* which Low took on his initial voyage after leaving Lowther and setting out on his own, had all been freed with the exception of the captain, one or two forced sailors, and Harris, who had signed on as a pirate. And even though Low brought the captain, James Flucker, to Nova Scotia where Ashton was captured, Low released most of the men from the dozen or so fishing boats he took there and set them free to sail back to Boston with the *Rebecca,* along with Flucker.

That meant, however, that the freed men could then report their encounter, and the pirates' last known location, to other ships, sometimes just hours after they were released. This is what happened only a month later as Low's crew made its way up the Atlantic coast toward New England. On Friday, June 7, 1723, a merchant vessel from Virginia met up with a British warship, the HMS *Greyhound,* that was cruising off the coast of New Jersey. That merchant ship had been overtaken and held by Low's fleet for several days and let go only the day before. The captain told the men on the *Greyhound* that the pirates were heading north toward Block Island. The *Greyhound,* under the command of a captain named Peter Solgard, immediately set off after the pirates.[12]

Three days later, in the faint light of daybreak on Monday, June 10, the *Greyhound* caught its first glimpse of Low's sloops. They were less than fifty miles south of the eastern tip of Long Island. The two pirate sloops were about seven miles away when the *Greyhound* first spotted them. At about five o'clock that morning, Solgard tacked and set a southerly course, keeping the pirates in view but not approaching, "to encourage them to give him chase." It didn't take long for Low and Harris to spot the *Greyhound,* and they set out after it. The winds were very light that morning, however. Making almost no headway under sail, the pirates were forced to row the sloops with long oars. More than two hours passed as the *Greyhound* and the two sloops moved slowly through the seas. At about 7:30 a.m., with slightly more wind, Solgard tacked again and started to close the distance between the warship and the pirates.

Aboard the *Fortune* and the *Ranger,* Low and Harris shouted orders for their crews to prepare for a battle as the *Greyhound* approached. The pirates brought gunpowder, shot, and their muskets from below deck and placed them at the ready, close enough for them to be within reach when they were needed, but set safely in a spot where they would be less likely to get soaked by splashing water or spray from the sea. Harris' sloop, the *Ranger,* had eight large iron cannon aboard, each mounted on four-wheeled wooden carriages and secured by ropes that were looped through wooden pulleys and fastened to the ship's walls near the port-holes. The sloop also had several swivel guns, smaller cannon mounted in yokes between the rails or on the edge of the rails themselves. Low's sloop had ten large cannon aboard. These large cannon were typically used to fire shot—small cannonballs—and the swivel guns often were loaded with musket balls. But in a pinch the guns could also be loaded with any number of potentially lethal projectiles, including nails, metal scraps, or even stones tightly wrapped in leather or cloth pouches.[13]

As the distance between the *Greyhound* and pirate sloops closed, the guns on all the vessels were loaded. On the *Greyhound,* the men probably loaded the cannon with cartridges—gunpowder wrapped in paper or cloth casings that the ship's gunner had prepared beforehand—but the men on the pirate ships may have used either cartridges or loose powder, depending on what they had available. After the gunpowder was forced down the long barrel of the cannon, the men loaded iron shot and then, using a long ramming pole, jammed in a wad of old rope, straw, or cloth to hold everything in place while they positioned the gun. Before firing, they would pull on the ropes that ran through the block-and-tackle pulleys attached to the vessel's inner walls, edging the cannon forward so that the nose of its barrel now stuck out from one of the portholes that dotted the side of the sloop.

By eight o'clock that morning, the pirates were within several hun-dred yards of the *Greyhound.* Both Low and Harris raised black pirate flags on their sloops. Low's crew flew a flag depicting a skeleton with two outstretched arms, one hand holding an hourglass, the other clutching a dart dripping with blood. Low and Harris gave the command to fire one shot each. The pirates on the two sloops poured loose gunpowder into the vent on the top of the cannon barrel, leaving a thin line of exposed powder running from the vent hole and along the iron gun. The cannon were fired by igniting this line of gunpowder and standing back. Timing the blast was tricky, however. Given the momentary delay between igniting the powder and the cannon firing, aiming a shot was difficult if the ship was rolling in the swell of the seas. A gunner might have to ignite the powder with his flame when the ship was at its lowest point in a downward roll so that, with any luck, the cannon would fire just as the ship was rolling back up and the gun was pointed squarely at the deck, mast, or rigging of the target.

The noise from the pirates' first two shots at the *Greyhound* shattered the morning. Each cannon blast sent a deafening boom across the water and filled the deck above the gun with a huge cloud of white smoke. The blast threw the cannon backwards on its wooden carriage into the sloop, but the powerful recoil was immediately restrained by the ropes and pulleys holding the cannon in place. The black flags the pirates had raised and the first two cannon shots were warnings; they signaled that the sloops were pirates, and they expected the *Greyhound* to surrender immediately. Many of the vessels Low's crew overtook did quickly surrender, and the ships and their crews were captured without a battle. But not today. The *Greyhound* was also heavily armed and ready for battle, and gave no sign of yielding.

The three vessels continued to maneuver slowly and cautiously through the water, changing course from time to time as they circled each other. At some points the pirates and the *Greyhound* were as much as three-quarters of a mile apart, but the men aboard each ship always kept the other vessels in their sight. After sailing for another half-hour, the pirates came within range and attacked again. Low ordered the black pirate flags to be pulled down and another—their "bloody" red flag—raised in its place. This meant the opportunity to surrender, and be given safe quarter, was gone and the pirates would now fight to the kill. "When they fight under the Jolly Roger, they give quarter, which they do not when they fight under the red or bloody flag," one sea captain wrote after he was captured by members of Low's crew.[14]

As the pirates' sloops closed in on the *Greyhound* again, they fired several more shots. Low's plan was to attack the *Greyhound* with a round of cannon fire, followed by a volley of gunfire from the armed pirates standing on deck. After blasting the *Greyhound,* he planned to bring his sloop, the *Fortune,* alongside the *Greyhound* to board the warship. Harris, in the *Ranger,* could then draw alongside the *Fortune* and his men could climb over the *Fortune* to board the *Greyhound* as well. But the *Greyhound* came alongside the sloops and, raising its royal flag, fired several rounds back, thwarting Low's plans of overtaking the warship. The blasts from the *Greyhound* included both cannon shot as well as a volley of grapeshot, a lethal mass of loose slugs packed into a canvas bag.

The pirates and the *Greyhound* now battled continuously, firing at each other with their cannon and muskets. The *Greyhound* had twenty guns and 130 men aboard, a formidable match for the two pirate sloops, which had about eighteen guns between them. Below deck, the men working at the guns ran frantically through the cycle of firing a gun, pulling it back into the ship from the porthole, wiping it clean, and then reloading. After each firing, the inside of the gun barrel had to be swabbed with sea water, using a sponge attached to a long pole, in order to extinguish any remaining embers that might still be smoldering inside the barrel, which could cause fresh gunpowder to explode when the cannon was immediately loaded again. That could be disastrous for the men loading the gun. "The poor fellow had discharged it several times," recalled one survivor of a cannon explosion aboard a ship. "But the reports were not sufficiently loud to please the captain, who ordered it to be again loaded and fired, which the mate thought he would do this time with effect, and therefore not only did he cram into its mouth a seaman's capful of powder, but commended ramming down the wadding with a handspike, which as he was doing, a spark that had remained in the breach of the gun from the previous firing ignited the charge, and the explosion which took place shattered his right arm to atoms."[15]

The first wave of fighting between the pirates and the *Greyhound* continued for about an hour that morning. Then the pirates broke away from the battle and tried to sail away. But there was still almost no wind that day, and even rowing with oars, the pirates were unable to put much distance between themselves and the warship. Between two and three o'clock in the afternoon, the *Greyhound* was again within range of Harris' sloop, the *Ranger,* and started firing on it again.

The battle continued for several more hours, and Harris' sloop took a number of hits from the *Greyhound.* Cannon fire shattered a ship's hull, snapped masts and rigging, and tore away at sails, often leaving a vessel helpless in the water. Guns aboard a ship could also be loaded with partridge—a wrapping of tin, leather, or cloth tied around a packet of musket balls, metal scraps, or stones—which also sent a blast of destruction at a vessel's sails or onto a deck full of men. Men stood on the deck of the ship armed with pistols and, if in range, fired across the water at their attacker. One of the men aboard the *Ranger* later said he was given more than a dozen pistols and told he "had better strike." With a volley of musket fire, the decks of a ship could quickly be cleared.

By now, after hours of fighting, Harris' battered sloop had its mainsail shot down. At least four men aboard Harris' sloop were dead or near death. The deck was splintered from the hours of cannon fire. In addition to the gunfire itself, shot hitting a ship caused explosions of chunks of wood and splinters torn from the masts and deck, which were just as often the cause of serious wounds. Guns that misfired or that fired too early also meant that burns were common during battles. The *Greyhound,* too, had sustained heavy damage during the battle. At least seven of its crew were wounded and the pirates' fire had done "much damage" to the warship's rigging and sails. By late afternoon, it became clear that the pirates aboard the *Ranger* were losing the fight but Harris could not manage to retreat. With so little wind and their mainsail practically in pieces, even by rowing Harris' crew could not get free of the *Greyhound.*

At about five o'clock that afternoon, Harris signaled his surrender. It had been a brutally long day, more than twelve hours since the pirates first spotted the *Greyhound,* and the mood aboard the pirate ships had gone from die-hard determination to desperation and outright panic. Earlier in the day Low, the ferocious pirate captain, had stood on the deck of his sloop, cutlass in hand, shouting orders at his crew. One member of the pirate crew had beat out a battle charge on a drum while the pirates stood up to the *Greyhound.* But by now Low had veered away in his sloop, and Harris was left alone. When Harris surrendered to the warship, one of the pirates aboard the *Ranger* refused to be taken prisoner. He ran across the deck toward the bow of the sloop, a flask in one hand and a pistol in the other. Then, shouting and cursing at the world, he pointed the pistol at his head and "shot out his own brains."[16]

Harris and thirty-five members of his crew who had survived the battle were taken prisoner by the *Greyhound*. Many of them were taken back to Newport, Rhode Island, in Harris' sloop. In the *Greyhound,* Solgard continued to chase after Low and Spriggs for several more hours, but lost sight of their sloop around nine o'clock that evening somewhere in the sea between Block Island and Martha's Vineyard. The *Greyhound* then returned to Newport that night. Harris' crew was put on trial a month later, and most of the pirates—including Ashton's former crewmate Joseph Libbey—were convicted and hanged in July.[17]

❈❈❈❈

Four days later, a merchant vessel leaving New England on its way back to Maryland was passing the island of Nantucket, about sixty miles east of Newport, when the men aboard the ship saw an abandoned sloop drifting in the sea. The sloop was a wreck. Its rigging was sliced, its sails were flapping loosely in the wind, hatches had been thrown overboard, and a hole was cut into the vessel by someone who apparently had tried to sink it. The sloop's cargo had been ransacked, and the deck was littered with broken boxes and wooden barrels. Casks of liquor had been left torn open. What hadn't been taken or drunk was still sitting in buckets on the deck of the sloop. The vessel was completely empty—there wasn't a single person, dead or alive, aboard.[18]

Nobody knows what happened to the men aboard the sloop. But given when and where it was found, it was almost certainly captured, destroyed, and then abandoned by an infuriated Low and his men. Low was undaunted by his battle with the *Greyhound* and the loss of Harris' ship and crew, and was now boarding ships with a rage that reached psychopathic proportions. Just months earlier, Low had captured a Portuguese ship sailing from Brazil. The captain of the Portuguese ship quickly dropped a bag of gold overboard as soon as his ship was cornered so the pirates would not be able to take it. Seeing this, Low had sliced off the captain's lips and broiled them over a fire, forcing the bloodied captain to stand watching the spectacle of his own flesh being cooked on the deck. Low's men then killed all thirty-two men aboard the Portuguese ship. Now, in the days and weeks following the *Greyhound* battle near Newport, Low continued his horrific rampage. Reports from up and down the Atlantic testified to Low's destruction, attacks characterized by "unparalleled insolence" as his crew caused "incredible damage to trade by taking, plundering, burning, or sinking all the ships, of what nation soever, which come in their way."[19]

Just a few days after the *Greyhound* battle, the pirates captured a whaling sloop from Nantucket, brutally torturing and then murdering the young captain, Nathan Skiff. According to survivors' reports, the pirates "cruelly whipped him about the deck, then they cut off his ears; and after they had wearied themselves with making a game and sport of the poor man, they told him that because he was a good master, he should have an easy death, and then shot him through the head." Low's crew also captured two other ships out of Plymouth, killing the captains in a similarly barbarous manner. One of the captains they cut open alive and ripped out his heart, which they then roasted and forced another sailor to eat. The pirates then attacked the captain of the second ship, "slashing and mauling him, and then cutting off his ears, they roasted them and made him eat them." Low had vowed "he would do the like by all he meets," a survivor of one of the attacks reported.[20]

Low and Spriggs then sailed back to the coast off Nova Scotia, where they captured several other fishing vessels and merchant ships from both sides of the Atlantic. The French captain of one of the captured ships asked Low for some way to prove that the pirates were taking several casks of wine and brandy so that when he returned home without payment, the ship's owner would not accuse him of taking the cargo himself and selling it on the side. Low said he would be happy to help the captain and went below deck, returning moments later with two pistols, one in each hand. Low pointed the first pistol at the captain's stomach, told him that was for his wine, and fired it. As the captain clutched his burned and bleeding stomach, Low pointed the second pistol at the man's head, told him that was for his brandy, and fired again.[21]

CHAPTER 7

The Bay of Honduras

By September 1723, Low's crew was back at the Azores, where the pirates captured a number of vessels and "barbarously used several persons taken by them, by cutting off their ears." A month later, in the last week of October, Low's crew had reached the coast of Africa. About two hundred miles northwest of Sierra Leone, the pirates captured a large slaving vessel, the *Delight Galley*, from London. This was a time when a constant stream of vessels hauled chained slaves in deplorable conditions from the African coast to ports on both sides of the Atlantic. These slaving ships were large and often heavily armed; the *Delight Galley* had previously been a British warship. The *Delight* had not yet reached the Guinea Coast, so it was not packed full of captured Africans. Low decided the large galley was worth keeping.[1]

One of the sailors working aboard the *Delight Galley* was Jonathan Barlow. Barlow would be among the last pirate captives ever taken by Low, and he found himself suddenly thrust into the world of threats and violence that awaited prisoners aboard Low's ship. Low insisted that Barlow give him a ring he was wearing and threatened to cut off his finger when he refused. Then Low demanded that Barlow sign the ship's articles and join the crew, but Barlow said he wouldn't. "Taking his pistol out," Barlow later recalled, Low "beat out one of my teeth and threatened to shoot me down the throat because I would not consent to his proposal which was to sign the Articles." Barlow was kept aboard the ship and forced to sail off with the pirates as they headed west back across the Atlantic toward the Caribbean.[2]

By now, Low had problems of his own to worry about. As violent as he was, Low's position as commander of the ship was a delicate one, and his support among the crew was crumbling. Pirate ships were organized in a manner that was, for the eighteenth century, remarkably democratic. The captain and quartermaster of a pirate ship were elected by the crew, a practice that stood in stark contrast to the nearly unlimited power of sea captains on naval or merchant vessels. Pirate captains were given absolute control during a chase or a battle, but all other decisions were made by a vote of the crew. "The captain seems to have no manner of command, but in time of chase or engaging," one pirate captive wrote in 1724. The pirate Sam Bellamy was elected as captain of his pirate ship after the crew dismissed the previous captain, Benjamin Hornigold, because he "refused to take and plunder English vessels." The first article aboard Bartholomew Roberts' pirate ship stated, "Every man shall have an equal vote in affairs of moment."[3]

Crews also elected a quartermaster, who enforced both discipline and equality aboard a pirate ship. John Rose Archer, who was the quartermaster of another pirate crew in 1724, later said that "the company thought him the fittest man for a quartermaster and so chose him." A captain who was captured by pirates that same year described the quartermaster as the "chief director" over the crew and said that at mealtime he "overlooks the cook, to see the provisions equally distributed to each mess." Often a quartermaster would take command of a new vessel after the pirates captured it. Spriggs had been put in charge of the schooner *Fancy* for some time when Ashton was sailing with Low's crew, and later that year Charles Harris was given command of the *Ranger* before it was captured by the *Greyhound* near Newport.[4]

Now, after taking the *Delight Galley* near Africa, Spriggs was given command of the vessel with a crew of eighteen men. But at about the same time, a man on Low's ship was killed; apparently one member of the crew murdered another one in "cold blood." Spriggs insisted that the murderer be hanged. But Low refused. So, with a new crew of his own, Spriggs deserted Low and headed for the Caribbean.

Not long after, sometime before the end of March 1724, the remaining members of Low's crew also decided they'd had enough of him and his brutal treatment of captives. The crew's repugnance at Low's barbarity may have been festering for the previous year. One report of the attacks following the battle with the *Greyhound* in June 1723 describes two incidents where Low wanted to kill all the men on vessels he captured, "but the rest of the pirates would not suffer his cruel order to put in execution." By early 1724, Low was finally outnumbered and lost his ship. Members of his crew later said they abandoned Low "on account of the barbarity he used those he took." The crew "disbanded Low from his office" and cast him off with two other pirates in a French sloop they had taken near Saint Lucia. The crew chose a pirate named Richard Shipton as their new captain.[5]

꧁꧂

The crew's desertion of Low that March was a remarkably peaceful event, but other pirates who tried to get rid of their temperamental captains were not so lucky. A month before, in early February 1724, a smaller band of pirates was cruising near the Chesapeake Bay, on the other side of the Atlantic. That crew was under the command of a man named John Phillips, who had begun his career as a pirate six months earlier. Phillips and four other men had been part of a fishing crew working near Newfoundland when, in late August 1723, they deserted their captain in a stolen schooner and set out as pirates. Since then, Phillips had made at least fourteen captures, a combination of fishing and merchant vessels, and had increased the size of his crew to about a dozen men, some of them willing recruits and others forced captives.

One of the first captives taken by Phillips after he set out as a pirate was a young fisherman named John Fillmore, who would become the great-grandfather of the future U.S. president Millard Fillmore. Just twenty-two years old in 1723, Fillmore had grown up near Ipswich, Massachusetts, a small coastal village about twenty-five miles north of Boston and just a few hours' sail up the coast from Marblehead. Built on the Ipswich and Chebacco Rivers, Ipswich had a number of farms, and its rivers powered several gristmills and sawmills. But situated along the Atlantic coast, Ipswich was, like Marblehead, a fishing village and seaport with several wharves along the cove. The stories brought back to the village by men who worked at sea had a powerful impact on the young Fillmore: "hearing sailors relate the curiosities they met with in their voyages, doubtless had a great effect, and the older I grew the impression became the stronger," Fillmore recalled. Fillmore's father had been a sailor and Fillmore himself spent his years growing up dreaming of going to sea.[6]

But Fillmore's mother hated the idea. She was determined that he should stay at home because her husband—Fillmore's father—had died at sea. Years earlier, his father's crew had been captured by a French privateer while sailing home from a voyage to the Caribbean. That was during the years of hostilities between England and France known as the War of Spanish Succession. French frigates captured hundreds of New England merchant vessels during the war, and many of the men working on these ships were taken as prisoners back to Martinique. Because of his father's experiences, the young Fillmore was forced by his mother to take work for several years on land as an apprentice to a local carpenter. It was not until the summer of 1723 that Fillmore took his first job at sea, working aboard the fishing schooner *Dolphin*.

The *Dolphin* was one of the pirate Phillips' first captures, on August 29, and Fillmore had sailed with Phillips since then. Phillips' growing crew now included the quartermaster John Rose Archer, a pirate who had previously sailed with the infamous Blackbeard. But by February 1724, many of the men aboard Phillips' ship—not just the captives but some of the pirates, too—were getting tired of the short-tempered captain. "Phillips was completely despotic," Fillmore later recalled, "and there was no such thing as evading his commands."[7]

It was in the first week of February that some of Phillips' crew tried to desert him. On February 4, the pirates were sailing off the coast of Maryland when they spotted a snow, a large, two-masted merchant vessel. They immediately started to chase it. But the snow was moving quickly through the water, making it difficult for the pirates to close the distance. The fiery-tempered Phillips was undaunted, however, and refused to give up. For three days the pirates chased the snow, at last coming within gunshot range and capturing it. Having seen how well the snow had sailed, Phillips decided to keep the vessel as a second ship. He sent three members of his crew and one of the forced men over to the snow to take command.

The men sent over to the snow were led by a pirate named Samuel Ferne, who had been with Phillips since he first formed the crew. But Ferne's loyalty to Phillips was crumbling. Like just about everyone else on the pirate ship, he was tired of dealing with Phillips' rage day in and out. "Phillips had now become so exceedingly arbitrary as to be hated by his own crew," Fillmore wrote. "But they stood in such dread of him that they durst no more contradict his orders than they durst to die." The night the pirates captured the snow, however, Ferne decided to abandon Phillips. Ferne and the other pirates extinguished all the lanterns aboard the snow and tried to slip away into the dark, open sea. But Phillips immediately suspected what Ferne was up to and put out all of his lights too. With both vessels darkened, neither had much of an advantage and Phillips was able to stay relatively close to the snow. At sunrise the next morning, Fillmore could still see the snow in the distance.

Phillips continued to chase the snow, trying to close the gap. It took two more days for Phillips to come within range of Ferne. By now he was fuming over the attempted desertion and ordered a cannon to be loaded with powder and shot. Drawing as close as he could to the snow, Phillips fired. That was enough to slow Ferne down. Phillips drew alongside the snow and shouted over to the other ship that the pirates should come back over to his ship immediately or the consequences would be deadly. Ferne refused. Instead, he cocked a pistol and fired directly at Phillips as he stood on the deck, but his shot missed its mark.

Fearing Phillips would fire again, the pirates and captured crew members aboard the snow hid below deck. Soon after, Ferne chose one of the four men who had come over with him from the pirate ship and sent him back up onto the deck. That unfortunate man was William Phillips, a sailor who'd been taken captive four months earlier and was no relation to the pirate captain. William Phillips had initially refused to sign the pirates' articles, but eventually he did; he later claimed he was forced to sign at gunpoint while the pirate captain Phillips threatened to "blow his brains out." He also said he had no part in Ferne's planned desertion and that Ferne had only told him they were going to sail to Martha's Vineyard, an island off the coast of Massachusetts, in order to escape. But Phillips the pirate captain had no way of knowing that. When William Phillips made his way back up onto the deck of the snow during the standoff, the pirates on the schooner assumed he was aligned with Ferne. One of the pirates fired with a pistol. The shot tore open William Phillips' left leg, and within a matter of days his wounded leg had to be cut off.[8]

By now, the pirates and captives below deck in the snow were starting to fear the rage of the captain Phillips. While Ferne and the others continued to hide out below decks, a boat full of captives, including some members of the snow's original crew, rowed over to the schooner, pleading to be taken on board. They also brought word that Ferne and his two accomplices were ready to surrender. Ferne had promised to faithfully serve Phillips again, they said, if Phillips would forgive them for the desertion.

Phillips sent a boat with eight men aboard back over to the snow to bring the three deserters back. When they returned, Phillips was waiting for them on the deck of the schooner, a sword in one hand and a pistol in the other. Ferne barely had time to take in the scene. The instant Ferne stepped onto the deck, Phillips drove his sword almost entirely through his body. A moment later, he shot Ferne in the head. He then killed another of the deserters, James Wood, in the same manner, and the bodies of both men were thrown overboard. Phillips then let the crew of the snow sail away, along with a few other captives, and the pirates continued to head north up the Atlantic coast.

❧❧❧❧❧

Just over a month later, on March 15, 1724, a ship with a cargo of logwood was slowly making its way through the cays off the coast of Belize, headed out into the Bay of Honduras. The ship was carrying close to one hundred tons of logwood cut by the Baymen and was finally setting out on its return trip to London. The ship's captain, Richard Hawkins, planned to head out of the bay in a northeasterly direction for Jamaica, stop there to resupply, and then head back to England. The first leg of his voyage, from England to the Caribbean, had already been difficult enough, struggling day after day to push the ship forward against contrary winds, and Hawkins was hoping for a smoother passage home. But the Bay of Honduras and the coves around the islands of Roatan and Guanaja continued to be popular hunting grounds for both pirates and Spanish vessels, and any passage through these waters was perilous for a merchant ship.

On March 22, exactly one week after Hawkins' crew set sail from Belize, they saw two vessels bearing down on them. One of them was a large, three-hundred-ton galley with three tall masts and several dozen men aboard. The other was a sloop. Hawkins immediately sensed that the men standing aboard the deck of the galley were pirates, standing ready to attack at the ship's twelve guns. And as he would soon learn, the man shouting orders from the deck was the quartermaster who'd just deserted Edward Low and was now a new pirate captain, Francis Spriggs.[9]

Two days earlier, Spriggs had captured the other vessel that was accompanying him, a sloop from Newport, Rhode Island. Spriggs' crew now came alongside Hawkins' ship and boarded it. The pirates ruthlessly ripped the ship apart, taking cable, rigging, several sails, and the ship's boat, then destroying everything else. "Every thing that pleased them not they threw overboard," Hawkins later wrote. "All my compasses, instruments, books, escritoire, binnacle, and in short, every individual thing they destroyed; broke all my windows, knocked down the cabin, seized all my small arms and ammunition, and then delivered me my ship in despicable condition." The pirates also plundered the captured sloop, then set it on fire and let the charred hulk sink into the sea.

Spriggs' crew surveyed the line of seamen from the captured ships, looking for likely recruits. They took several men from each of the ships, including Hawkins' first mate, a man named Burridge. Within a matter of days, however, the men who were taken apparently decided to sign on as members of Spriggs' crew. Late one evening, around eleven o'clock at night, Hawkins and some of the other captives were on the dark deck when a series of shouts erupted from inside the ship's cabin. A crowd of rowdy pirates then came out onto the deck, raised their black flag, and "fired all the guns in the ship, with repeated shouts." Hawkins asked "the reason of this joy" and was told his former mate, Burridge, had just joined the crew.

As many pirate captives learned firsthand, men who resisted the pirates' offer to join the crew or who got on the wrong side of the pirates while they were being held captive quickly became the target of all kinds of abuse. After holding Hawkins and the other prisoners for about ten days, Spriggs prepared to let the men go free. The captives got ready to sail away in Hawkins' battered ship. The pirates asked one of the captives if he wanted to stay on with the pirates or to go free. But the question couldn't possibly have been serious; in fact it was a cruel joke, since the pirates already knew what the answer would be. The sailor was a quiet man who kept to himself, "sober and grave," and he had refused to take part in any of the drinking or celebrations. Even now, in the face of the pirates' questioning, he was too scared to speak. But the pirates pressed him, so he answered that he had a family and "a small estate" back home—none of which was true—and that he preferred to leave with Hawkins. "Yes, yes," the pirates shouted. "You shall go, and we will give you your discharge on your back." The pirates took up a leather strap and whipped the captive repeatedly, striking him with ten lashes from each of the dozens of pirates aboard the ship.

Hawkins was then allowed to depart in his ship, along with the remaining members of his crew and the captain and crew from the Newport sloop the pirates had burned. Hawkins sailed away from Spriggs' galley, and about four hours later, the pirates were out of sight. Hawkins and the other freed captives set out again for Jamaica. The very next day, however, Hawkins saw a large ship in the distance. It looked like it could be a Spanish vessel and Hawkins immediately set a course away from it. By nightfall he had lost sight of the ship and believed he was safe. It was a clear night, however, and the stars were shining brightly over the dark Caribbean Sea, which made it possible for the other ship to spot Hawkins. Before long, the ship came alongside. Hawkins could make out dozens of men lining the deck in the dark night. The crew then blasted Hawkins' vessel, shattering the night with two broadside cannon blasts and several loud volleys of musket shot from the men standing on the deck. Hawkins and the others shouted out for the men to stop firing, saying they would surrender, begging to be given safe quarter. The attackers then ordered Hawkins to row over to their ship.

Hawkins climbed into a canoe—Spriggs had taken his boat and left the canoe in its place—and paddled over. Drawing closer, he realized it was Spriggs' crew, the same pirates who had released him only a day earlier. Standing on the deck, Spriggs' crew had thought they were only moments away from the plunder and spoils of a newly captured ship. Their hopes were instantly dashed. The pirates were furious to learn they'd spent close to a day chasing down a ship they'd already destroyed. Hawkins had barely climbed up onto the deck when the pirates jumped on him in a rage. "As soon as I was over their side, they were so incensed that I was not a Spaniard or some other vessel to their purpose that I was surrounded by fifteen men with cutlasses in their hands, who all made at me and soon laid me on the deck, some giving me the edge, others favored me with severe blows with the flat," Hawkins wrote.

Lying helpless on the deck, it seemed to Hawkins as though the enraged pirates were going to stab him until he died, but his former mate, Burridge, spoke up and asked the men to spare the captain. The pirates backed off, but were still in a drunken, raucous mood, "being then very merry, as it is customary for them at that time of night," Hawkins wrote. Spriggs' crew brought the rest of the captives back onto the ship and then set fire to Hawkins' ship. The blaze lit up the dark night until eventually the ruined ship sunk into the sea. The pirates then turned their fury back to the recaptured group of prisoners.

❧❧❧❧

The cohort of pirates who sailed under Low were among the most successful and most violent in history. While the legends of infamous pirates like Edward Teach (Blackbeard) and Bartholomew Roberts ("Black Bart") live on today, the names of Low and Spriggs are little-known. But in the years between 1722 and 1725, Low and Spriggs captured more ships than just about any other pirates of the era, and the impact of their bloody rampage was felt throughout the Caribbean and Atlantic. After deserting Low, Spriggs and Shipton would continue to cruise the Caribbean, reuniting and sailing together for much of the next year and capturing a number of merchant vessels in the area. Spriggs would meet up and sail with Low again as well. And within a year's time, the pirates would be hiding out again at Roatan, just miles from where Philip Ashton was still living on a cay with the Baymen.[10]

Low and Spriggs were known more than anything for the horrific torture of their victims. Their violence could be ruthless. They tortured captives to learn where money and treasures were hidden aboard a ship, to punish captains who'd mistreated their crews, to force captives to join their crews, and, as Hawkins would witness that night, sometimes just for fun. Just three days before Hawkins was captured by Spriggs, the colonial governor of the Caribbean Leeward Islands, John Hart, urged the British government to offer a large reward and even a pardon for members of Low's crew, if that would help put an end to Low's reign. "This Lowe is notorious also for his cruelty even to the subjects of the British Nation," Hart wrote, "and as a greater monster never infested the seas, I submit it to your Lordship's superior judgment, whether it ought not to be recommended to H.M. that a Proclamation be issued, even with pardon to his accomplices, offering an ample reward to such as should bring him in alive or dead."[11]

Low's tortures typically involved slicing off—and often roasting over a fire—parts of a captive's body. Low cut off and broiled the lips of a Portuguese captain and he cut the ears or nose off other captains and roasted them, as well, sometimes forcing the victim to eat his own cooked flesh. Low even sliced the heart out of one of the sea captains he captured. Low and his former partner, George Lowther, were both known to touch flaming matches to the thin piece of flesh between captives' fingers to force the men to reveal the location of any money or other valuables aboard a ship. Lowther burned the fingers of two captives aboard a ship he captured in September 1723, and Low had burned many captives the same way after he took several ships near Cuba earlier that year. By comparison, Spriggs' treatment of captives could seem mild. But the night the pirates burned Hawkins' ship, Hawkins and the other prisoners were taken below deck and run through Spriggs' terrifying gauntlet known as the "sweat."

First the pirates gave Hawkins a plate of candles. "I was sent for down to the cabin to supper," Hawkins wrote. "What should be provided for me but a dish of candles, which I was forced to eat, they having a pistol at my head and a naked sword to my breast, whilst others beat me with swords called tucks." Then Hawkins was taken to the dark, cramped space between decks. A group of men—both captives and pirates— stood around the base of one of the ship's tall masts. Each of the masts ran vertically through the middle of the ship, from above decks down through the vessel and into the base of the ship's hull. A section of the thick, round mast filled the center of the compartment where the men now stood. A ring of candles was placed around the mast and, a few feet further out, "about twenty-five" pirates who were gathered there formed a circle. The pirates all held sharp objects in their hands, an assortment of swords, knives, pitchforks, and sticks.

One of the captives was brought into the circle formed by the ring of pirates and a member of the crew began playing a jig on his fiddle. As the music started, the captive was told to start running in circles around the mast. As he ran, the pirates each jabbed and poked him with their weapons, "the villainous crew all the time striking the poor man with penknives in a miserable manner," one survivor recalled. The man ran circles for about ten minutes before he was released, sweaty, exhausted, and more than likely bleeding from the cuts and gashes on his body. A new captive was then brought into the circle and the ritual was repeated. When it came time for Hawkins to step into the ring, once again his former mate Burridge came to his defense, saying the captain "never did any man any ill." Another forced man, Joseph Cooper, who'd been captured shortly before Hawkins, then spoke up as well. Hawkins had done nothing against the pirates, the men argued, and the crew had already destroyed his ship and left him with nothing. He deserved to be spared, they said.[12]

Life aboard Spriggs' ship could be rough even for members of his own crew. Hawkins noticed that the pirates would take a vote each morning to determine who among them was drunk the night before, and whoever it was would be punished either by getting ten lashes from every member of the crew or by having to stand a four-hour watch atop the ship's mast. The daily ritual struck Hawkins as something of a farce, however, since the pirates seemed to choose the same few men as the drunkards to be punished each day. "I observed it generally fell on one or two particular men," Hawkins wrote, "for were all to go aloft that were fuddled overnight, there would be but few left to lookout below."

Now that they had burned Hawkins' ship, the pirates had no way to get rid of the captives. But they found a solution two days later when their ship neared the island of Roatan. Spriggs decided to dump the men there on the remote island. Of course, the island was not entirely uninhabited since, at the time, Ashton was still living there somewhere near Roatan's eastern end. This is one of the incredible coincidences of Ashton's story—one, unfortunately for Ashton, that he never knew about. For at least a week's time, a small group of other captives were living on Roatan at the same time Ashton was. But Roatan is almost thirty miles long and heavily wooded, and the men were probably marooned on a faraway shore, miles from Ashton.

The pirates left nine men on the island: Hawkins, the captain of the other captured and burned ship, who was named Samuel Pike, and seven other men, which could have included one passenger and one member of Spriggs' crew that the pirates wanted to get rid of. The men were put on the island with a few supplies, so initially they were much better off than Ashton was when he was first marooned. Hawkins was wearing a shirt, pants, shoes, and an old hat. He had a cutlass, a musket, and a small supply of gunpowder and shot. The men also had some flour and about a week's supply of beef and brandy. "The manner of our living on the island was tolerable considering our circumstances, for we were not sent away empty-handed," Hawkins wrote.

But their good fortune was short-lived. Most of the flour they had with them was soon ruined when it got wet in a rainstorm. One of the castaways, the passenger, died on the island. And on their second day ashore, two of the men from Pike's ship told the group they had plenty of experience living in the wild and they were certain they could kill enough hogs to keep them all well fed. They left the next day, taking the musket, gunpowder, and cutlass with them, but they never came back. Hawkins and the remaining men were forced to forage for food by hand. They combed the beach for shellfish, which they cleaned off in the sand and seawater and then boiled in a pewter bowl filled with whatever muddy water they could find.

The men stayed on Roatan for only a short time, however. They soon met up with two men who were living on a nearby cay and had come over to Roatan in their canoe. One of them, James Farmer, was probably a Bayman who had escaped from the Spanish on several occasions. The other man had escaped from another crew of pirates. Making several trips back and forth, the two men brought Hawkins' group to several other cays where they had camps, although conditions there were only slightly better. The men suffered from the constant biting of the vicious insects that lived on the wild islands, and finding clean drinking water continued to be a struggle. In addition to shellfish, the men also killed and roasted many iguanas, which Hawkins said tasted "as sweet as any rabbit."

The men's condition improved a week or so later when the group moved again to a small island just off Guanaja. Here they found clean drinking water and a good supply of iguanas and shellfish. They also were able to eat coconuts they found on Guanaja and they beat an old nail from the canoe into a fishhook, which allowed them to catch a good-sized rockfish.

The men had been living on the islands for twenty-nine days when they finally spotted a sloop in the distance. The men raced to their fire and sent up a huge plume of smoke as a signal. The ship saw them and turned toward shore. The next day, a second ship came in as well. Hawkins and his men sailed with one of the ships to Jamaica and from there to England, arriving back home in August. Pike and his men sailed in the other ship for Bermuda and then arrived back in Newport in July. The two men who'd abandoned Hawkins' group shortly after they'd been cast away stayed on the islands. They had apparently lost their musket and broken their cutlass in the woods and decided to stay with the Bayman, James Farmer, for a while longer.

By the middle of the summer of 1724, Spriggs met back up with the rest of his former crewmates, now led by the pirate Richard Shipton, who had been chosen as captain after the crew set Low adrift. After leaving Hawkins and the other captives on Roatan, Spriggs had sailed in a northerly direction past Florida, where he captured several more ships off the coast of the Carolinas and Virginia in the last few days of April and the first week of May. He took one or two men from each of these three ships as forced men. By June Spriggs had returned to the Caribbean, where his crew continued to ransack the trading ships they captured. After taking a vessel near the island of Saint Kitts around the first of June, Spriggs' crew found several horses aboard the ship, a diversion too good to pass up. "The wanton pirates rode the horses backward and forwards upon the deck," a survivor reported. But Spriggs' men were apparently frustrated by the lack of riding equipment aboard.

The pirates "swore they wanted boots and spurs, and whipped the men very cruelly because they had not brought them those accoutrements, whereby they might ride like gentlemen." Not long after that Spriggs, now somewhere near Aruba, met up again with Shipton. After Spriggs careened his galley, he and Shipton decided to sail together back toward the Bay of Honduras.[13]

The crews were sailing north through the channel that separates Cuba and Hispaniola (present-day Haiti and Dominican Republic) when they spotted a ship making its way out of Hispaniola. The pirates overtook the ship and Spriggs ordered the crew to lower its boat and row over to his galley. One of the captives who came over was a man named Nicholas Simmons, who had spent the past several months working on merchant vessels sailing in the Caribbean. Simmons was trained as a navigator, a valuable skill aboard a ship, and Spriggs tried to convince him to join the crew. Spriggs first fed Simmons and gave him a drink or two, but the pirates soon turned vindictive when Simmons still refused to sign the ship's articles. Like Hawkins, Simmons was forced to eat a plate of candles. "They treated me very plentifully and having eat and drank enough to satisfy me they discovered their minds unto me and persuading me to sign their Articles, which I refused," Simmons later wrote. "He [Spriggs] said he would fill my belly with other sort of diet and he sent the boy to fetch two candles in a plate which he made me eat. . . . He leaving me, the rest of the company fell upon me and beat me, some saying I should go with them and some saying I should not."

Simmons was in for a taste of a "sweat" by Spriggs' crew as well. Simmons saw some members of Spriggs' crew holding weapons, wooden sticks that had needles or nails protruding from the end of each one. He asked the pirates what their weapons were for and they said they were for "sweating." "I asked them the meaning of that," Simmons recalled, "and they told me to run round the mast and they to prick me as I ran around." Simmons decided to take his chances swimming for the other ship rather than subjecting himself to more torture. Dashing away from the pirates standing around the deck, he jumped overboard into the water. A boat was sent to pick Simmons up and he was eventually brought onto the second ship, under Shipton's command, where he would be held for the next several months.

By the end of August, the pirates had reached the western edge of the Bay of Honduras, off the coast of Belize. The ships were running low on supplies and had less than a week's worth of food on board and very little gunpowder. But the busy logwood trade meant there was a steady stream of ships in the area, and it looked as though the pirates would end the summer with a successful run of luck. On August 27, 1724, the pirates closed in on a well-armed ship, called the *Joseph Galley*, from London. Almost immediately before or after that capture, they also took about nine more vessels from London, France, and the New England colonies. Shipton decided to keep one of the ships, the London-based *York*, as part of his fleet, and the pirates set about moving the eighteen cannon mounted on the newly captured *Joseph Galley* over to the *York*.

On the morning of August 31, the pirates awoke to a calm day with very light winds in the bay. Spriggs was still in the former *Delight Galley*, which he now called *Bachelor's Delight*, mounting twenty-four guns. Shipton's sloop was named *Royal Fortune* and had twenty-two guns, though Shipton and some of his men had just moved over to the *York* after its capture. Shortly after noon, the pirates spotted four more ships in the distance and set out after them. It wasn't until they got closer that they realized one of them was a British warship, the HMS *Diamond*, heavily laden with men and arms. Spriggs was in for the battle of his life.[14]

❖❖❖❖❖

The man in command of the *Diamond* that summer was James Windham, whose life was already colored by a bumpy, up-and-down career both on land and at sea. The next twenty-four hours would prove to be one of Windham's closest encounters with Caribbean pirates during his time as captain of the warship. Sadly, it was also the last voyage of his life. Windham was thirty-seven years old, born in England in 1688, the youngest of eight children. He had gone to sea at an early age and seemed to enjoy sailing with the Royal Navy for several years, but by the time he was twenty-six he was still a lieutenant and was frustrated that he could not get promoted. "Really I am ashamed to be Lieutenant any longer," Windham wrote in 1714. Not long after, Windham returned to London and took a job in the office of Commissioners of the Duties Upon Salt. But his luck wasn't any better there, and by 1721 he was financially ruined.[15]

The end of Windham's career on land was sparked by London's South Sea Bubble of 1720. The South Sea Company had existed since 1711, but it took off in 1720 when, after an intense lobbying effort that included bribes to members of Parliament and a government payment of more than seven million pounds, the company outbid the Bank of England for the right to take over the bulk of the loans that comprised the British national debt. Investors like Windham quickly got caught up in enthusiasm for the company's plans, and the South Sea stock price jumped almost daily. The frenzied financial speculation surrounding the South Sea Company was, in James Windham's eyes, a get-rich-quick opportunity that seemed too good to pass up.[16]

Windham invested heavily. For several months the stock price continued to soar, at one point selling for ten times its initial price. Windham was practically giddy; "I grow rich so fast that I like stock jobbing of all things," he wrote to his brother. He also began looking to buy himself an estate. But the boom was too good to be true. By August of 1720, the South Sea Company stock price crashed. Windham was overextended, and his own finances collapsed along with the company's. Blaming the leadership of the South Sea Company, Windham had no money to pay his bills and was forced to default on loans, including one debt of twenty thousand pounds. "The directors have brought themselves into bankruptcy by being cunning artful knaves, I am come into the same state by being a very silly fool," Windham wrote. Perhaps sensing he might have better luck at sea, the man who would one day battle pirates in the Bay of Honduras decided by January of 1721 to return to the Royal Navy. "The sea is fittest for an undone man, and so I am for that," he wrote.[17]

Windham's failure as an investor nearly put him face-to-face with Low and Spriggs only days after they first captured Ashton. Now thirty-three years old, Windham was given command of the British warship *Solebay* in May 1721. He cruised in the North Atlantic for several months and captured at least twelve smuggling vessels that his crew brought back into Newcastle and Yarmouth. The *Solebay* then sailed for America, where it arrived at Newfoundland by the end of May 1722. The *Solebay* came close to battling Low and Spriggs just a month later when the pirates, sailing into Saint John's harbor in a thick fog, mistook the frigate for a merchant ship. But by that time Windham was no longer serving on the *Solebay*. He had since been given command of a larger ship and was soon on his way to the Caribbean.[18]

By August of 1724, Windham was in command of the HMS *Diamond*. The *Diamond* had arrived in the bay from Jamaica only the day after Spriggs, but Windham had already heard several reports about the pirates' activities in the area. The constant threat posed by both pirates and Spanish ships meant the *Diamond* would spend much of the next several years patrolling the bay and leading convoys of ships between the coast of Belize and Jamaica. In fact, it was the *Diamond*'s patrols in the bay that would soon lead to Ashton's rescue.

Nearing Guanaja on the evening of August 28, the crew of the *Diamond* saw smoke rising from a fire on the island. Windham was already on high alert, ready to chase down anything suspicious he saw. Just a week earlier, sailing past the Cayman Islands after leaving Jamaica, the *Diamond* had spotted a ship to the northeast and had immediately set off after it. But the ship had turned out to be one of the vessels that was accompanying the warship to the bay and had been separated from the fleet in a heavy rainstorm. Now, after spotting the smoke at Guanaja, some of the ship's crew took a yawl ashore to investigate, but they did not find any pirates, although they did meet up with some men who told them two pirate ships had passed by a few days earlier and were apparently headed for Roatan. The *Diamond* spent the next day sailing along the length of Roatan but saw no sign of pirates. On August 30, the *Diamond* reached the outer bay off the coast of Belize. The large warship was unable to find a place to anchor among the dozens of cays that border the coastline and had to spend the night in the channel between the Turneffe Islands and Glover's Reef, about thirty miles off the coast.[19]

The next morning, the *Diamond* headed inland toward the mouth of the Belize River. At about eleven o'clock that morning, the warship met up with some men in a canoe who told them about the flurry of recent ship captures by Spriggs and Shipton. Only a few hours later, the crew aboard the *Diamond* spotted the two pirate ships heading in their direction. The warship loaded its cannon and prepared for battle. A little over a year after surviving the battle with the *Greyhound,* Spriggs was now in for another bloody fight. The *Diamond* was heavily armed, with as many as forty large guns. As the *Diamond* came within range of the pirate ships, Spriggs could see some of the iron guns jutting out from the two rows of portholes that ran the full length of the battleship, one set of portholes on the upper deck and another on the lower deck. The men aboard the *Diamond* hunched over in the cramped space around the guns, ramming shot into the cannon and preparing to ignite the touchhole of each cannon as soon as the command to fire was given.

As soon as they were within range, Spriggs and Shipton both ordered their men to fire on the *Diamond*. Windham was facing a formidable enemy in Spriggs, who had been seeking to avenge the capture of nearly half of Low's crew the previous summer. Pirates never felt anything but hatred for the Royal Navy—even before the battle with the *Greyhound,* Low's crew once whipped a captive because he had previously served on a warship—but since losing many members of Low's crew after being defeated by the *Greyhound,* Spriggs made it known he planned to kill the warship's captain, Peter Solgard. After separating from Low, Spriggs told the men on vessels he captured that he was planning to go "to the banks of Newfoundland and get more men and then come upon this coast and take Captain Solgard." Another report claimed Spriggs punished men for even knowing Solgard. "He asked one man he had taken if he knew Captain Solegard, who answered no," the report stated. "He asked another the same question, who answered he knew him very well. On which Spriggs ordered him to be sweated."[20]

Spriggs' crew, in *Bachelor's Delight,* initially fired seven or eight shots at the *Diamond*. In the *York,* Shipton's fired at least twice. But the *Di-*

amond returned fire on Spriggs and came close to ending his career as a pirate then and there. At least two of the *Diamond*'s cannon blasts struck Spriggs' ship head-on, ripping off his bowsprit and tearing away the front edge of his foresail. Half a dozen men aboard the *Bachelor's Delight* were killed. A number of other pirates were seriously wounded, some of them losing an arm or a leg. Clearly outmatched, Spriggs turned to flee. The light winds made it hard for him to pick up any speed, but they also made it impossible for the *Diamond* to catch up to him. The bay off the coast of Belize is dotted with dozens of islands, cays, and reefs, and eventually Spriggs navigated his ship into some shoal waters among the cays that, at many points, were only twenty feet deep or less. As a result, the *Diamond* was unable to capture Spriggs in the *Bachelor's Delight*. "We gave her chase," Windham recorded in his logbook, "but by reason of the shoal water she got away." Spriggs escaped once again.[21]

Spriggs and Shipton both decided to clear out of the area. After firing several times on the *Diamond,* Shipton had abandoned the *York* and moved back onto his own sloop, the *Royal Fortune,* and sailed away. The next morning Shipton was sailing relatively close to the coastline when he spotted another ship that had been sailing with the *Diamond* the day before but had been separated. With the *Diamond* now some distance away, Shipton captured this new vessel, brought its captain over to his ship, and ordered the remaining men aboard the captured ship to follow him as they continued to make their way out of the bay. But by about three o'clock that afternoon, Shipton had a change of heart. The pirates released most of the prisoners they still had aboard from the recent captures and sent them off in a small boat. They then burned the ship captured that morning and sailed away.

Shipton planned to head north toward the American colonies, but he never made it. Sailing near what is today Key Biscayne in Florida, Shipton's sloop was shipwrecked. Most of the men aboard drowned, but about a dozen members of the crew—including Shipton, some pirates, and the captives Barlow and Simmons—survived. They had two small boats or *piraguas* with them at the time of the wreck and they took as much food, water, weapons, and ammunition as they could carry with them. Barlow and Simmons made it into one of the boats with one other member of Shipton's crew. They describe him as a pirate, but he may have been a reluctant one. Either by choice or because he was banished, he stayed with the two captives. Shipton and a handful of other pirates escaped in the second boat. Although they were close to the Florida coast, the men were worried about encountering natives if they went ashore, so they stayed at sea. Barlow, Simmons, and their companion eventually separated from Shipton and the other pirates and drifted in a southwesterly direction for about five days. By the evening of their fifth day at sea, they were off the Florida Keys. Coming near the shore to anchor for the night, the three men met up with Shipton and his crew again, and the pirates forced the men to stay with them when they headed out again the next day.

Shipton was probably more concerned about holding onto the second boat than he was with keeping Barlow and Simmons, since he let them go again in a few days. It was now December of 1724. Still in two small boats, the men made their way from the Florida Keys down to the western end of Cuba, where they found another small craft. Shipton put Barlow, Simmons, and the other man into the boat and tied it to one of their own boats so the three of them could not escape. The crew then made their way further west toward the Yucatan Peninsula. But when they were only about twenty-five miles off the coast of Cuba the weather took a turn for the worse. The pirates cut the captives' boat loose and let them fend for themselves in the rough seas. Riding out the storm, the three of them landed near Cape Catoche, the northernmost point of the Yucatan Peninsula, two days later. The next day, the men saw Shipton and his crew passing in their two boats, but Barlow, Simmons, and their companion stayed hidden from their view. The three men continued to hide out for another seven days, hoping the pirates would by then have gone some distance. But that plan did not work out. The men headed out again in a southerly direction, back toward the coast of Belize, where they hoped to find a logging sloop that would give them passage to New England. Before long they met up with Shipton's crew yet again.

Still in their *piraguas,* the band of pirates continued to move south along the coastline of Belize. One day in the third week of December, three of the pirates went out fishing and came back to the boats with word that two vessels, a sloop and a ship, were anchored in a cove near the Turneffe Islands, which lie directly off of what is today Belize City. This was precisely what Shipton and his men needed. If they could capture either of the vessels, Shipton could get his crew out of the *piraguas* and into a larger, more seaworthy craft and then get as quickly as possible out of the area in case the *Diamond* was still patrolling there. Though there were only about a dozen members of Shipton's crew, the pirates were well-armed and were able to capture both the sloop and the ship on December 22. Shipton took command of the sloop and brought the captain of the ship, the *John and Mary*, on board with him. He sent three of his pirates, along with Barlow and Simmons, to take command of the *John and Mary*, with orders to follow him. All five of the men sent over to the *John and Mary*, including Barlow and Simmons, were armed with several pistols to prevent any kind of uprising among the crew. The pirates struck the first mate of the *John and Mary*, Matthew Perry, wounding him in two places on his head, and tied his hands behind his back.[22]

At about eight o'clock on the morning of December 23, the pirates set off again in their two newly captured vessels. Shipton planned to get out of the area and head east for Roatan, but because of the extensive series of islands and cays scattered along the coast, they were forced to start out sailing in a southerly direction for most of the day. By nightfall, what had started out as a clear day had turned stormy. It was now raining hard and the winds had picked up considerably, making their navigation through the maze of cays and reefs all the more treacherous. Around ten o'clock that night, Shipton's sloop tacked to the east to head out of the bay. He signaled with a lantern for Simmons, who was navigating the *John and Mary*, to follow. But Simmons was worried that turning at that point would put them dangerously close to Glover's Reef, a large atoll about thirty miles off of Belize, and he did not change his course.

The next morning the men on the *John and Mary* thought they could make out Shipton's sloop in the distance, but they soon lost sight of it in the stormy weather. The hard rain and wind continued for another twenty-four hours. By the morning of December 26, the men were well south of Glover's Reef and spotted the island of Utila, another of the larger islands in the Bay of Honduras. Shipton had ordered the men to meet him at Utila if they got separated again. But Barlow and Simmons had other plans.

✻✻✻✻✻

Twice in 1724 captives aboard a pirate ship were able to overthrow the crew and sail their vessel to safety. In March of that year, shortly after the pirate John Phillips had executed two members of his crew for trying to escape, Phillips was sailing past the coast of Virginia in a northeasterly direction, heading toward New England. With the executions of Ferne and Wood, Phillips' crew was made up of seven other men, along with about a dozen captives, including John Fillmore.

Phillips' violent temper was still in full force. One of the vessels the pirates captured as they made their way north had some geese and hogs aboard, which offered the mouth-watering prospect of fresh meat to men who spent virtually all of their time at sea eating dried and salted food. Phillips demanded the live animals, but the ship's captain refused and struck Phillips with a handspike, a long pole used on board the ship. Phillips quickly drew his sword and plunged it into the captain, killing him. Phillips also killed one of his own captives when he tried to sail away in the pirates' schooner while the pirates were aboard the two new captured ships.

The pirates then continued their sail up the Atlantic to the Isles of Shoals, off the coast of New England, where they found and captured close to a dozen fishing vessels. Boarding one of them, the quartermaster Archer and several other pirates beat and whipped the fishermen and then bound all the men except the captain and brought them back aboard their ship. Phillips and his men fired their guns repeatedly at the fishing schooner and cut a hole in its hull in order to sink it, although the hole was later patched and the fishermen were let go. In all, the pirates' run up the coast had been ruthless. "It is almost incredible to think what dreadful havoc, mischief, and wickedness the above four pirates and a few of their accomplices have acted and done in about eight weeks' time," the *Boston News Letter* would write a few weeks later, "robbing and taking out whatever they pleased, forcing, killing, beating and abusing them, and often killing some of their own crew."[23]

Amid the flurry of destruction and violence, however, Fillmore saw a glimmer of hope. Several of the new captives who had recently been brought aboard refused to join with the pirates. Within a day or two Fillmore decided they could be trusted. One of these new captives was Edward Cheesman, the carpenter aboard one of the ships taken near Virginia. Like Fillmore, Cheesman was willing to risk an escape. But the discussions among the captives, even in the darkened corners below decks, were dangerous. Even the slightest whisper caused the ever-watchful Phillips to suspect the men were up to something. One day Phillips accused one of the other captives of being in a plot to kill all the pirates. The man repeatedly denied the accusation, but Phillips only became more enraged. He thrust his sword into the man's chest, pushing it in as far as he could and then twisting it so sharply that the point of the sword broke off in the victim's spine. The man did not die immediately and continued to plead his innocence even as he lay bleeding on the deck, begging to be spared. Phillips was unmoved. He raised his pistol and shot the man in the head. The pirate captain then looked around at the men standing nearby, searching for Fillmore, whom he also suspected of being in on a plot. "I have sent one of the devils to hell, and where is Fillmore?" Phillips shouted. "He shall go next."

On Saturday, April 11, 1724, the British warship HMS *Seahorse* arrived in Boston Harbor from Saltertudas and immediately started restocking to set sail in search of Phillips, leaving nine days later. But the warship would never have a chance to catch up with the pirates. The break Fillmore and the other captives were desperately looking for came only a few days later, on April 14. By now, Phillips' crew had sailed as far north as Nova Scotia. They captured a sloop, the *Squirrel*, and took the new vessel as their own, moving their equipment, supplies, and weapons over the next day. The pirates allowed most of the captured sloop's crew to go free, but kept its young captain, Andrew Harradine, from Gloucester, Massachusetts. Within a day of Harradine's capture, Fillmore quietly approached him with the idea of planning an attack on the pirate crew. There were seven captives in on the plot, including Fillmore, Cheesman, and Harradine, and it seemed possible that they might be able to overpower the eight pirates if circumstances were right.[24]

Two days after moving over to Harradine's sloop, the pirates were in an especially raucous mood as they continued to sail north toward Newfoundland. They had captured as many as eighteen vessels in less than three weeks' time and had brought on board a huge supply of food and drink. The crew spent most of April 17 celebrating their success, eating and drinking late into the night. Sometime that evening, Phillips gave two orders: for Cheesman, the carpenter, to bring his tools up onto the deck so he could start work on some repairs early the next morning, and for the crew to make sure they took an observation of the sun at noon the next day to determine their position at sea. This gave the captives the opportunity they needed to form a plan.

Later that night, the pirates finally passed out. Some went to sleep in Phillips' cabin near the back of the ship and two others—the quartermaster Archer and a pirate named William White—lay down in the cook's area near the fireplace on deck. The two of them must have been drunk beyond comprehension because after they'd been asleep for a while, Fillmore was able to sneak up to Archer and White with a hot stick from the fire and burn the soles of their bare feet so badly that they would not be able to walk on the deck the next day. Nonetheless, the captives apparently decided not to try and overpower the pirates that night, either because some of them were still stirring or because they thought it would be better to wait until daylight.

When morning broke, the captives woke up and began their work, but there was no sign of the pirates, who remained fast asleep. By late morning, Cheesman had finished his repairs on the deck. The captives started to worry that if the pirates did not wake up in time to take the midday observation, their plan would fail. Finally, Fillmore stuck his head into Phillips' cabin and tried to wake the men, telling them the sun was almost at the meridian. Phillips swore at him and told him to go away. The pirates slept for another hour or so.

Finally, close to noon, Phillips and several other men stumbled out of the cabin. With barely a glance between Cheesman and Fillmore, the captives saw their chance. Most of the crew was now on deck. One of the pirates got ready to measure the angle of the sun with a wooden quadrant, its arm-length slats connected in the shape of a long and narrow triangle. Cheesman was standing with him. The pirate needed to hold the quadrant in front of him, his back to the midday sun, and measure the angle of the sun to the horizon by reading the position of the sun's shadow on the quadrant. That angle, when checked against a set of tables, would give them their approximate latitude, or how far north of the equator they were. As the men focused on measuring the ship's position, Phillips went back into his cabin to mold some lead slugs. The sails were full and the ship was moving through the water at a good rate, with one of the captives at the helm. Fillmore and Harradine were standing on the deck with several of the other pirates. Cheesman had intentionally left a broad axe resting on the deck after finishing his work that morning, and Fillmore stood casually spinning the broad axe with his foot.

In an instant the men attacked. First Cheesman grabbed the pirate standing next to him and threw him overboard. Fillmore bent over and picked up the broad axe at his feet and bore down on another of the pirates who was busy cleaning his gun, striking him over the head and killing him. Alarmed by the shouts and commotion on deck, Phillips came out of his cabin to see what was going on. The captive who was manning the tiller, a Native American named Isaac Lassen, jumped at Phillips and grabbed his arm while Harradine struck him over the head with an adze. Finally, two French captives jumped a fourth pirate, killed him, and threw him overboard.

In less than two minutes' time, four of the most active pirates on the crew, including Phillips, had been killed. The remaining pirates were now far outnumbered and immediately surrendered. The captives took control of the ship and headed home. They may have stopped briefly at Gloucester, Harradine's hometown, and then they sailed the ship down to Boston Harbor, arriving there on Sunday, May 3. As the ship passed the dozen or so islands that ring Boston Harbor, the surviving pirates White and Archer might have caught sight of Bird Island, one of several smaller mounds of land that were used at the time for the burial of executed pirates. It would have been an ominous sight for the men. Back on shore, the captives' stunning overthrow of the pirate crew fascinated the town. The *Boston News Letter,* the *Boston Gazette,* and the *New England Courant* each published accounts of how Fillmore, Cheesman, and Harradine brought down Phillips and his men. One report even suggested that the captives brought Phillips' head back to Boston with them. The men were put on trial nine days later, on May 12. Two members of Phillips' crew, William White and the quartermaster John Rose Archer, were convicted and hanged. After the execution, the bodies of White and Archer were hauled back out to Bird Island in Boston Harbor. White was buried on the island, while Archer's body was hung there in a gibbet "to be a spectacle, and so a warning to others."[25]

The village of Marblehead, Massachusetts, during Philip Ashton's lifetime. This 1763 painting by Ashley Bowen depicts a view of Marblehead from the harbor of the small fishing village. The church steeple at the far right of the painting is the First Church in Marblehead, which was then located on Franklin Street, where the minister John Barnard dedicated a sermon to Philip Ashton's amazing ordeal the Sunday after the young fisherman returned home. *Courtesy of the Marblehead Museum & Historical Society, Marblehead, MA.*

A fishing crew working on a schooner off the Canadian coast. It was in a schooner like this one that Philip Ashton and his five-man crew had spent the week fishing for cod off Cape Sable, at the southern tip of Nova Scotia, before their fateful sail to a secluded harbor on a Friday afternoon in June 1722. Drawing by H. W. Elliot and Capt. J. W. Collins. *Courtesy of National Oceanic and Atmospheric Administration/ Department of Commerce.*

A 1733 map of Acadia, present-day Nova Scotia. Along with a number of other Marblehead fishing vessels, Philip Ashton and his crew sailed into Port Roseway, near the southern tip of Nova Scotia, not realizing a pirate ship was already waiting there. *Courtesy of the David Rumsey Map Collection, www.davidrumsey.com.*

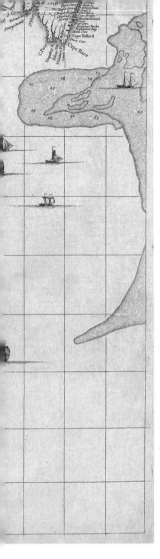

The official notice of Philip Ashton's capture by Edward
Low's pirate crew. This advertisement, printed in the *Boston
News Letter* on July 9, 1722, publicized the depositions
recorded by several Marblehead fishermen concerning the
capture of Philip Ashton, Joseph Libbey, and Nicholas
Merritt several weeks earlier. Nothing more would be
heard about Ashton for nearly three years. *Courtesy of the
Massachusetts Historical Society.*

The pirate captain Edward Low, as depicted in a book printed in 1736. While it is impossible to know exactly what Low looked like, one ship captain described the pirate, best known for his horrific forms of torture, as "a little man." *Courtesy of the John Carter Brown Library at Brown University.*

The pirate George Lowther, Low's first partner. Low began his pirate career sailing with Lowther, but the two separated after they captured the *Rebecca* in May 1722, only weeks before Ashton was captured. Low's crew would often stop at secluded islands and set up temporary camps, as shown here, while their ship was careened and repaired near the shore. *Courtesy of the John Carter Brown Library at Brown University.*

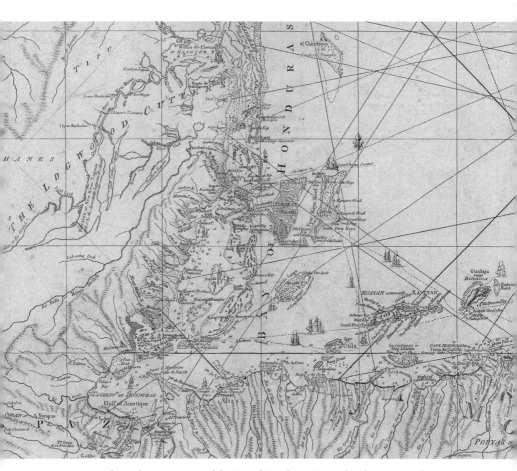

An eighteenth-century map of the Bay of Honduras. Located at the western edge of the Caribbean Sea, the bay was one of Low's favorite hunting grounds and hideaways. The island of Roatan ("Ruatan"), where Ashton escaped, is visible at the lower right part of the map. The coastal area of modern Belize, labeled "Logwood Cutters," is where the Baymen who would eventually rescue Ashton worked harvesting logwood. *Courtesy of the David Rumsey Map Collection, www.davidrumsey.com.*

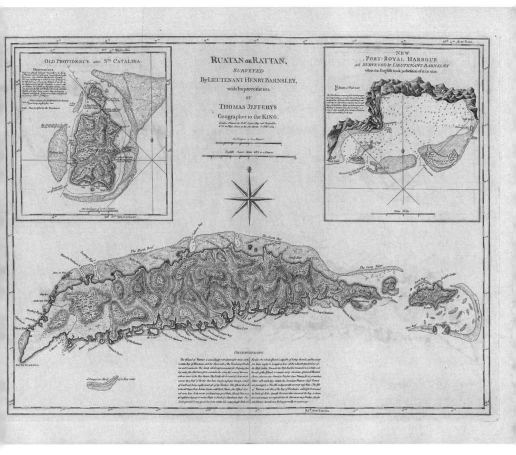

An early map of Roatan and Port Royal harbor. On this 1775 map of Roatan Island in the Bay of Honduras, Port Royal harbor, where Ashton was marooned, is to the far right, near the eastern end of the island. The survey of Port Royal harbor on this map dates back to 1742 and shows the location of several "rivulets of fresh water" that provided the opportunity for Ashton's escape. *Courtesy of the David Rumsey Map Collection, www.davidrumsey.com.*

OPPOSITE TOP The shore of present-day Port Royal, Roatan. When seven members of Low's crew went ashore to get fresh water on March 9, 1723, Ashton finally escaped. The mouth of a small creek is visible to the left of the photograph. This location was marked as a source of fresh water in a 1742 survey of the area by Lieut. Henry Barnsley. *Photograph by the author.*

OPPOSITE BOTTOM A small, windswept cay in Port Royal harbor. For many of the months he lived on Roatan, Ashton spent countless days on these small cays, which lie several hundred feet off the island's shore and atop the reef that borders the wide harbor. Ashton swam out to these cays to escape the mosquitoes and sand flies on the island and spent hours gazing at the empty the sea and waiting for help. *Photograph by the author.*

Torture aboard a pirate ship. Several of the captives taken by one of Low's quartermasters, Francis Spriggs, described being run through a gauntlet called the "sweat." Taken below deck, they were forced to run in circles around the mast while a group of pirates poked at them with pitchforks, knives, and swords. *Lebrecht Music and Arts Photo Library.*

A British warship attacks a pirate vessel at sea. One of Low's two sloops and about half his crew were captured by the warship HMS *Greyhound* after a brutal, day-long battle near the eastern tip of Long Island in June 1723. © *National Maritime Museum, Greenwich, London.*

The harbor at Newport, Rhode Island, in the early 1700s. The thin strip of land that extends into the harbor from the left is Gravelly Point, where Joseph Libbey and twenty-five other condemned men from Low's pirate crew were hanged in July 1723. The island in the foreground, with the fort, is Goat Island, where the men were buried after the execution. *Lithograph by John Perry Newell, courtesy of the Newport Historical Society.*

Ashton's Memorial.

A N

H I S T O R Y

OF THE

Strange Adventures,

A N D

Signal Deliverances,

O F

Mr. *Philip Ashton,*

Who, after he had made his Efcape from the
P I R A T E S, liv'd alone on a Defolate
Ifland for about Sixteen Months, &c.

W I T H

A fhort Account of Mr. *Nicholas Merritt,*
who was taken at the fame time.

To which is added

A S E R M O N on *Dan.* 3. 17.

By J o h n B a r n a r d, V. D. M.

——*We fhould not truft in our felves, but in God ;*
—— *who delivered us from fo great a Death, and doth
deliver ; in whom we truft, that he will yet deliver us.*
II. Cor. I. 9, 10.

B O S T O N, N. E. Printed for *Samuel Gerrifh,*
at his Shop in Corn-Hill, 1 7 2 5.

Cover page of *Ashton's Memorial,* first Boston printing, 1725. A second
edition of the narrative was printed in London in 1726 and may even have
been read by Daniel Defoe. Several details about Low's crew from *Ashton's
Memorial* appeared in a new book about pirates that has been attributed to
Defoe. *Courtesy of the Massachusetts Historical Society.*

Edward Low's treasure map. A map of Isle Haut in the Bay of Fundy that was acquired by the historian Edward Rowe Snow in 1947, which bears the inscription "E. Low" at the bottom. Based on this map, Snow found Spanish and Portuguese coins of gold and silver buried on the island, near the spot marked "The Place." *Map originally published in Edward Rowe Snow,* True Tales of Pirates and Their Gold *(Dodd, Mead, and Company, 1966); used with permission of Dolly Snow Bicknell.*

CHAPTER 8

As One Coming
from the Dead

Back in the Bay of Honduras, Jonathan Barlow and Nicholas Simmons were hatching a plan to take control of the *John and Mary.* Shortly after setting sail and separating from the pirate Richard Shipton, Barlow and Simmons had untied Matthew Perry, the first mate of the *John and Mary,* but the men then had to find a way to catch the pirates who were aboard their ship off guard. While Barlow and Simmons had been given pistols when they came aboard, the three pirates that Shipton sent over were also heavily armed; one of them had four pistols with him. Now that the captives were separated from Shipton, they saw their chance. Rather than sailing to Utila as Shipton had ordered, they decided to sail to the island of Guanaja. Once there, they planned to have several of the pirates go onto the island to hunt for food and, while they were ashore, steal away in the ship.

But that plan fell apart when they unexpectedly caught up with Shipton once again. Sometime between two and four o'clock on the afternoon of December 27, they arrived at a cay on the southern side of Guanaja. Approaching the shore, they saw Shipton was already there, anchored just a short distance away. Shipton and three members of his crew soon came over to the *John and Mary* to take stock of the situation. They also plundered the ship; in their rush to get away from the coast of Belize four days ago, the pirates probably had not taken the time to thoroughly search the ship. Now they did.

Before heading back to his vessel for the evening, Shipton gave orders for the next day. He was apparently tired of repeatedly getting separated from the captives' ship in bad weather, so they would wait to see what the morning brought. If the weather was good, they were to sail in consort to nearby Roatan, where Spriggs was anchored with five captured ships. But if the weather was bad, they were to load all of the captives onto Shipton's sloop and then burn the *John and Mary*. They would then sail in a single ship to meet up with Spriggs. What is striking about the congregation of all these vessels near Roatan is that Philip Ashton was still in the area too, living with the Baymen not far from Guanaja, on the Pigeon Cays. While Barlow and Simmons were planning their escape, Ashton had no idea that Spriggs and Shipton were back at the islands. But that would change in a matter of days.

When Shipton and his crew rowed back to their ship that evening, Barlow and Simmons realized time was running out. Once they reunited with the temperamental Spriggs, any chance of escape would be lost. In desperation they decided to take on the pirates that evening. Barlow gave Perry one of his pistols, and at about seven o'clock, only hours after arriving at Guanaja, Perry approached the most heavily armed pirate, cocked his pistol, and snapped it. But the gunpowder loaded in the pistol must have been damp, perhaps from the heavy rains of the past few days, and the pistol misfired. Hearing the snap, the pirate immediately grabbed one of his own pistols and fired at Perry, but his first shot misfired as well. Perry then scrambled away toward the stern of the ship.

At that point Simmons stepped out of the ship's cabin and fired his pistol at the pirate. Simmons' pistol went off, and the bullet killed the pirate instantly. Simmons then pointed a pistol at another of the pirates and told him to surrender. But the warning was too late. Barlow and several other captives were already jumping toward the pirate and killed him as well. The only remaining member of Shipton's crew who was still alive now surrendered. Barlow, Simmons, and Perry had control of the *John and Mary*.

The men needed to move quickly. Shipton was only a short distance away and it was likely someone had heard the pistol firing. With not even minutes to spare, the men didn't take the time to haul up their anchor but instead cut their cable, loosened the sails, and headed out. They were able to slip around the island of Guanaja and sail off, and they arrived back in Newport, Rhode Island, just four weeks later.

While the *John and Mary* made it safely home, it sailed back into Newport as a plundered ship that had no cargo and a missing captain. The unusual circumstances surrounding the ship's return led to a flurry of legal activity. Even though they were not pirates, the ship's crew had some explaining to do. One week after arriving in Newport, Matthew Perry, the first mate of the *John and Mary*, gave a sworn statement describing the crew's capture by Shipton and the crew's efforts to escape. Perry's statement sought to make it clear that the pirates—not any negligence on his or his crew's part—were responsible for the failure of the voyage. The "aforesaid crew and company of the pirates," Perry stated, was the "only and sole occasion of hindering the aforesaid ship from prosecuting her said intended voyage for Honduras and also of the damage done in the loading and cargo of said ship."[1]

Three weeks later, Perry, Simmons, Barlow, and seven other members of the crew on the *John and Mary* were brought to trial at the Newport townhouse. The trial began on February 24 and was held because the men, with "force and arms," had killed "two of the subjects of our Lord the King," but because these two "subjects" were by all accounts pirates, there never seemed to be any question of the crew's innocence. The men recounted their capture and escape, and all of them were found not guilty.

A number of the men captured by the pirates petitioned the government in Rhode Island, seeking compensation for their ordeal. Three of the crew members from the *John and Mary* claimed they should be compensated for the expense of their trial and because "they rescued the barque from the pirates." They were awarded ten pounds each. In one of the more unusual statements ever given by a pirate captive, three months after the trial Simmons also filed a petition in Boston claiming his capture by the pirates had terrorized him so much that he couldn't go back to working on ships. "And in as much as the said Nicholas Simmons is now under a necessity to leave off his employment of a mariner for fear of the said pirates and has a new employment to seek for his support, he being in but low circumstances," Simmons' petition stated, "he therefore most humbly prays your honors would be pleased to take the premises into your most just and wise consideration and bestow of your bounty upon him as in your accustomed goodness you shall see meet."[2]

While Barlow and Simmons made it safely to Newport after sailing away from Guanaja on the evening of December 27, 1724, the pirates they'd left behind, Francis Spriggs and Richard Shipton, were still anchored near Roatan. That would prove to be nearly fatal for Philip Ashton, who in December 1724 was still living with the Baymen not even thirty miles from where the pirates had gathered.

Ashton had been with the Baymen for about seven months. By December, however, the Baymen were getting ready to leave. They had decided to take their boats back to the mainland to see if it was safe to return there and, if not, to collect more of their supplies. To prepare for the journey of anywhere from thirty to one hundred miles across the open bay, the men hauled their *piraguas* up onto the shore to dry them out and seal them with a fresh coating of tar to close any leaks.

Meanwhile, Ashton and three of the Baymen took a *piragua* over to Guanaja to go hunting. The *piragua* they took was fitted out with a sail, which reduced the amount of paddling they would need to do in order to make the crossing. Ashton had previously encountered the Spanish on his solitary trip to Guanaja, and on this trip Ashton and his companions barely missed Shipton's two vessels there. They saw nobody on the island and had a successful hunt, filling their canoe with both tortoise and a good supply of meat.

It was late in the evening, well after dark, when the men returned to their camp at the small cay. Suddenly, the quiet of the night was shattered by a flash of light and loud gunshot. The shot came from a small swivel gun mounted on a *piragua* that was riding in the water just off the Baymen's small island. A minute or two later, they heard more firing, eighteen to twenty gunshots in all. It sounded to Ashton like the shots were coming both from aboard the *piragua* and from the beach. It was clear the Baymen's camp was under attack.

Hoping to remain hidden in the night, Ashton and his three companions tore down their sail and paddled as quickly as they could away from the cay, heading toward another of the smaller islands less than two miles away. They didn't escape unseen, however. "But they either saw us before we had taken our sail down, or heard the noise of our oars as we made out of the harbor, and came after us with all speed," Ashton wrote. A group of four or five of the attackers set out after them in a *piragua,* quickly closing the distance between the two boats. The attackers fired at the men from the *piragua* but their first volley of bullets overshot the canoe. Ashton and his companions paddled as fast as they could, finally reaching the shore of the small island. They scrambled out of their boat, but the attackers started firing at them again with their muskets. Abandoning their *piragua* on the beach, the men tore into the woods.

The attackers then called out to them, saying they were pirates, not Spaniards, and would not hurt them. This only made Ashton run faster. "But they could not have mentioned any thing worse to discourage me from having anything to do with them, for I had the utmost dread of a pirate," Ashton wrote. "And my first aversion to them was now strengthened with the just fears that if I should fall into their hands again, they would soon make a sacrifice of me for deserting them."

The pirates did not spend much time searching for Ashton and the three Baymen after they fled into the woods, satisfied instead to take the *piragua* left on the beach and paddle away. Though he was no longer alone, Ashton was again marooned on an uninhabited island, hiding out from nearby pirates. While the Baymen had guns to hunt with, they didn't dare use them or even light a fire to cook any food because they were worried about giving away their location. So they remained hidden in the woods and ate raw food for five days until they saw the pirates sail away from the islands.

Shortly after the pirates had left, the remaining Baymen—those who'd survived the attack back on their camp on the cay—paddled over to search for Ashton and the other missing men. As the man they called "Father Hope," the leader of the Baymen, started to describe the attack, it became clear that Ashton's escape a few days earlier was even narrower than he could have imagined. The pirates who had attacked them were from Spriggs' crew. When several of Spriggs' men had noticed the Baymen's camp on the nearby cay, Spriggs had sent a party to investigate, and they ended up attacking the Baymen who were there. Only when Spriggs' vessels had set sail from Port Royal harbor on Roatan—the same secluded harbor on Roatan where Ashton had first escaped—did the Baymen come in search of Ashton and the men he was hiding with on the island where they had fled.

It was a perilously close call for Ashton. " 'Tis very apparent that if I had been with my companions at the usual residence, I had been taken with them; and if I had, it is beyond question (humanely speaking) that I should not have escaped with life, if I should the most painful and cruel death that the madness and rage of Spriggs could have invented for me," Ashton wrote.

As it was, the attack by Spriggs' men on the Baymen's camp had been nothing short of brutal. The pirates had killed one of the Baymen and tossed his body into a tar-covered *piragua* the Baymen had been repairing. Lighting the boat on fire, the pirates burned the victim's corpse in it. The native woman the Baymen had brought with them was taken and "shamefully" abused. The rest of the Baymen were taken aboard one of the two ships in Spriggs' fleet and subjected to more barbarous treatment. At least one of the Baymen turned pirate and revealed that their leader, Hope, had supplies or valuables hidden on the island. The pirates then beat Hope violently to force him to reveal the location of his hiding place and then, once he did, retrieved his stash and took it with them.

After they'd spent about five days in the harbor, the pirates gave the

Baymen a "flat," possibly a square, barge-like craft, and prepared to leave. They made Hope and his crew swear that they would not rescue the men they had seen flee to the nearby island. But Hope quickly abandoned that promise and came searching for the men as soon as the pirates sailed off.

Despite the loss of several of the *piraguas,* Hope and the other Baymen were still determined to make the return trip to the mainland as planned. Ashton's first inclination was to go with them. But Hope, despite the kindness he had shown toward Ashton, argued against it. There was barely enough room on the flatboat for all of his men, and if Ashton came along that would mean crowding on one more person. They also had a scarce supply of food for the journey, and making the long trip over open water in the flat was likely to be dangerous. In addition, Hope argued, if the situation back at the logging camps seemed safe, the Baymen were likely to remain for some time, probably moving inland in search of logwood, which would stand in the way of Ashton's goal of finding passage back to New England. Hope told Ashton he should stay with two other men who were remaining behind at the islands, a man named John Symonds and his African slave.

Symonds wanted to stay on the islands because he hoped to trade with ships from Jamaica as they passed through the bay. Symonds also urged Ashton to stay with him, arguing that Ashton stood a greater chance of encountering a ship bound for New England at the islands than he did back on the mainland. Symonds planned to go back to the mainland himself once the rainy season had ended in the hopes of meeting up with traders. In that event, Symonds argued, Ashton could secure passage to Jamaica on a vessel bound there and, once in Jamaica, could easily find a ship headed back to New England. "I thought, upon the consideration of the whole, that there seemed to be a fairer prospect of my getting home by the way of Jamaica than the Bay; and therefore I said no more to Father Hope about going with him, but concluded to stay," Ashton wrote.

The Baymen set off, leaving Symonds with a boat and two dogs. The three men—Ashton, Symonds, and the African—spent several more months on the island. With the boat and Symonds' musket, they were able to go hunting on nearby islands and keep themselves fed, but due to the stormy rains of the winter season, the men did not go far nor did they ever have an abundance of food. Symonds was passing the time, waiting for the end of February when the rains would subside and the trading ships were likely to return to the bay.

Near the beginning of March—Ashton's two-year anniversary at the islands—Symonds decided to go searching the nearby islands for sea turtles. Turtle shells were a valuable commodity, and Symonds was confident he could get new supplies and clothing from the traders in exchange for them. After gathering a good supply of shells, Symonds then suggested going over to Guanaja again. Ashton and Symonds spent about five days on the island without incident, until the last week of March 1725. It was then that a hard tropical storm hit the area.

❧❧❧❧

That storm turned out to be a remarkable blessing for Ashton. At the same time Ashton and Symonds had decided to go over to Guanaja, the HMS *Diamond* had been getting ready to lead another large convoy of ships from the bay back to Jamaica. The *Diamond* was still spending much of its time in the bay since its battle with Spriggs the previous August, and the warship would continue to hunt for pirates in the area for the next year or so. Cruising among the cays at the mouth of the Belize River, the heavily armed warship chased down—or at least chased away—any unknown vessels that it saw. The *Diamond* had been riding in the bay since at least February. Around the beginning of March, the warship began preparing for the voyage back to Jamaica. The crew spent the second week of March cleaning the ship's hull. Anchoring the ship alongside one of the cays in the bay, the men careened the huge warship much as the pirate crews did, heeling the ship onto its side, then scraping the hull clean and applying a coat of tar. The *Diamond* also used the first few weeks of March to signal to the many English and colonial ships working in the area that the convoy would soon be heading out.

Every few days—and sometimes twice a day—the *Diamond* would fire its cannon and raise a pendant signaling that ships should get ready to depart, if they wanted to sail along with the warship back to Jamaica.

But even with the *Diamond* guarding the harbor, both pirates and Spanish patrols were still a threat. One day in the early part of March the *Diamond* met up with a vessel carrying four sea captains whose sloops had recently been taken by Spriggs. A little more than a week later, the *Diamond* got word that a Spanish half galley was in the area. That night, the warship fired a cannon and raised a light as a warning to other vessels. A few days later, at about eight o'clock in the morning, the crew of the *Diamond* spotted a small but heavily armed ship, carrying at least a dozen cannon and four swivel guns, sailing into the bay. The ship was flying an English flag, but as it came closer to the *Diamond* and the fleet of vessels that had gathered in the area with it, the men aboard the warship grew suspicious. The *Diamond* fired a warning shot at the approaching ship, but it did not stop. The *Diamond* fired a second shot at the ship. At this point the ship "sprung his luff and made what sail he could," attempting to sail away. At the same time it lowered the English flag it was flying and raised a Spanish flag in its place.

The *Diamond* quickly set out after the Spanish ship. Around midday, the crew of the Spanish ship decided to stop running from the *Diamond* and dropped anchor in very shallow water. The *Diamond* drew alongside and blasted the ship with several more broadsides from its cannon. Eventually the Spanish flag was lowered in surrender. A crew of men from the *Diamond* rowed over to the ship. Some of them stayed on board to take command of the ship, while several others brought the Spanish captain back to the *Diamond*. Most of the men aboard the Spanish ship would be taken back to Jamaica as prisoners, but at least two of them escaped by jumping overboard and swimming ashore to the mainland of Belize.[3]

Three days later, on March 29, the *Diamond* set off on its voyage back to Jamaica. The warship was leading a large convoy of more than two dozen vessels, including the newly captured Spanish ship. But the fleet did not get far before being jolted by a tropical storm. The voyage had started out under cloudy skies with little breeze, but by the time the ships were navigating the tricky channel off the coast of Belize that runs between the Four Cays and Glover's Reef, heavy weather—"squally with much rain"—hit the area, making it impossible for the vessels to keep within sight of each other. Several ships were separated from the fleet. Heading under still cloudy skies, the *Diamond* passed just north of Roatan and by March 31 was just off the coast of Barbaret, one of the smaller islands that lie between Roatan and Guanaja. Two days later, the *Diamond* was anchored just off Guanaja. By now, the storm had passed. With clearer skies, the ships that had separated from the fleet caught sight of the *Diamond* again and were able to fall back in. "In the morning," the captain of the *Diamond* noted in the ship's logbook, they could see "sails to the northwestward of us which proved to be of our fleet, having lost company."

Philip Ashton—who was on Guanaja with Symonds at the time—noticed the ships anchored offshore. The largest of the ships, including the *Diamond,* were anchored some distance away, beyond the cays and coral reefs that bordered the island. But a single brigantine had been able to navigate closer to shore and was anchored not far from the island. Before long, Ashton saw a boat from the brigantine coming toward land with its water casks. Based on the clothing and appearance of the three men in the boat, Ashton was confident that they were English, not Spanish, and since there were only three men in the boat, Ashton felt it was unlikely they were pirates. He stepped out into the open on the beach. Symonds, suspecting the men would be less likely to come ashore if they saw two men rather than one, remained hidden about a half-mile down the beach.

Seeing Ashton on the beach, the three men stopped rowing. Ashton called out to the men and they exchanged greetings, each asking who the other was and assuring each other that they were not a threat. Ashton told the men to come ashore.

The meeting with the three men on the shore of Guanaja was a moment Ashton would never forget. The men told Ashton the vessels anchored offshore were sailing with the *Diamond* for Jamaica. A number of the men aboard the *Diamond* were sick and had drunk most of their water, so the brigantine had been sent closer into the island to restock with fresh water. Even more remarkable was that the brigantine Ashton could see resting in the bay was from Salem, Massachusetts—the very next town to his hometown of Marblehead—and the ship's captain was a man Ashton knew. He was almost certainly going home.

"I sent off to Captain Dove to know if he would give me a passage home with him and he was very ready to comply with my desire," Ashton recalled. "And upon my going on board with him, besides the great civilities he treated me with, he took me into pay, for he had lost a hand and need me to supply his place."

The brigantine sailed away from Guanaja with the *Diamond* and the other ships on April 3 and stayed in the company of the *Diamond* for a week or so as the fleet sailed in a northeasterly direction toward Cuba. By April 6 or 7 they spotted the Isle of Pines just off the southwestern end of Cuba. At some point, the Massachusetts-bound brigantine broke away from the *Diamond,* which turned to the west and arrived in Port Royal, Jamaica, by April 25. Ashton's ship sailed north up past the coast of Florida and toward New England.[4]

On Saturday, May 1, 1725, the brigantine sailed past the small islands off Marblehead's rocky point and, rounding the bend, arrived back in Salem harbor. For the first time in nearly three years, Ashton set foot on the soil of his New England homeland. He did not linger in Salem. Almost immediately he made his way back across the harbor to his house in Marblehead. "I went the same evening to my father's house, where I was received as one coming to them from the dead, with all imaginable surprise of joy."

CHAPTER 9

Ashton's
Memorial

Philip Ashton's remarkable story might have ended there, fading
into obscurity, if it weren't for an adventurous young minister who was
in Marblehead when Ashton returned home. One of the first people
Ashton sat down with after coming home to the fishing village was his
forty-three-year-old minister, John Barnard. Everything about Ashton's
story appealed to Barnard, who was well-traveled himself and had a
lifelong love of fishing, ships, and adventure. But more than that, Barnard saw in Ashton's journey a story he could use to demonstrate to the
people in Marblehead a real connection between the teachings of the
Bible and their everyday lives. As a minister, Barnard had significant
concerns about the fate of religion in his small colonial fishing village.
As he heard the details of Ashton's journey and safe return home, he
realized it was an amazing story. But Barnard saw that it might also give
him a chance to show skeptics in his seafaring community how God
did protect those who were faithful, even intervening in the life of an
ordinary fisherman like Ashton.

Barnard was not the first New England minister to bring sensational
stories about pirates into the pulpit. The exploits of pirates and the adventures of captives who returned safely home were used time and again
during this era by religious leaders who wanted to illustrate their stark

warnings against a sinful lifestyle. These Puritan leaders saw piracy as a vivid and gruesome symbol of everything that was wrong with colonial New England at a time of deteriorating social and religious values. As Barnard sat down with Ashton and handwrote his story so that he could prepare a historic sermon in early May 1725, he was following in the footsteps of his former teacher, a relentlessly religious man and one of the most famous figures in colonial America at the time.

❧❧❧❧❧

A few hours before sunrise in the early morning of Tuesday, November 14, 1721, someone standing on a dark street set fire to a crude homemade grenade and threw it at the window of a house in Boston's North End. The grenade was filled with a mix of gunpowder and turpentine and encased by an explosive ball. The grenade was so heavy that its impact alone could probably have killed the person sleeping in the room where it struck, if it had hit him. The concoction of gunpowder and turpentine would surely have swept the room with fire. But by chance the grenade ended up hitting the ironwork around the window and simply fell onto the floor of the room, where the burning fuse slipped out. The grenade never exploded.

Tied to the grenade with a piece of string was a handwritten note. The person who'd written the note and thrown the grenade at the house was apparently a disgruntled member of Boston's North Church, and the bomb had been intended for the church's minister. "Cotton Mather, I was once of your meeting, but the cursed lie you told of _____ you know who, made me leave you, you dog," the note read. "And damn you, I will inoculate you with this, with a pox to you."[1]

Cotton Mather, a third-generation Puritan, was not only Boston's most prominent religious leader, but also an outspoken and frequently controversial force in colonial New England. Mather was deeply engaged in the church, politics, and science. He was a prolific writer, publishing more than 380 sermons, books, and pamphlets during his lifetime, and he was extremely well-read, with one of the best private libraries in

America at the time. By 1721, Mather's interest in science had convinced him that inoculation, as crude as it was then, could be effective in preventing the further spread of smallpox, which had once again struck Boston that year. Mather's arguments in favor of inoculation won him few friends, however, and the references to "inoculate" and "pox" in the note attached to the grenade were meant to be a warning.[2]

Smallpox was one of the most feared diseases in the world at the time. It was often fatal—about one-third of those who contracted smallpox died—and it was highly contagious. Smallpox victims would become very sick, suffering from high fevers, vomiting, and stomach pains. Several days later, after the pox broke out, their bodies would be covered from head to toe with small, red blisters or pustules filled with a pussy liquid. A smallpox epidemic tended to hit Boston about once every two decades, but it was nearly endemic in London and was known throughout the world. Ashton's cousin, Nicholas Merritt, had contracted smallpox while in prison in the Azores. When a new wave of smallpox hit Boston earlier that year, brought there by the crew of a ship arriving from the Caribbean in April, Mather published a paper encouraging doctors to try inoculations. Smallpox inoculation had been practiced as folk medicine for centuries in Africa, India, and China and was then gaining some proponents in the Western world. The basic principle behind inoculation was the same then as it is today—expose a healthy person to a small amount of the virus so the body builds up a resistance to it—but the practice was much simpler, less precise, and far riskier.

To perform an inoculation in 1721, several of the raised bumps on the skin of someone suffering from smallpox were pricked to release a small amount of the pus and fluid within them. The fluid was collected in a bottle or bowl and carried to an uninfected person awaiting inoculation. Several cuts were made in that person's arm with a lance or needle and the drops of the smallpox fluid were put into the cuts and mixed with the person's blood. The cuts were then capped with a protective cover, like a walnut shell, and bandaged. The person who was inoculated might break out with some sores, but in successful cases these would dry up and fall off and the person would not get smallpox.

How often inoculation was successful—and how often it simply spread the disease even faster—was a matter of vicious controversy that year in Boston. As one of the leading promoters of inoculation, Mather was in the middle of the debate. In early 1721 Mather had written an address describing inoculation and encouraging Boston doctors to try the "wonderful practice." But there were many who saw inoculation as reckless and deadly, describing cases where the practice spread the disease more than it prevented it. A month after Mather's letter promoting inoculation was published, a group of Boston doctors adopted a resolution opposing the practice.

The doctors were harshly critical of at least one other doctor who had attempted to inoculate his patients. As the number of smallpox cases in Boston continued to rise, the vicious debate over inoculation was played out in a string of letters and newspaper commentaries. James Franklin, the older brother of Benjamin Franklin, started publishing a new newspaper that summer, the *New England Courant,* with one of its primary objectives to "oppose the doubtful and dangerous practice of inoculating the small pox." For his part, Mather complained in his diary about the "prodigious nonsense, and folly, and baseness ever now and then expressed by the people." Mather may also have argued with publisher James Franklin on the streets of Boston one winter day in late 1721, warning him that there are "many curses that await those" who are so critical of the ministers in town.[3]

Cotton Mather's defiant stance in favor of what he believed to be right was nothing new. New England's most forceful minister, Mather was never afraid to promote his beliefs and to criticize what he thought was wrong. He held himself to the highest standards of faith. He prayed daily, sometimes setting aside an entire day for fasting, reading, and reflection. Mather's faith was so intense that he sometimes prayed lying down on his stomach, weeping as his face touched the dusty floor of his study. Carrying on the Puritan tradition of both his father and his grandfather, Mather expected religious faith to dominate public life as well, but so often during his lifetime he was sorely disappointed.

Barely three generations after the first Puritans had come to New England, life there had changed. Today, Puritans are remembered as a stern and hard-working community of settlers who came to New England to get out from under the restrictions imposed on them by Church of England. Puritans came to New England to establish a devout community that reflected a covenant with God. Yet three generations later, the heavenly aspirations of John Winthrop's "city on a hill" had been steadily eroded by the surge of New England's rapidly expanding and increasingly diverse population. By the 1720s, after nearly a century of steady growth, New England was a much larger, thriving commercial center. Boston was now a bustling city of twelve thousand people, America's largest city and its busiest seaport. Much to Mather's disappointment, New Englanders were doing much more than working and going to church, and many were not going to church at all.

Religious leaders issued warning after warning about the propensity for drunkenness, adultery, blasphemy, church skipping, and other aspects of wayward lifestyles within their communities. Boston had at least one brothel as early as 1672, and the decades leading up to the 1720s saw a growing number of prosecutions for drunkenness, skipping church, nighttime riots, and a range of sex crimes, including prostitution and illegitimate births. Hundreds of taverns sold beer, hard cider, and liquor in smoke-filled tap rooms throughout the colonies, especially in seaport communities. In the eyes of their ministers, people were visiting these taverns too often and staying out too late. Within a matter of a few years, in 1726, concern about drinking and drunkenness would be so widespread that Mather and twenty-one other Puritan ministers, including Barnard, were compelled to jointly publish a diatribe against abuse called "A Serious Address to Those Who Unnecessarily Frequent the Tavern."

Despite their reputation today, Puritans were not in principle opposed to any form of leisure or fun. But religious leaders like Mather felt that too many New Englanders were having too much fun and forsaking their commitment to faith along the way. This was particularly true among the men who worked at sea, who were notorious for their swearing, drinking, irreverence, and promiscuous lifestyles. These men spent long stretches of their lives at sea, weeks or months at a time, so they rarely attended church services or felt as though they were under the watchful eye of their minister. Some sailors rejected even the slightest hint of religion aboard their ships. On a voyage to New York in 1725, a minister who was sailing aboard the vessel gave Bibles to some of the crew. The men responded by sneaking up to the minister while he was sleeping and cutting down his hammock so that he crashed down onto one of the ship's iron cannon. The sailors also beat the minister over the head with his Bible, complaining that he "would not swear and drink as fast as they, and seemingly showed his dislike of those vices."[4]

Cotton Mather complained repeatedly about the rampant disregard for religion among seafaring men. "And now, if I begin with seafaring," Mather had written in his diary a few years earlier. "Oh, what an horrible spectacle I have before me! A wicked, stupid, abominable generation; every year growing rather worse." Mather had also warned New England fishermen about their sinful ways, which included profanity, Sabbath breaking, and drunkenness. "Intemperance is another of those errors whereinto Satan often draws too many fishermen," Mather scolded in 1712. "Too many of them drink too much, are the slaves of the bottle. Fishermen, I wish you would soberly ponder on those words."[5]

But the absolute worst symbol of the "horrible spectacle" at sea, in Mather's mind, was the pirate. Pirates were notorious for their blatant hatred of religion, and even Ashton had noticed that aboard Low's ship "every thing that had the least face of religion and virtue was entirely banished." Mather had been railing against the evils of piracy for more than two decades. He'd personally gone to the Boston jailhouse in January 1700 to meet with the infamous Captain Kidd, shortly before Kidd was shipped back to London to be hanged for piracy. Mather had delivered a blistering sermon at the execution of crew members who'd served under the pirate John Quelch in 1704. Thirteen years later, when six members of Samuel Bellamy's crew who survived the Cape Cod shipwreck were condemned in 1717, Mather made the "long and sad walk with them from the prison to the place of execution," where he delivered final words before the pirates were hanged.[6]

Mather had also taken up the story of the twenty-six members of Low's crew hanged in Newport, Rhode Island, in July 1723 after they were captured by the *Greyhound.* Mather was sixty years old that summer, nearing the end of his life. The corpses of the executed pirates strung from the gallows became a gruesome symbol of how badly things would end for those who gave in to the vices of the pirates. Page after page of Mather's sermon detailed the pirates' sins. He railed not only against the violence for which they were convicted, but also their sins of sexual promiscuity, drunkenness, blasphemy, and irreverence. "It was the hand of the Glorious God which brought these criminals to die," Mather proclaimed in his sermon about the pirates executed in Newport. "Take a due notice of what you have seen in the way which these wicked men have trodden, and in the fearful end in which their way has brought them to."[7]

Only a year later, when John Fillmore and his fellow captives returned to Boston after overthrowing Phillips' pirate crew, Mather again preached at the executions of Archer and White. But this time, the story had a new twist: Fillmore and several other captives had overpowered the pirates and brought the ship safety back home. This was, for Mather, proof of God's direct intervention in human affairs. "It is among the admirable works of the Divine Providence that the glorious God fetches good out of the greatest evil and makes the sins and woes of the wicked an occasion of benefits unto His chosen," Mather wrote.[8]

Like Mather, Marblehead minister John Barnard would also put Ashton's dramatic tale of piracy and survival to use in his own enduring battle against religious indifference and a wayward lifestyle. But in many ways, Barnard's retelling of Ashton's story lacked the fire and brimstone fury of Mather's sermons on piracy. The different ways Barnard and Mather interpreted the stories of the pirates and their captives reflect generational differences between a student and his teacher and, to a large degree, the evident strains of a maturing and evolving Puritan community during these years. Barnard had spent his first years as a minister under the eyes of both Cotton Mather and his equally stern father, Increase Mather. But Barnard was part of a new generation of ministers, and he was anything but a strict and stuffy old Puritan.

⊰⊱⊰⊱⊰

John Barnard had been born in Boston in 1681. After graduating from Harvard College at age eighteen, he joined the Mathers' North Church in Boston. There, however, the fresh young minister found himself caught in the midst of a religious hornet's nest. His tutors at Harvard, Thomas Brattle and John Leverett, had recently written a three-page manifesto that sharply challenged the Mathers' conservative religious leadership in Boston and called for the establishment of a new and more inclusive Brattle Street Church. The Brattle Street Church, built only a short walk from Mather's North Church, was not only a competing house of worship that drained away some of the Mathers' congregation, it was also a more open and progressive church that broke tradition with Mather's church in several ways that seemed minor but that nonetheless enraged both Mather and his father.

The new Brattle Street Church had a full tower and spire at one end of its roof, rather than the central turret that was traditional among New England churches at the time. The new church also broke with the tradition of having the minister read Bible passages without providing comments or explanations about the scripture to the congregation, and with the custom of alternating, line by line, between singing and reading psalms. Mather was beside himself. He claimed that the founders of the Brattle Street Church, in laying out their manifesto, sought to "utterly subvert our Churches" and he wrote privately in his diary that the group was "ignorant, arrogant, obstinate, and full of malice and slander, and the fill the land with lies."[9]

While the young John Barnard was at first viewed as a "mimic and tool" of the Mathers, within a matter of a few years he was invited to preach at the new Brattle Street Church, and he began to align himself more closely with the new church's minister, Benjamin Colman. Compared to the reproachful Mather, Colman seemed like a spirited and forgiving friend. Colman was well-traveled, well-dressed, and soft-spoken. He was described as "pious but polished," a tall man with a "tuneful" voice. Barnard soon became close to Colman, whom he called a "kind father and intimate and fast friend."[10]

Barnard's devotion, his faith that God had the power to save people from danger—and even from certain death—was based in part on his own experiences in life. Years later, Barnard would preserve Ashton's story not only because of his love of ships and his fascination with life at sea, but also because of a lifelong belief in divine intervention in human affairs. This belief was based in part on his firsthand experiences, including several near-death escapes in the early part of 1707, when the twenty-five-year-old Barnard sailed as part of a New England military campaign against the French in Nova Scotia.

❦❦❦❦

Early in the morning of May 13, 1707, just around sunrise, a huge fleet of more than two dozen ships made its way out of Boston Harbor. The ships were sailing north to attack a French fort at Port Royal (now Annapolis), located on the western edge of Nova Scotia facing the Bay of Fundy. While England and other Protestant countries fought with the Catholic nations of Spain and France in the European War of Spanish Succession, the conflict in the Americas was known as Queen Anne's War and was being fought largely over control of present-day Nova Scotia. The fort at Port Royal, the first ever built in the history of Canada, was a major French stronghold in the region, and England intended to capture the fort and take possession of Nova Scotia.

The fleet sailing out of Boston that May was the first of two expeditions sent to Nova Scotia in 1707. Although there was later some bickering over the campaign's specific objectives, the army of more than one thousand men was headed north to attack the fort. Barnard was one of five ministers appointed by Governor Joseph Dudley of Massachusetts as chaplains for the expedition. Due to light winds during the journey, it was about a two-week sail before the ships made their way into the Bay of Fundy and through the half-mile-wide channel that opened into the large river basin that led to the fort. The fleet split into two groups, with most of the ships landing on the southern side of the basin, some distance from the fort, while the remaining ships, including Barnard's, made their way further north to anchor and go ashore. Barnard and the rest of the men in his group were able to land by about five o'clock on the afternoon of May 26. The men then started hiking in the direction of the fort, but made slow progress, "partly through hideous woods, and fallen trees across our way, which sometimes we climbed over, at other times crept under," Barnard recalled. Within a few hours it was nightfall and the men stopped to make camp.

Early the next morning the men set out again. They had not gone far before reaching a deep gully, where they were ambushed by about sixty French soldiers. Two of the New Englanders were killed by the gunfire. After the skirmish, the men continued on their way and by midday they were less than a mile from the fort, where they stopped to make another camp. Meanwhile, the other contingent from New England, marching from the south, was also attacked by about three hundred French soldiers hiding in the brush near a creek. The two sides fought but eventually the French turned and retreated up a hill toward the fort, firing as they went. The New Englanders then camped out in some houses at the foot of the hill and positioned guards to keep a lookout for attackers during the night.

The troops learned from some deserters who came to their camp from the fort that there were about five hundred men inside the walls, as well as two hundred women and children. The fort was not a traditional structure of vertical stone walls, but a Vauban-style ring of high, earthen walls towering above deep gullies below. The rock and soil that had been removed from the perimeter was used to fill in the tall, sloping walls, and the excavation created a series of ravines that looked like a deep moat encircling the fort. The walls were more than a hundred feet high from top to bottom and rose so sharply that it was nearly impossible for the men to run or climb up, and if they had tried, they would be completely exposed to anyone standing at the peak of the fort walls. Cannon dotted the tops of the walls, particularly to the west facing the basin and the mouth of a river known as Allain's Creek. Barnard and the other men could also see the roofs of a powder house and other buildings that lay in the sunken ground behind the fort walls.

The New Englanders decided that firing several cannon blasts up over the fort walls and into the center area where the French were hiding out would be enough to force them to surrender. They planned to move some of their heavy artillery up to their camp the next day, but when the time came to move the weapons, several officers decided it would result in disaster. To bring the artillery into position, the men would have to haul the heavy guns directly past the fort, which itself was fitted out with more than forty cannon. So instead, the troops decided to burn a church, a storehouse, and a number of homes near the fort and then hike back to where their ships were.

Barnard kept busy during the week the army spent at Port Royal, too curious to simply spend his time ministering to the troops. Barnard met several times with the officers leading the campaign to talk about their strategy. He also set out alone one day to sketch a map of the area around the fort and the roads and pathways leading up to it. But this left Barnard vulnerable to gunfire from behind the fort's walls, which resulted in several narrow escapes.

For most of his life, Barnard had come to believe that times when he—or someone else—was saved from a dangerous situation, those experiences were proof of divine intervention. He called these events "signal deliverances." When as a young man he survived a dangerous fall from an eighteen-foot-high scaffold, somehow landing directly between two large pieces of timber on the ground (landing directly on top of them would have killed him), that safe landing was a "signal deliverance." When Barnard recovered from the scarlet fever as a young boy, that too was evidence of a God that watched over and protected him. Barnard saw even more evidence of divine intervention during the fighting at Port Royal.

One day, Barnard was crossing a river in a canoe when some French soldiers in the fort fired a cannon shot at him and narrowly missed his boat. Later, on the day Barnard was walking around the fort to sketch his map, he was standing at the end of a narrow pathway leading up to the fort when he was nearly hit by another shot. The cannonball struck the ground so close to where Barnard was standing that he was brushed by the dirt kicked up by the impact. "While we lay at Port Royal, I experienced signal deliverances," Barnard later wrote. "I thought with myself that I had no business here, and retreated slowly backward out of danger; and thank God I escaped what was designed against me."

The campaign to Nova Scotia was short-lived, and the fleet left in the first week of June. The day before the ships left there had been one more decision to haul out their artillery and launch an attack on the fort, but once again the leaders changed their mind the next day. So the fleet sailed from Nova Scotia, stopping for about a month at Casco Bay off the coast of present-day Maine, and returned to Boston later that summer.

Once back in Boston, Barnard continued to align himself more closely with his friend Benjamin Colman. Barnard's relationship with Cotton Mather could be tense at times, and it wasn't helped by his time away in Port Royal. Mather had learned that Barnard took part in a card game with some of the men during the expedition to Port Royal. This did not sit well with the stern and pious Mather, and he publicly disciplined Barnard for the "scandalous game of cards." For his part, Barnard seems to believe the rebuke had as much to do with the infighting between the Mathers and their adversaries in the church as it did with a minister who played a game of cards with some troops. "Nor did I go without my share of obloquy for a little piece of imprudence while I was absent, for which my pastors treated me cruelly for reasons best known to themselves; by which my reputation sunk among some people," Barnard recalled. "But the more thinking persons looked upon it as a vile treating of me and continued their respects to me, especially the excellent Mr. Colman, so that I was almost constantly employed in preaching."

Barnard struggled for more than a decade after graduating from Harvard to find a church of his own. He was forced to spend his time filling in as a visiting minister or accepting short, temporary appointments at churches throughout the Massachusetts Bay colony. Opportunities would come his way every now and then, but none of them worked out. So when he wasn't filling in at the Mathers' church or some other meeting house, Barnard took full advantage of any opportunity to get away. Two years after the Port Royal campaign, Barnard set off again on a roundabout journey to England. In July 1709 he sailed as chaplain again, this time aboard a large ship under the command of Captain John Wentworth. The vessel stopped at Barbados for five weeks and then continued on to London. Barnard lived in London for about a year before sailing back to New England in August 1710 and arriving home in Boston three months later.

Several years after Barnard's return from London, it appeared as though he would finally land his own church, but the Mathers put a stop to that too. A new meeting house was being built in Boston and Barnard's name had been suggested by church leaders as a candidate for the pulpit. But the Mathers worried that if Barnard were named to lead the new church, his popularity as a preacher might draw some of the Mathers' congregation from their own church. That was Barnard's interpretation of the events, at least. Increase Mather apparently met with each of the church elders and successfully lobbied against Barnard, whom he described as an ally of Colman and other church members who had been critical of the Mathers.

It was two years later, in November of 1715, that Barnard arrived in Marblehead. He moved to the fishing village three days after his thirty-fourth birthday and was ordained as minister of his own church in July 1716. In many ways, Marblehead was a world apart from Boston. Barnard found that his new community was little more than a fishing outpost, a collection of simple wooden houses clustered along roads that were "narrow, and rugged, and dirty." The busy harbor reeked of drying fish. "When I came, there was not so much as one proper carpenter nor mason nor tailor nor butcher in the town, nor any thing of a market worth naming," Barnard wrote in his autobiography. "They had their houses built by country workmen and their clothes made out of town, and supplied themselves with beef and pork from Boston, which drained the town of its money."[11]

The fighting in Nova Scotia and the threat of French attacks had smothered Marblehead's fishing fleets during Queen Anne's War. When Barnard arrived in 1715, the town was just coming out of a two-decade-long slump in trade. Even with the rapid growth of cod fishing in the years that followed the war, very little of the profit from the catch stayed in Marblehead. Most of the fish hauled back to the village during the time Ashton was fishing was sold by merchants in Salem or Boston, who kept the profits for themselves. Many fishermen and their families borrowed heavily on credit to pay for food and clothing, and they spent most of their lives in debt.[12]

Barnard described the fishermen in his new community as "slaves that digged in the mines," and in time he set out to change this. As a man who loved to fish himself and who was fascinated by the trade, Barnard found it easy to talk to the men who worked in the harbor, including captains from foreign ports who came to Marblehead to load their ships with fish. He learned as much as he could about the business side of the salt cod trade and urged local ship owners to start exporting their own catch themselves rather than through middlemen in Salem or Boston. After some initial reluctance, Marblehead ship owners began exporting their catch directly to Europe and the Caribbean. Not long after, Boston merchants would be complaining that they were "almost entirely stripped" of cod exports because the trade was now "confined to the fishing towns who generally send it abroad in their own vessels, especially Marblehead, Salem, and Plymouth."[13]

But Marblehead's economic troubles were not the only problems Barnard encountered. Barnard had moved to Marblehead to take over as minister of the First Church to help make sure the village did not fall further into the clutches of drunkenness and disregard for religion that was rampant in fishing communities. Though he had his differences with Cotton Mather, Barnard soon saw that Marblehead was overflowing with all the impurities Mather and other Puritan leaders were so concerned about in Boston. Marblehead had an abundance of taverns, many of them unlicensed. Drunkenness and brawls were common in the town. Court records detail the frequency of sexual misconduct, theft, and other crimes, and Barnard himself held several disciplinary hearings during his tenure against member of his congregation who had engaged in sexual promiscuity or domestic disturbances. "They were generally as rude, swearing, drunken, and fighting a crew as they were poor," Barnard wrote of the village during his early years there.[14]

When Ashton arrived back in Marblehead that first week in May and told Barnard about his journey, Barnard immediately realized it combined all the elements of a perfect story for a community that lived by the sea, a narrative filled with danger and adventure that he could also use to demonstrate God's influence over the lives of ordinary people. This was not a story based on the unknown characters and faraway lands of the Bible. It was based on the actual experiences of a fisherman in their own village, a person everyone in the community knew and could see, hear, and talk to in person. This, Barnard surely thought, would drive home what he saw as a profoundly important message.

Given his strong belief in a protective God and "signal deliverances," it was frustrating for Barnard that many people in Marblehead had so little faith of their own. To Barnard, it made no sense that men who worked at sea would have little regard for God. Nobody should have appreciated the need for divine protection and the importance of "signal deliverances" more than the fishermen who lived in danger every day, miles away from land, working in the deep, cold, and often stormy ocean. But like Mather, Barnard found just the opposite. Many of the sailors and fishermen in his community were a rough, faithless bunch, notorious for swearing and blasphemy. "The seafaring business (which is very much the business of the town), which one would think should teach them to pray and live like dying persons, but tends to encourage them in their insensibilities and immoral practices," Barnard wrote.

So Ashton's remarkable journey gave Barnard, who had the largest congregation in Marblehead, another chance to deliver this message. The very Sunday after Ashton arrived home, on May 9, 1725, Barnard devoted his sermon at Marblehead's First Church to telling the remarkable story of Ashton's experiences as a pirate captive and castaway. Ashton attended the service that Sunday with his parents. The backdrop for Barnard's sermon was the Old Testament Book of Daniel. Barnard compared Ashton to the biblical Daniel, who is best known for the story of his survival in the den of lions. Barnard chose this story that day for other reasons too. The parallels between Ashton and his fellow pirate captives, on the one hand, and the Biblical captives in the Book of Daniel, on the other, are striking.

In the Book of Daniel, the idol-worshiping Babylonian king Nebuchadnezzar gave instructions for carefully selecting captives to serve him, much as the pirates had when boarding a newly captured ship: those "in whom was no blemish, but well favored, and skilful in all wisdom, and cunning in knowledge, and understanding science, and such as had ability in them to stand in the king's palace." And like Ashton and other captives aboard pirate ships, the biblical captives were pressured to adopt the lifestyle of their captors—to eat their food and to worship their idols. But the biblical captives refused to go against their beliefs, even when threatened with death. Barnard's sermon that Sunday centered around a critical confrontation in the Book of Daniel when Nebuchadnezzar, "furious with rage," demands that the captives kneel before his ninety-foot-high golden idol or, if they refuse, be thrown into a blazing furnace. The captives refuse, telling the king that even if they were dragged into the flames, God would protect them. "If it be so," the captives told Nebuchadnezzar, "that is, if thou should cast us into the fiery furnace, yet our God whom we serve is able to deliver us from the burning fiery furnace, and He will deliver us out of thine hand." Moments later, Nebuchadnezzar is amazed to see that the captives are, in fact, unharmed by the raging fire.

What is striking about the story that Barnard told that Sunday is how it differed from Cotton Mather's sermons on piracy. Clearly, Barnard was not a "tool" of the Mathers, and standing in the pulpit of the First Church, his sermon struck a remarkably different tone. Mather's execution sermons walked through the trail of sins pirates committed, one by one: gambling, adultery, drunkenness, profanity, thievery, and murder. Mather's message to his congregation was a stern warning: turn away from sinful ways before it's too late. The pirates standing before him offered all the evidence anyone needed that God saw and punished peoples' sins. "By departing from God you are brought into such a deplorable state that there can be nothing, verily nothing, so necessary for you as a recovery from that state by a conversion to God," Mather said in sermon a year earlier, the Sunday before the execution of the two pirates from Phillips' crew. "In your departure from God, you are in those ways that lead you down to the chambers of death—destruction and misery are in your ways."

Barnard's words the Sunday after Ashton returned to Marblehead were noticeably less stern. He told a story of life rather than death, of a God that saves rather than a God that punishes. In fact, Barnard even titled his sermon "God's Ability to Save His People Out of All Their Dangers." Barnard recounted the series of events in Ashton's journey that he believed represented signal deliverances: a pirate's pistol misfiring three times as it was held to Ashton's head (but igniting on the fourth snap, when it was no longer pointed at Ashton's head), the mysterious arrival of the Scotsman who left Ashton with a knife, food, and fire, and that a merchant ship from Salem, the town next to Marblehead, appeared off the island of Guanaja on a day when Ashton happened to be there. Barnard wondered at the fateful turn of events that brought Ashton home. The Salem ship had not planned to be anywhere near the Bay Islands but was blown far off course by the storm. A few sailors from the ship had rowed over to the island, where they met Ashton only because some of the crew aboard the *Diamond* were sick and were running out of water. "In you, we see that our God whom we serve is able to deliver out of the fiery furnace and from the den of lions!" Barnard proclaimed. "In you, we see that nothing is too hard for the Lord and that 'tis not in vain for us to call upon Him!"[15]

Barnard continued to emphasize this theme when he went on to publish the text of Ashton's narrative later that summer. In the weeks following the Sunday sermon, Barnard sat down with Ashton several more times to write out the full narrative of his journey in more detail. The result was a sixty-six-page tract, also including Merritt's experiences, that Barnard called *Ashton's Memorial: An History of the Strange Adventures and Signal Deliverances of Mr. Philip Ashton*. Barnard's published text has three sections in it. The main section recounts, in Ashton's own words, his full journey from Port Roseway to Roatan and back to Marblehead. Barnard added a second short section describing Nicholas Merritt's escape and imprisonment at the Azores. Finally, Barnard concluded the book by reprinting the text of the sermon he delivered the Sunday after Ashton came home.[16]

When he gave his sermon, Barnard spoke repeatedly about the three brave captives from the biblical story of Nebuchadnezzar. These "three Jewish worthies, Shadrach, Meshach, and Abednego, steadily adhered to the worship of the True God of Israel," Barnard said. The captives "utterly refused to bow the knee and give any religious worship to the golden image." But in Barnard's book, he tells the story of only two captives, Philip Ashton and Nicholas Merritt. The tragic story of the third captive—Joseph Libbey, Ashton's crewmate who was captured along with him—fades from Barnard's text. Libbey is listed in the first pages of Ashton's narrative as one of the Marblehead fishermen taken captive. And Libbey's name is mentioned once again at the point where Ashton describes his near drowning during the sinking of Low's pink, when Libbey reached out his hand and saved him. But Barnard includes no other references to Libbey in his text or sermon, despite the well-publicized trial and hanging of Libbey and twenty-five other condemned pirates in Newport, Rhode Island, less than two years earlier.

Even so, while Barnard did not use Libbey as an example of a wayward seaman, his sermon was not without warnings. Barnard reminded Ashton of all he had been saved from and urged him to spend time thinking about his experiences with the pirates and on Roatan, to read the Bible daily, and to avoid the temptations that lured so many others in the community. "Allow me to say, basely ungrateful and deeply guilty beyond almost any man in the world you will be, if now you do not become one of the most humble, holy, faithful, active servants of God,"

Barnard said. "Watch against all sin, even the least, and those especially which your age and company may most of all addict you to, and be not drawn away by the evil example and enticements of others."[17]

Word of Ashton's journey soon spread far beyond Marblehead. Within a week the *New England Courant* ran an item about Ashton, reporting that he had been "taken by Low the pirate some years since, and ran away from him when he went ashore at a maroon island to take in water, where he had been above two years." Sensing the potential appeal of the story of a real-life Robinson Crusoe from the American colonies, Samuel Gerrish, one of Boston's most important and prestigious printers, published *Ashton's Memorial.* An advertisement announcing its sale was printed in the *Boston News Letter* on October 7, 1725.[18]

Ashton's Memorial benefited from the widespread popularity of colonial captivity narratives; in many ways it closely resembled the traditional captivity narrative. In a day when Puritan beliefs frowned on novels and other fiction, true and at times gruesome stories of adventure, suffering, and survival provided colonial New Englanders with an enticing read. Captivity narratives and other similar tracts typically told a sensational story of danger and survival, detailing weeks or months of captivity, torture, starvation, and death. During Barnard's lifetime, these stories were often compiled by Puritan ministers who infused the narrative with religious themes, demonstrating how faith and divine intervention leads to captives' release or rescue. The most famous of these captivity narratives, compiled under the direction of Increase Mather, was Mary Rowlandson's journal *A True Story of the Captivity and Restoration of Mrs. Mary Rowlandson.* Published in 1682, it told the story of the eleven weeks Rowlandson spent as a captive of Native Americans after an attack on her home in Lancaster, Massachusetts. Mary Rowlandson's captivity narrative was an immediate bestseller, and fourteen more editions of the book were published over the next century.[19]

It is likely that *Ashton's Memorial,* with its spectacular first-person account of sailing with pirates and castaway survival on a remote island, was also a popular book in New England. In fact, Gerrish was advertising a new edition of the book in October 1727, two years after its initial publication. News of Ashton's journey soon made its way across the Atlantic, and the story drew attention in London. A note about the book's publication in Boston and a long reprinting of some of Ashton's experiences were published in London in the *Weekly Journal/British Gazetteer* on March 5, 1726. That summer, a second edition of *Ashton's Memorial* was printed in London.[20]

⁂

It was sometime in late 1725 or early 1726 when the first copies of *Ashton's Memorial* reached London from Boston, and it is likely that the book was then read by the most famous person to pick up a copy of the volume: Daniel Defoe. Just seven years after he wrote *The Adventures of Robinson Crusoe,* Defoe was able to read the true story of a man who, like Crusoe, had survived encounters with pirates and led the solitary life of a castaway on an uninhabited island. The similarities between Ashton's experiences and the fictional Robinson Crusoe were impossible to ignore, even more so because Barnard incorporated several subtle references to *Robinson Crusoe* in *Ashton's Memorial.*

By 1725, Defoe's novel was well-known in the American colonies. Cotton Mather had alluded to the book in one of his political tracts published in 1720, titled "News from Robinson Cruso's Island." As Barnard compiled Ashton's story, he included several references to the novel, perhaps to draw a contrast between Ashton and Crusoe. While Robinson Crusoe taught a parrot to say his name, for example, Ashton notes dryly in his narrative that "the parrots here had not been taught to speak." Barnard also drew a significant contrast between the fictional Crusoe and the real-life Ashton, whom he held up as a devout and ever-faithful young man. While Crusoe recalls his "original sin" of ignoring his parents' advice, *Ashton's Memorial* included Ashton's explicit affirmation that, despite his troubles, he had not sailed off without his parents' approval. "It wonderfully alleviated my sorrows to think that I had my parents' approbation and consent in my going to sea," Ashton wrote.[21]

When the book reached London, the rich details in *Ashton's Memo-*

rial about sailing aboard a pirate ship undoubtedly fascinated Defoe, who'd had a lifelong interest in piracy and life at sea. In fact, Defoe seems to have taken a number of these details from *Ashton's Memorial* and used them in his next book, published in the summer of 1726.

Defoe was sixty-five years old when Ashton's narrative was published. He had led a full and prolific life. While best known today for his fiction, Defoe had spent most of his life working as a journalist, historian, and commentator. His political pamphlets had at times made him the target of persecution, but *Robinson Crusoe,* first published in 1719, was instantly a popular success. The second of many subsequent editions of the novel was published just two weeks after the first, and within a year the book had been translated into French, Dutch, and German. As reflected in his story about Robinson Crusoe's life as a castaway, Defoe was fascinated by shipbuilding, life at sea, and maritime trade. He was an avid reader of the journals written by men who sailed the seas and of news reports about pirate encounters. *Robinson Crusoe* is widely believed to have been based on the experiences of Alexander Selkirk, which were later recorded by Woodes Rogers, the captain who picked Selkirk up from the island where he had lived as a castaway. Another Defoe novel, *Moll Flanders,* may have been based on trial records and newspaper accounts of the female pirates Anny Bonny and Mary Read.[22] Under the pseudonym of Captain Charles Johnson, Defoe is also believed to have authored several editions of *A General History of the Pyrates,* which remains even today a widely referenced source of information about the leading pirates of the early 1700s. Given Defoe's interests, *Ashton's Memorial* was bound to capture his attention.

In July of 1726, Defoe published a new book called *The Four Years Voyages of Capt. George Roberts.* This book told the story of a sea captain, George Roberts, who is forced to overcome a series of Crusoe-like predicaments in the course of his journey. Sailing near the Cape Verde Islands, Roberts' sloop is captured by the pirate crew of none other than Edward Low. Roberts is held for ten days and spends much of that time with the pirates. In Defoe's book, the pirates on Low's crew quarrel amongst themselves about whether or not to keep Roberts as a captive, and even when he is finally set free his sloop had been emptied; the pirates had taken all the cargo, food, and water aboard the sloop and stripped it of almost all its sails.[23]

Defoe used a number of details about Low's crew in his novel, and the pirates that captured Ashton and the other Marblehead fishermen seem to come alive on the pages of the book. The capture of Roberts' sloop, in October 1722, occurs at a time when Low's crew, with Ashton aboard, was actually in the area near the Cape Verde Islands. The key figures in Roberts' encounter with the pirates—Low and his two quartermasters, Francis (Farrington) Spriggs and John Russel—are familiar faces from Ashton's story.

It's clear that Defoe read *Ashton's Memorial* because several key details in Roberts' story could only have come from Ashton's narrative; they were never published anywhere else. A leading scholar of Defoe's work, Manuel Schonhorn, carefully compared what Defoe knew and wrote about Low before *Ashton's Memorial* was published and what he wrote after. In 1724, while Ashton was still marooned on Roatan, Defoe published his first edition of *A General History of the Pyrates,* which contained a biography of Low that was based largely on newspaper reports. Two years later, after Ashton had returned home to Marblehead and his narrative has been published, Defoe wrote *The Four Years Voyages.* In his detailed analysis of Defoe's books, Schonhorn concludes that "*The Four Years Voyages of Capt. George Roberts* owes its dramatic core to *Ashton's Memorial.*"[24]

For example, Defoe had previously referred to Charles Harris as Low's quartermaster, probably based on the reports from Harris' 1723 capture, trial, and execution in Newport, Rhode Island. But in his 1726 novel, Defoe identifies John Russel—the enraged pirate who had tried to shoot Ashton after he was captured at Port Roseway—as Low's quartermaster. Russel plays a prominent role in Defoe's story about Captain Roberts' capture. He is the pirate who argues most vehemently against setting Roberts free and then, once the decision is made to release him, insists that his ship be completely stripped of its food and supplies. Defoe also uses the details about the ship Nicholas Merritt used to escape from

Low and flee to the Azores, also revealed in *Ashton's Memorial,* as part of the story line in the *Four Years Voyages,* in this case correcting erroneous information from the first edition of his *History of the Pyrates.* Most significantly, however, Defoe learned from Ashton's narrative about Low's unique habit of refusing to force married men to join his crew. This is a critical detail in Defoe's novel. After Roberts is captured, a member of the pirate crew secretly tells Roberts about Low's aversion to taking married men as captives. Sure enough, when Roberts later tells Low, perhaps dishonestly, that he is married and has children, Low sets him free.

Back in Marblehead, Barnard, Ashton, and Merritt might have been amazed to learn that their story had made its way to the man who wrote *Robinson Crusoe* and onto the pages of his newest novel. But they probably never did. It's likely that they went on with their lives in the small fishing village, almost as if nothing had happened at all.

CHAPTER 10

Pirate
Executions
and Pirate
Treasure

In early February 1726, about nine months after Philip Ashton finally returned home to Marblehead, the pirate Francis Spriggs was back on Roatan yet again. He was asleep one night on a cay just off of Roatan near Coxen Hole, about fifteen miles to the west of where Ashton had probably spent most of his time on the island. Suddenly, around two o'clock in the morning, Spriggs woke with a start when the quiet night was shattered by the barking of his hunting dogs.

The HMS *Diamond,* which cornered and nearly captured Spriggs more than a year earlier, was still chasing him. In the dark of the night, fifteen men from the *Diamond* had quietly approached the cay in a canoe and were now launching an attack on Spriggs' camp. The instant the dogs started barking, Spriggs and the six men with him jumped to their feet and ran. The tables had completely turned: now it was Spriggs who was forced to dash from a cay over to Roatan and hide out in the thick woods bordering the shore. The men from the *Diamond* captured two of Spriggs' men who were unable to get away and took a number of possessions left behind, including his *piragua,* a turtle net, five dogs, and a gold watch. But Spriggs and four of the other pirates who were with him escaped again.[1]

By 1726, the war against piracy was beginning to pay off. Captures were becoming more the rule than the exception. Twenty-six members of Low's crew had been caught and hanged at Newport, Rhode Island, in 1723, and eleven pirates from the crew of Low's first partner, George Lowther, were hanged on the Caribbean island of Saint Kitts a year later. (Rather than face trial, Lowther shot himself with a pistol when his crew was captured while careening their ship.) In all, more than four hundred pirates were executed in the decade between 1716 and 1726.[2]

The *Diamond* had been back in the Bay of Honduras since January of 1726. Despite narrowly missing Spriggs in the midnight attack, the royal warship was in the midst of its most successful campaign yet. The *Diamond* was now familiar with the pirates' favorite hideouts in the bay and was waging an aggressive hunt. Constantly on alert, the warship would regularly fire a warning shot at any vessel it saw that was not flying a flag and could not be identified. Several men from the *Diamond* had recently spent a day searching Guanaja for pirates, but returned to their ship that afternoon empty-handed. The pirates were not far away, however. Only two days later, the *Diamond* met up with a Spanish sloop that appeared to be under the control of a band of pirates. The *Diamond* set out after it, "gave chase, fired a shot at her, and brought to." Boarding the sloop, the men from the *Diamond* found "eleven naked Spaniards ready to perish, and their sloop leaky." The Spanish men said they had been captured eight days earlier by a band of twenty to thirty pirates who had been part of Spriggs' crew and were now under the command of a man named Joseph Cooper. Some of the pirates took control of the Spanish sloop while Cooper and the rest of the crew stayed aboard their own sloop. The two vessels had sailed together for about six days until, on the night of January 11, they were separated in a storm. When the pirates aboard the Spanish sloop saw the *Diamond* chasing them down, they had quickly loaded their food and water into a *piragua* and escaped.[3]

Some men from the *Diamond* took the leaky sloop into Port Royal harbor on Roatan for repairs and several days later set out again in the

Spanish sloop to hunt for the pirate Cooper and his crew. Sailing near Guanaja on January 16, they spotted the pirates. Believing Cooper's sloop was faster than the repaired Spanish sloop, the men from the *Diamond* decided not to chase the pirates, but sailed toward the shallower water near the island. Recognizing the sloop and thinking the Spanish captives had killed the pirates he had put aboard, Cooper came alongside and shouted a warning from the deck "threatening to cut the Spaniards to pieces, supposing that they had overcome and murdered the pirates they left in her."

At that point, one of the bolder men from the *Diamond* went up onto the deck near the stern of the Spanish sloop, "flourished and whetted his cutlass," and dared Cooper to come aboard. The pirates realized their mistake and tried to get away, but more men from the *Diamond* quickly boarded the pirate sloop. Cooper and the others fired several times, wounding four men from the *Diamond,* but they soon realized they were doomed.

Pirate crews were often heard to say they'd rather die at their own hands than be captured. "They have no thoughts of ever being taken," wrote Captain Richard Hawkins after his capture by Spriggs' crew, "but swear, with the most direful imprecations, that if ever they should find themselves overpowered, they would immediately blow their ship up, rather than do *Jolly Roger* the disgrace to be struck, or suffer themselves to be hanged like dogs." Ashton had heard a similar pledge when Spriggs came close to being captured by another warship, the *Mermaid.* "When he saw the danger they were in of being taken, upon the man-of-war's out-sailing them, was afraid of falling into the hands of justice," Ashton wrote. "To prevent which, he and one of his companions took their pistols and laid them down by them, and solemnly swore to each other and pledged the oath in a bumper of liquor that if they saw there was at last no possibility of escaping, but that they should be taken, they would set foot to foot and shoot one another to escape justice and the halter."[4]

When the men from the *Diamond* climbed onto the deck of Cooper's sloop, the pirates ran into their cabin, touched a flame to gunpowder, and blew the cabin up. One man from the *Diamond* was killed during the explosion, and more than a dozen other men from both the warship and the pirate crew were severely burned or injured. The pirates were brought back to the *Diamond,* and a number of those who survived the explosion died aboard the warship only a few days later.[5]

Not long after taking Cooper's sloop, the *Diamond* saw a *piragua* alongside a schooner with what appeared to be a group of pirates tearing through the deck and plundering the ship. The *Diamond* immediately dispatched a boat, but the pirates quickly left in their *piragua* and escaped among the cays. About a week later, the sloops set out again to hunt for pirates near Guanaja and Roatan. It was then, in early February, that the men came within inches of catching Spriggs during their nighttime raid. The two pirates who were captured at Spriggs' camp said that Spriggs had been off the coast of Belize ten days before and that Shipton was still near the Black River, just thirty miles from Guanaja on the coast of Honduras.

The crew set sail for the Black River in their sloop and found some Miskito Indians to lead them to Shipton. They found Shipton during the night, fast asleep, and easily captured him. They took at least seventeen other men along with Shipton. The men then set out in the canoe they'd taken from Spriggs and captured three more of Spriggs' men in the area. On the heels of several successful captures, the men decided to stay in the area for a few more days to try and bring in some of the Baymen, who they suspected were supplying the pirates with vessels, gunpowder, and shot. But a heavy storm hit the coast and tore the sloop loose from its anchor. Cast adrift, the sloop was forced to sail back to the *Diamond,* meeting back up with the flagship on February 19. About twenty prisoners captured that January and February—including Shipton and other pirates from his and Cooper's crew, as well as several Spaniards—were taken back to Jamaica and put on trial in the first week of May 1726.

Joseph Cooper was not the only member of Spriggs' crew to strike out on his own. When Spriggs captured the sloop *Susannah* he put a quartermaster, Philip Lyne, in command of the ship. By early 1725, Lyne was capturing ships independently, although he and Spriggs may have followed the same course up the Atlantic coast of the American colonies during the first part of the year. Like Low and Spriggs, Lyne built his small crew by enticing recruits or forcing captives from the ships he overtook as he sailed north. By May, Lyne had about a dozen men aboard, both crew members and captives. Off the coast of Florida, Lyne captured a sloop on its way back to Virginia, forcing two more men and taking about half of the ship's cargo of rum and sugar.[6]

Sailors who were skilled in a trade—carpenters, coopers, navigators, and doctors—were often desperately needed aboard a pirate ship, and attempts to force these men could be ruthless. On June 3, Lyne captured a sloop sailing from Rhode Island to Martinique. Lyne shouted for the captain of the captured sloop, Edmund Casey, to row over to his ship. Casey took with him a crewman named James Salter and the ship's cooper, Ebenezer Mower. Mower was a short, thin man from Boston, about thirty years old. Once the captives were on Lyne's ship, the pirates started beating them. Mower was struck several times in the head with the handle of an ax, but he resisted the pirates' demands that he join their crew.

Lyne and his men forced Mower to lay his head down on the top of a hatch and then raised the ax again, holding it over his head. If he did not sign the ship's article at once, the pirates shouted, they would chop his head off. Mower pleaded with them, begging for his life. He then was taken back into one of the ship's cabins with the pirates. A short time later, they came back out. Mower told Salter he was "ruined and undone." He had been forced to sign the pirate's articles and he would sail away with Lyne.[7]

Lyne captured two more ships several weeks later, by this time further up the coast near Newfoundland. Lyne now had about forty men on board and a formidable number of guns—ten large cannon and sixteen swivel guns. He forced another tradesman, a carpenter, from one of the ships captured off Newfoundland. But Lyne's luck would run out in a matter of months.[8]

Sometime before November 1725, Lyne's ship was captured in a bloody battle with two sloops and brought back to the Dutch island of Curacao at the bottom of the Caribbean, just north of South America. Many of the pirates had been wounded during the capture and their injuries had barely been treated or bandaged. They were a dismal group as they were marched to their trial and, according to bystanders, they "were very offensive and stunk as they went along." Lyne was the most gruesome of the pack. He'd taken a blast head-on. One of his eyes was shot out and his nose hung down on his face. Lyne and four other pirates were convicted and hanged at Curacao.[9]

But in the end, nobody ever knew what happened to Spriggs and Low themselves. The two pirates separated in 1724 when Spriggs stole away in the newly captured galley off the coast of Africa with some of his followers. Not long after that, the remaining members of Low's crew decided they'd had enough of him and he was cast away in a boat near the Caribbean island of Martinique. It was then that Shipton was chosen as the new captain. Some reports suggest that Low was soon captured by the French and taken back to Martinique to be hanged. But those reports are contradicted by news brought back to the colonies by several sea captains returning from voyages to the Caribbean, as well as by sightings by the men from the HMS *Diamond* in the early part of 1726. Some of these reports even suggest that Spriggs and Low may have been sailing together again.

At the same time Ashton was on his journey back to Massachusetts— between April 1 and May 1—Spriggs was also cruising off the Atlantic coast. Off the coast of Florida in the middle of April, Spriggs captured a brigantine on its way back to Boston. Spriggs' crew held the brigantine for five days, rifling through its cargo and taking two carpenters on the ship as captives. But by mid-August, Spriggs was back down at one of his favorite hideaways, Roatan. He captured a sloop from Jamaica and stopped at the island to careen his flagship, the *Delight*. That stay at Roatan gave two disgruntled members of his crew, a quartermaster and a ship's doctor, a chance to abandon the ship. The two men convinced the captain of the captured Jamaican sloop to join them and together they overpowered the remaining pirates aboard the sloop one day while Spriggs was off in his canoe. The men were able to sail away in the sloop, although the former pirates were afraid to go back to Jamaica, where they would likely be put on trial. They decided instead to go ashore somewhere along the Central American coast.

A ship captain returning to New York in late November 1725 with news about Spriggs' activities near Roatan, and the subsequent capture of some other members of Spriggs' crew, said Spriggs was now aboard a sloop being commanded by Low. This and several other reports of the pirates' activities hint that not only was Low still alive and roaming as a pirate, but that he and Spriggs had joined up again. Only a day or two after returning from capturing Shipton in February 1726, some of the crew of the *Diamond* spotted Low with eight other men in a *piragua* off the west end of Guanaja. The canoe the *Diamond* had taken from Spriggs was being repaired that day, so the men weren't able to launch it and go looking for Low until that evening. The crew planned to attempt a nighttime attack on Low in the cays, but they got caught up in another storm and weren't able to launch the boat. By now, the sloop was running low on food and water and needed to head back to the *Diamond*. They caught one last glimpse of Low on their sail away from the island, brazenly navigating his *piragua* amongst the cays and along the shore; "he stayed till the sloop came so near as the people on board could see his swivel guns mounded on the bow of his *piragua*." The sloop followed for some time in the shallow water, "but their being many shoals in their way he got from them, just out of reach of the sloop."

What may be the last report of the whereabouts of Spriggs and Low places them off the coast of Virginia as late as June 1726. They may have sailed for a few more months, but they were not capturing and terrorizing ships at the rate they once were. The number of pirate crews sailing in the Atlantic and Caribbean was dwindling fast, due in part to the aggressive patrols by Royal Navy warships like the *Diamond*. Within a year or two after Ashton returned home, the golden age of piracy was over.

❦❦❦❦

When pirates like Low and Spriggs went to Roatan three hundred years ago, they usually went to the eastern end of the island, where Port Royal offered a protected harbor and fresh water. There was little reason to go to the western end of the island. But over time, the pattern reversed. Most of Roatan's year-round population of sixty thousand now lives closer to the western end in small towns like Coxen Hole and French Harbor. The tourists who come to the island, both by jet and on huge cruise ships that stop there each week, also tend to flock to the west end of the island in search of postcard-perfect sandy beaches, shops, restaurants and bars, and remarkable scuba diving sites. Roatan is a popular diving destination today because of the extensive coral reef that surrounds the island. But few people head east toward Port Royal anymore. The main roads on Roatan run only as far as Oak Ridge, and Port Royal is typically reached by boat. There are a few secluded vacation homes along the shore, and one or two dive resorts, but much of the mountainous eastern end of Roatan is still wild and untouched. It is a peaceful, solitary place. It might even still be recognizable to Ashton today.

Because so many pirates—including Morgan, Blackbeard, Low, and Spriggs—stopped at Roatan, there has always been speculation that there is buried treasure there. In the early 1930s, an English adventurer named Frederick Mitchell-Hedges and several of his companions went searching near Port Royal and on several neighboring islands for native artifacts. The men found some stunning items, including jade figurines, pottery, and sculptures, some of which are still housed today at the National Museum of the American Indian in New York.[10] But as the story goes—at least as told by several other treasure hunters generations later, for Mitchell-Hedges does not mention this discovery in his own book—one of the explorers took a ship's compass with him as he walked along one of the cays. Suddenly the needle on the compass swung wildly. The men started digging at that spot and soon, about a foot down, they unearthed a large iron chest. They broke off the rusted hasps and found that the chest was full of gold and jewels. Mitchell-Hedges soon discovered two more treasure chests on that cay.[11]

The explorers are said to have reburied the chests and planned to return to them in a few days, but later that same day they were told that the Honduran police on the island had heard about the discovery and were planning to come out to investigate. Mitchell-Hedges and his companions spent the night digging the chests back up and, just before daybreak the next day, sailed for Belize, where they disguised the treasure as Mayan artifacts and brought them back to New York.

The next treasure hunters said to have explored Port Royal were two men named Howard Jennings and Robin Moore. They had heard the story of the Mitchell-Hedges discovery and Jennings had contacted Mitchell-Hedges' stepdaughter, who told him about the location of a third treasure chest that the men had been unable to take during their midnight escape. Jennings and Moore went to Roatan in 1963, exploring the area around Port Royal and the cays in the harbor. The men found a number of old discarded items—cannonballs, brass buttons, shoe buckles, and a flat iron—as well as one buried chest holding a gold necklace, a gold ring, and some silver Spanish pieces of eight, or *Reales*, blackened from years of exposure to moisture. Jennings and Moore claimed that the dates on the silver coins ranged between 1635 and 1687. The explorers also searched Careening Cay and the largest of a pair of two rocky islands that lie within Port Royal harbor, known as the Cow, and claimed to have found another box containing a pair of old leather boots, a corroded navigational quadrant, some silver ingots, and a small leather pouch containing several handfuls of gold nuggets. The rumors of buried treasure persist on Roatan today, though not everyone who is familiar with the island and the treasure hunters is convinced that these stories are true.[12]

Another treasure hunter believed he had discovered buried gold and silver coins actually hidden away by Low himself, but that find was thousands of miles to the north of Roatan. In 1947, Massachusetts historian and author Edward Rowe Snow bought what he believed was a treasure map that may have belonged to Low. The one-page map was really nothing more than a simple, hand-drawn sketch on a torn piece of paper. The strip of land drawn on the map is labeled "Island Haute." At the bottom of the paper is the name "E. Low." The word "Victoria" is also written on the map, which may have referenced a Portuguese ship that Low captured in 1723 called the *Nostra Signiora de Victoria;* it was that ship's captain whom Low had tortured by slicing off his lips and broiling them over a fire. Snow identified the land depicted on the map as Isle Haute, a one-and-a-half-mile-long island just off the Nova Scotia shoreline at the top of the Bay of Fundy. The name written on the map, Snow believed, belonged to the pirate Edward Low.[13]

There are four places marked on the map, three of them apparently navigational markers on the island: a rocky formation just off the island's western end called "Boar Head," the island's long rocky tail of shallows at the eastern end marked "Dangerous Bar," and another spot to the southeast called "Wrack Point." An arrow points to the fourth point on the map, just to the east of a small lake near one end of the island, labeled "The Place."

In June 1952, Snow took a boat out to Isle Haute to explore the site marked on the map as "The Place." He stayed with the island's lighthouse keeper, the only resident on the rocky island, and spent his days digging in several spots near the lake, scanning the dirt, gravel, and stones with a metal detector. On his first day of digging, Snow found a large iron spike and the broken ribs and skull of what he believed was a human skeleton. After digging for several more hours the next day, Snow found what we was looking for—eight small, blackened disks buried in the soil. When Snow cleaned the disks off, they were Spanish and Portuguese coins of gold and silver.

Based on his map, Snow believed the coins were part of the pirate treasure buried by Edward Low. One of the pieces was a Portuguese coin dated 1710, which is consistent with the time when Low was sailing. It's possible, as Snow believed, that Low stole up the Bay of Fundy after his disastrous battle with the *Greyhound* off Newport, Rhode Island, in the summer of 1723 and hid away some of his spoils on the secluded Isle Haute. In fact, some members of Low's crew who were captured in the battle with the *Greyhound* claimed Low had "150,000 pounds in gold and silver" aboard his sloop at the time. When Snow returned to Boston, his discoveries captured widespread public attention and were even featured in an article in *Life* magazine in July 1952.[14]

❦❦❦❦❦

After returning to Marblehead in 1725, Philip Ashton seems to have settled back into the routines of life. He may well have gone back to cod fishing not long after he came home. Barnard mentions that during the several months leading up to the publication of *Ashton's Memorial,* Ashton "has necessarily been so much absent." This seems to suggest that Ashton may have already gone back to sea on extended offshore fishing trips. Fishing was Marblehead's principal industry and it was likely the only trade Ashton knew. If Ashton did return to the fleet of fishing schooners, the camaraderie of the crew and the familiar routine of hauling in cod and packing it in salt might have been a comfort to him. But there must have been nervous moments aboard his first trips to sea too. What would have passed through Ashton's mind the first few times he looked up from his fishing lines and saw a passing brigantine or other large ship on the horizon? What did it feel like to sail with his crew back into the fateful harbor of Port Roseway in Nova Scotia?

When he was not working, whether on a fishing boat or not, Ashton went on to marry and raise a family. About a year and a half after coming home, he married a young woman named Jane Gallison, just seventeen or eighteen years old. Their marriage was tragically short, however. They had a daughter, Sarah, born a year later, but Jane died just days after the baby's birth in December 1727. A year and a half later, Ashton married Sarah Bartlett, a young woman who was closer to Ashton's age. Ashton had many more years with his second wife. The couple had six children together—a girl and five boys, though one of the boys died at a young age—in the twelve years between 1730 and 1742. There is no surviving record of Ashton's death, but the birth of his youngest son in 1742 indicates Ashton lived at least into his forties.[15]

Ashton's minister, John Barnard, lived a long life, remaining in Marblehead until his death at age eighty-eight in January 1770. In addition to his daily duties of baptisms, funerals, attending to sermons, and visiting the sick, Barnard continued to work with Marblehead fish captains to develop the town's fishing trade and keep it independent of the merchants in Salem and Boston. Ironically, given his at times testy relationship with the Mathers, later in his life Barnard was asked if he would consider coming back to the North Church in Boston to fill the shoes of Cotton Mather and his father, both now dead. But Barnard said he was too attached to Marblehead to leave. "I look upon myself so strongly engaged to Marblehead, from their kind treatment of me, that no prospect of worldly interest shall prevail with me to leave them," Barnard later wrote.[16]

Barnard was proud of his many sermons and religious writings over his lifetime. Some of them, he wrote, drew "high expressions of commendation from some of the most judicious ministers" and the words from one of his tracts "sounded in the pulpits in Boston and in the country churches many months after." But he makes no mention in his autobiography of *Ashton's Memorial,* and it is almost certain that Barnard never knew of its influence on Daniel Defoe or anyone else. As interesting as Ashton's encounter with the pirates was, for Barnard the true message in the story was "God's ability to save," which he continued to profess throughout his time in Marblehead.

At some point soon after returning home, Ashton would have finally learned about the final days of his former crewmate, Joseph Libbey. About three months after Ashton had escaped on Roatan, Libbey was aboard Low's second sloop, the *Ranger,* when it was attacked and captured during the day-long battle with the HMS *Greyhound* off the coast of Newport, Rhode Island, in June 1723. The accused pirates had spent several weeks under armed guard in a musty jail cell in Newport, shackled in chains. At one point three of the prisoners managed to get out of their chains and attack the jail keeper, his daughter, and a servant when they came to bring the men their breakfast. The three prisoners "knocked down the gaol-keeper with their irons, got out of the gaol and ran a little way to the outskirts of town." But the three pirates were soon caught, brought back to the jail, and put in the dungeon. Another of the men who was wounded during the battle with the *Greyhound* died after several weeks in jail.[17]

Ironically, if Ashton had stayed aboard with Low instead of running ashore on Roatan, he might have gotten back to New England almost two years earlier. But it's impossible to know if he would have survived. Ashton could have been on Harris' sloop and ended up in the Newport jail, but he could just as likely have been held on Low's sloop and sailed north with the crew and back across the Atlantic again. Even if Ashton had been brought in with the surviving members of Harris' crew, only a handful of the men aboard the pirate ship—even those initially taken as captives—were acquitted.

The judges needed to hear consistent testimony from shipmates that a man was never involved in the pirates' activities—never held a weapon and never took anything off a captured ship—before they would find him not guilty. Ashton may have lucked out, like Joseph Swetser, another quiet, melancholy young man who kept to himself, or Thomas Mumford, a Native American who cooked for the crew. Swetser, according to shipmates who testified at the trial, "refused to go on board any vessels," and even during the devastating battle with the *Greyhound* Swetser had simply "sat unarmed in the range of the mast." Many of the other men aboard the pirate sloop who claimed they were forced men were still convicted, however. In fact, John Valentine, the advocate general who prosecuted the case, took a cynical view of the captives' repeated arguments that they were "forced" men. "The plea of constraint, or force (in the mouth of every pirate) can be of no avail to them," Valentine told the court, "for if that would justify or excuse, no pirate would ever be convicted."

The Newport trial started on July 10, 1723, a month after the pirates were captured. The captives who were believed to be innocent were tried first and typically acquitted. These men could then serve as witnesses when other, presumably guilty, members of the crew were called to the bar. Many of the prisoners claimed they were forced but heard other shipmates testify that they'd been active members of the pirate crew. John Brown, a twenty-nine-year-old seaman from England, told the court he had been captured at the Cape Verde Islands and that Low had "beat him black and blue to make him sign the articles." But another seaman testified against Brown, describing a conversation the two of them had when Low was capturing a ship in the West Indies.

During the encounter, the man said, Brown told him "he had rather be in a tight vessel than a leaky one, and that he was not forced." William Blades, a thirty-two-year-old sailor from Rhode Island, also claimed he was forced aboard, never signed the ship's articles, and only took what the pirates gave him, but he was still convicted.[18]

It wasn't until the third day of the trial that Libbey was called up, along with two other prisoners. All of them pleaded not guilty to the charges brought against them of "piracy, robberies, and felonies." Libbey insisted that he was forced to join the pirates and held against his will, and he presented as evidence an advertisement published in a Boston newspaper containing sworn statements about his capture, along with Ashton and Merritt, by Low's crew at Nova Scotia. But four witnesses—all men who had also been forced aboard Low's ships but had been acquitted by the court earlier in the trial—came forward to testify against Libbey. The witnesses' accounts painted a picture of Libbey as an active participant in attacks while aboard with the pirates, firing weapons and participating in the plunder of captured vessels. John Kencate, the doctor who'd been taken by Low near the Cape Verde Islands, told the court that "Joseph Libbey was an active man aboard the *Ranger*, and used to go on board vessels they took and plundered, and that he saw him fire several times." Thomas Mumford, one of several Native Americans captured off Nantucket shortly before Libbey and Ashton were taken aboard, also testified that he'd seen Libbey plunder captured ships and once that he once came away with a pair of stockings.

The verdict came quickly. Before lunchtime, the court had handed down a guilty verdict against Libbey and one of the other two prisoners tried that morning. Similar evidence was presented at the trial against other crew members, including Low's quartermaster, Charles Harris, who was in command of the *Ranger* when it was captured. The twenty-six convicted pirates were taken back to the jail for another seven days.

As the execution day drew near, two of the condemned men were granted a reprieve. William Dummer, the acting governor of the Massachusetts Bay Colony, who presided at the Newport trial, wrote to London requesting pardons for them. One of these men was Patrick

Cunningham, who'd been captured by the pirates a year earlier. Cunningham's case was similar to Libbey's. He'd been taken captive the same weekend as Libbey and Ashton at Port Roseway, Nova Scotia, and several witnesses testified against him at the trial. One told the court he'd seen Cunningham aboard the pirate ship with a gun in his hand, and another said Cunningham had taken a share of plunder from captured ships. But the testimony of John Welland, the Boston sea captain whose ear was sliced off by a pirate's cutlass after his capture in May, may have swayed the court in Cunningham's favor. Cunningham had come to Welland's rescue as he lay bleeding below decks, bringing him some water, going to get the ship's doctor, and helping the doctor to bandage Welland. In fact, Welland testified, Cunningham "was the means of saving his life." So while Libbey and the other condemned pirates were marched to their execution, Cunningham and one other reprieved man, a seventeen-year-old John Brown (the youngest of two men named John Brown aboard the *Ranger*), were held in jail for close to a year. Their pardon was issued in London in March 1724, and the men were released when the news finally reached New England.[19]

Cunningham's close call was similar to the case of another pirate captive, William Phillips, who was forced aboard the pirate ship under the command of John Phillips in 1723. William Phillips was the man whose leg was shot—and later sawed off—during the standoff between John Phillips and the small band of pirates who tried to escape from the crew in the captured snow. At the trial of the surviving members of the John Phillips' crew, held in Boston in May 1724, William Phillips told the court he at first refused to sign his name to the ship's articles and in the end did so only when forced at gunpoint. But despite that, Phillips found himself in the same frightening situation as many of the captives from Low's crew, since he knew that anyone seen holding a weapon or taking a few simple articles of clothing from a captured ship—even when ordered to do so—could be convicted of piracy.

Phillips knew this, and even before the trial he was worried this might happen. After his left leg was cut off, the pirate captain John Phillips tried to send him back to shore. But the one-legged Phillips didn't want to risk it. The captain of a fishing schooner captured by the pirates in April near southern Nova Scotia was willing to take Phillips home with him. But despite his injury, Phillips refused to go, "saying if he should they would hang him."[20]

At the trial in Boston, the testimony by several of Phillips' crewmates seemed to raise doubts about the extent to which Phillips was an active member of the pirate crew. Fillmore, for example, told the court that he did not see Phillips board a brigantine the pirates captured and robbed shortly after he came aboard. Fillmore testified that Phillips boarded the captured snow along with Ferne and several other pirates, and he described the turn of events that resulted in Phillips' being shot in the leg. Fillmore said Phillips was carrying a cutlass when he went aboard the snow, although another sea captain taken by the pirates testified that he did not know whether Phillips actually helped carry any food the pirates took off the snow back to their schooner.

The court split over Phillips' case. When the judges voted, he alone was narrowly convicted by a plurality of the panel, even as six other captives were unanimously acquitted. Phillips then heard the fateful judgment of the court, words that could only drown him with regret: "You, William Phillips, are to go from hence to the place whence you come and from thence to the place of execution, and there you are to be hanged by the neck until you are dead, and God of His Infinite Mercy save your Soul." Luckily for Phillips, however, he was somehow spared. At the last moment, Williams and one of the other convicted pirates were granted a reprieve, and Governor Dummer wrote to London asking for a royal pardon of the two pirates. The pardon was granted a year later.[21]

❦❦❦❦

Libbey and the other condemned pirates from Low's crew were hanged in a celebrated Newport execution just after noon on Friday, July 19. The gallows where the men were hanged had been built on a narrow strip of land called Gravelly Point that extended out from the harbor's edge. The crowd that gathered to watch the execution could see flying above the condemned men a dark pirate flag, the same flag the men had aboard their ship when it was captured, now fastened to one corner of the gallows as a mark of their crimes. Hundreds of people had come to watch the spectacle that was about to unfold. "Never was there a more doleful sight in all this land," one witness wrote, "than while they were standing on the stage, waiting for the stopping of their breath and the flying of their souls into the eternal world."[22]

Nobody knows what went through Joseph Libbey's mind during the final moments in Newport before he closed his eyes for the last time. Some of the other men with him had, the day before, dictated letters to their parents, brothers, and sisters, gushing with regret. "I desire you all in general to take warning by me, for you see what a greedy eye brings a young man to," wrote one of them, John Fitzgerald, a twenty-one-year-old sailor from Ireland. "Beware how you disobey your friends. Beware of drunkenness, for it is the inlet of all other sins. I must confess that I was not guilty of murder, nor of striking men as others were; but of all other sins I was guilty, of which I ask God's pardon." Libbey, too, may well have thought in his final hours about the sequence of events that led him from the fishing vessel he shared with Ashton to the gallows at the edge of Newport harbor. After the execution, the men's bodies were taken just across the harbor to Goat Island where they were buried along the shore between the high and low water marks.[23]

The capture and hanging of the twenty-six pirates from Low's crew was celebrated throughout New England. The newspapers in Boston published detailed descriptions of the historic execution. Cotton Mather delivered a sermon on the fate of the pirates hanged in Newport that July, and he published a copy of his exhortation shortly after. "If you will not hear the warnings of your faithful pastors," Mather said in his sermon, "hear the roarings of twenty-six terrible preachers that, in a ghastly apparition are now from the dead, calling you to turn and live unto God."[24] Two hundred miles to the southwest, in New York City, the celebration of the pirates' capture was less religious than in Puritan Boston, but there was plenty of gloating nonetheless.

The *Greyhound,* the royal warship that captured the pirates in June, was stationed out of New York, and the ship's captain, Peter Solgard, was honored by the city council when he returned to port less than a week after the execution. Low and his crew "have been remarkably cruel, and have done vast damage in the West Indies," wrote New York governor William Burnet, "but the honor of destroying them has been reserved for Captain Solgard, whose merit makes everybody glad it has fallen to his share, at the same time that they rejoice at the public deliverance." The mayor presented Solgard with the "Freedom of the City," a certificate of gratitude that symbolically conferred the privileges of residency to the captain from England. The certificate was presented along with a gold box praising his efforts in the "war against the enemies of the human race" and engraved with both the coat of arms of New York and a depiction of the *Greyhound*'s battle against the pirates. The city council also adopted a resolution praising Solgard for his "signal services done against the enemies of mankind."

The captured pirate sloop, the *Ranger,* did not survive for long. Brought back to New York by Solgard, it was anchored in the harbor in the last week of July when a violent storm struck and the sloop was blown out to sea.[25]

For Ashton, the irony was that his own life may have been saved by Libbey's apparent decision to join the pirate crew. The scene at the disastrous careening of Low's pink, *Rose,* off Devil's Island suggests Libbey was by then already seen as a member of the crew. It was off Devil's Island that the pirates tipped over Low's pink while trying to clean it. The pink sank in the bay, and two men drowned. Ashton himself had been working on high on one of the vessel's masts when it tipped, and he jumped overboard even though he did not know how to swim. Clinging to the ship's buoy, Ashton struggled to keep his head above water. The pirates who were circling the sunken pink in a small boat to pick up survivors refused to take Ashton aboard. But Libbey was allowed on the crowded boat, most likely because he had decided to join with the pirates during the sail across the Atlantic. Libbey signaled to Ashton to swim over to him and then, grabbing him by the hand, pulled him aboard, possibly saving his life.

While Ashton may have gone back to fishing when he came home, another pirate captive, John Fillmore, did not. The one fishing trip he took in his life, which resulted in his capture by Phillips' pirate crew, apparently put an end to Fillmore's desire to work at sea. Fillmore was not alone. Nicholas Simmons, one of the captives taken by Spriggs, also decided he could not bear to go back to work at sea. About five months after he returned home to Newport with Barlow and the other captives, Simmons filed a petition with the governor of Rhode Island seeking financial compensation because, he claimed, he was "now under a necessity to leave off his employment of a mariner for fear of the said pirates."[26]

For his part, Fillmore returned briefly to Ipswich, on the north shore of Boston, after the trial and execution of the surviving members of Phillips' crew. Fillmore married a woman named Mary Spiller only six months after returning home. But Fillmore and his new wife moved almost immediately to a seventy-acre farm in Franklin, Connecticut. Fillmore and his first wife had four children before her death in late 1733 or early 1734. Fillmore soon married again and had twelve more children with his second wife, Dorcas Day.

Fillmore was the great-grandfather of U.S. president Millard Fillmore. The line to the future president was through Fillmore's fourth child with Dorcas, a boy named Nathaniel, who was born in 1739. Nathaniel would go on to survive a brush or two with danger of his own. By the time he was fifteen, England and France were fighting again in what would come to be known as the French and Indian Wars. Nathaniel went into battle with other New Englanders but was wounded during a skirmish and left in the woods on his own. He survived for about a week by eating only a few kernels of corn he had with him and, when that was gone, by chewing on pieces of his shoes and a blanket. Anguishing in the woods, though, Nathaniel had with him a reminder of his father's struggle aboard the pirate ship: Phillips' sword, which had been given to Fillmore at the end of the pirates' trial, along with some silver buckles, two gold rings, and a tobacco box. Nathaniel is said to have used the sword given him by his father in both the French and Indian Wars and later the Revolutionary War.

It was the second of Nathaniel's six children, a son also named Nathaniel, who would grow up to be the father of Millard Fillmore, who became the thirteenth president of the United States in 1850, following the death of Zachary Taylor. President Fillmore was apparently familiar with his great-grandfather's experiences as a pirate captive and kept a copy of John Fillmore's narrative for many years. The president may also have owned the infamous sword that once belonged to the pirate captain John Phillips.[27]

Unlike Fillmore, one other captive who helped overthrow Phillips' pirate crew—the carpenter Edward Cheesman—did return to sea. Cheesman sailed to England after the trial in Boston and by early 1726 was serving as the carpenter on a British warship, HMS *Kingsale*.[28]

Fillmore and Cheesman were not the only captives to overthrow a pirate crew during the 1720s. Within a year, pirates—as well as Puritan ministers and Marblehead fishermen—were again thrust into the public eye on the occasion of one of the last pirate executions held in Boston, on July 12, 1726. Those events poignantly symbolize the end of the widespread piracy that Ashton, Libbey, and Fillmore got caught up in during the early American colonial era, and they provide the last hint of the whereabouts of the pirates Spriggs and Low.

It was just six weeks earlier when several rebellious crew members led by a man named William Fly took control of an English slaving vessel that was sailing from Jamaica to the coast of Africa. Just after midnight on May 27, Fly and his partners had crept into the ship's cabin and dragged the captain, John Green, out onto the deck. Green begged for mercy as the men picked him up and heaved him over the ship's rail. Fighting to the end, the captain reached desperately for something to hold onto, grabbing onto a rope or the mainsail. One of Fly's men then picked up an axe and chopped off the captain's hand, and he fell to his death into the sea. The mutineers then threw the ship's first mate overboard as well and took control of the ship.[29]

Fly's crew became pirates and headed north. In all, they had a little more than twenty men on board. The ship was armed with six cannon— four large carriage guns and two swivel guns—as well as a good supply of muskets and pistols. Seven days later, they captured a sloop that was anchored off the coast of North Carolina. One of the captives they took was William Atkinson, a ship's captain who was aboard as a passenger traveling back to Boston. The next day, off the coast of Virginia, Fly's crew met up with two sloops under the command of Spriggs and Low. Fly's brief encounter with the two pirates, reported by a New London ship captain Fly captured four days later, remains the last surviving report of the activities of Spriggs and Low.

Fly's crew went on to capture two more ships over the next week or so. As they sailed toward New England, the pirates forced Atkinson to serve as their pilot, but Atkinson gave the appearance of cooperating and Fly came to trust him. This trust would allow Atkinson to lead an uprising of his own, although his revolt against the pirates was nowhere near as bloody as Fillmore's.

By June 23 the pirates were near Martha's Vineyard, just off the southern edge of Massachusetts. The pirates caught up with and captured a fishing schooner from Marblehead. Fly sent several of his men over to take command of the schooner, and the vessels then set off to look for other ships. Standing on the deck, Atkinson told Fly he could see several more ships in the distance. Fly said he couldn't see them. Atkinson told Fly it was because of where he was standing; if he moved over next to Atkinson, he would be able to see the ships. Fly walked across the deck, briefly stepping away from his guns and cutlass, and peered through his spyglass in search of the ships. In an instant, Atkinson and several other men grabbed the unarmed Fly, held him at gunpoint, and tied him up on the ship's deck. The ship was then brought back into Boston harbor and the pirates were arrested.

All the men aboard the ship, including Atkinson, were brought to trial five days later. But only Fly and three others—Samuel Cole, Henry Greenville, and George Condick—were convicted. Exactly a week later, on July 12, all but Condick were executed before a large crowd in Boston Harbor near the mouth of the Charles River. Condick, a "drunken, ignorant fellow who served as ship's cook," was granted a last-minute reprieve at the gallows.[30]

Two days before the men died, a Sunday, was a momentous day in the pulpits of Boston. Benjamin Colman and Cotton Mather both gave sermons on the pirates that day. The themes were by now familiar ones: a reciting of the crimes against man and against God that had been committed by the condemned men and a warning to other young men who worked at sea not to fall to the temptations of piracy. But the pirates' leader, William Fly, refused to attend church with the other condemned men. Fly didn't show even a hint of guilt or remorse. Fly's irreverence even in the face of death seemed to underscore that in some ways the ministers were fighting a losing battle. Mather, now sixty-three years old, met several times with Fly to offer religious counsel and to pray for forgiveness. But Fly steadfastly refused. He confessed to nothing, showed not even the slightest fear of dying, and saw no reason to repent.[31]

William Fly was one of the last pirates of the golden age of piracy, and his complete disregard for the law and morality offered a fitting end to nearly three decades of colonial discourse on the exploits of pirates. Fly's unrepentant death came at a time when the Puritan battle over social and religious order was also dying out. The same year Fly died, twenty-six Puritan ministers—including Mather, Colman, and Barnard—jointly published their final warning on the dangers of drunkenness and time wasted in taverns. When Mather's sermon and notes from his meetings with the pirates was published several weeks later, it would prove to be his last criminal narrative. Mather's death in two years would mark the passing of a third generation of Puritan leaders. New England was becoming less a place singularly devoted to Puritan ideals and was increasingly more secular and materialistic.[32]

When Fly was led out of the Boston jail to be brought to the place of execution on July 12, he did not quiver with fear or hang his head in shame. He acted as though he did not have a care in the world. Fly briskly jumped into the cart that would carry the men down to the water's edge. He rode to the gallows with a bunch of flowers in his hand, greeting and bowing to onlookers who lined the road as he passed. Fly jumped enthusiastically up onto the scaffold. Asked if he had any final words, Fly simply warned other ship captains that they had better treat their crews well or risk the same violent death he had brought upon his master. Around three o'clock that afternoon, the moment came for the men to die. The hangman stepped up to place the noose around Fly's neck. But carefully watching the man's work, Fly told him he wasn't doing it right. Fly then took the noose in his own hands and fastened it around his neck himself.

Later that same day, several men steered a boat out of Boston Harbor. The wooden craft rode low in the water, weighted down by its cargo. Their destination was Nixes Mate Island, a small patch of land less than six miles from Boston. Today, Nixes Mate Island is little more than a mound of rocks capped by a cone-shaped harbor marker with black and white stripes. But in July 1726, before much of the slate on Nixes Mate had been dug up, there was more to the patch of land. The men were headed there in a boat loaded with the corpses of the three executed pirates. Two of the pirates, Cole and Greenville, were buried.[33] But like John Rose Archer before him, Fly was hung in chains on the small harbor island to rot, a gruesome symbol of the pirates that sailed the Atlantic during this bloody era.

Acknowledgments

At the Point of a Cutlass began with Philip Ashton's fascinating narrative written in 1725, but filling the gaps in this firsthand account required searching for a number of details long hidden away in a wealth of colonial newspaper reports, ship's logbooks, trial records, and other archival documents. Many people and organizations were incredibly helpful in my search for these materials. I am grateful to the staffs of the Massachusetts Historical Society and the Boston Public Library, as well as to a number of archivists, including Karen Mac Innis, curator of the Marblehead Museum & Historical Society, Wayne Butler of the Marblehead Historical Commission, Ken Carlson of the Rhode Island State Archives Division, Jennifer Robinson of the Newport Historical Society, David Rumsey and the David Rumsey Map Collection, Dolly Snow Bicknell, Pat Libbey Davis, and Lee Casey. Philip Schwartzberg created the map of Low's voyages for this book. At the National Archives in London, Simon Neal was extremely helpful in obtaining sections of the logbooks from several British warships, including the *Greyhound,* the *Mermaid,* and the *Diamond,* and other pieces of correspondence from this period.

Ashton's odyssey carried him to the far reaches of the Atlantic and Caribbean, and helpful hosts and guides enhanced my visits to key locations in this story. In Nova Scotia, I was welcomed by Shelburne Harbor Boat Tours and the Fort Anne National Historic Site of Canada. On Roatan, Matt and Corrine Cavanaugh at the Royal Playa Resort did everything they could to facilitate my exploration of Port Royal and the surrounding area. I am especially indebted to my wonderful guide, Randy Matute, who spent a day with me using a 1742 map to hunt down the creek where Ashton escaped and even went so far as to climb a sapote tree so I could see and taste the rare fruit that sustained Philip Ashton during his time on the island. I am also grateful to the writer Anne Jennings Brown, who lived for many years in Port Royal and is the author of *Roatan Odyssey*. Anne offered both encouragement and additional insights into the history of Roatan.

Several writers and accomplished historians provided valuable feedback on sticky questions or sections of this book in draft form. I appreciate the assistance of Daniel Finamore at the Peabody Essex Museum, Marcus Rediker at the University of Pittsburgh, Michael Jarvis at the University of Rochester, Daniel Vickers at the University of British Columbia, and Manuel Schonhorn, professor emeritus at Southern Illinois University–Carbondale. Brendan Dubois provided early encouragement and, like the accomplished journalist that he is, helped me focus the narrative in important ways. David McKean provided a powerful critique that helped put this project on a sure course. I am grateful to two wonderful colleagues with deep experience in the publishing world: my agent, Roger Williams, and my editor at the University Press of New England, Stephen Hull, who repeatedly prompted me to think, question, and clarify.

My family is a constant source of support and joy. My parents instilled in me a passion for exploring and writing early on. My brother Sean has been a constant fan of this project. I am especially grateful to my son, who continues to tolerate countless stories about pirates and ships and who endured a long cruise around Shelburne Harbor and the Nova Scotia coastline so that I could conduct some of my research.

Cod fishing lies at the very heart of Massachusetts' history. There is, even to this day, a Sacred Cod that hangs high above the floor of the House of Representatives in the State House in Boston. When I was working there many years ago, it never occurred to me that the history of Massachusetts cod fishing would uncover the amazing story represented by Philip Ashton's journey. I also never dreamed I would marry and spend my life with the wonderful young woman who worked just down the hall from me at the State House—but I did. Just about everything I have accomplished since then, including this book, has been perfected by the advice and support of my wife, Laura. This book is for her.

Notes

PROLOGUE: JULY 19, 1723

1. The July 19, 1723, hangings are often described, as in a site marker located near the place of execution in Newport, Rhode Island, as the "single, largest, mass public execution in the history of America." In fact, the hangings do represent the largest mass execution of pirates on American soil during the colonial period. But there were several larger mass executions, almost entirely of African American men, that occurred in prerevolutionary America in 1740 and 1741 as a consequence of slave revolts. Blackman and McLaughlin, "Mass Legal Executions in America." Additional details regarding the Newport execution are from "Trials of Thirty-Six Persons for Piracy," in Updike, *Memoirs of the Rhode Island Bar; Boston News Letter,* July 25, 1723, and August 1, 1723; *New England Courant,* July 22, 1723; Cotton Mather, *Useful Remarks: An Essay Upon Remarkables in the Way of Wicked Men,* 1723; and Banner, *The Death Penalty,* pp. 44–48.

2. Hart to Council of Trade and Plantations, Calendar of State Papers Colonial, America and West Indies, vol. 34: 1724–1725, pp. 71–76.

CHAPTER 1: THE *REBECCA*

1. Reports of the warehouse fire on Long Wharf are in the *Boston News Letter,* January 8, 1722 and January 15, 1722. The "extreme cold for six days" of that January are from the diary of Jeremiah Bumstead, published in the *New England Historical and Genealogical Register* 15, no. 3 (July 1861).

2. The *Rebecca*'s departure for Saint Kitts in January of 1722 was reported in the *Boston News Letter,* January 8, 1722.

3. Drake, *Life and Correspondence of Henry Knox,* p. 125.

4. Bridenbaugh, *Cities in the Wilderness,* pp. 155–56, 184. The population in Boston in 1720 was estimated to be approximately 12,000, compared to 10,000 in Philadelphia and 7,000 in New York.

5. Neal, *The History of New England,* pp. 224–25.

6. Vickers, *Young Men and the Sea,* pp. 62–67; *Boston News Letter,* June 18 1722.

7. There is almost no documented evidence concerning Low's early years before he became a pirate, other than the dates of his marriage and birth of his child in Boston. The background details concerning the lives of both Edward Low and George Lowther before they sailed as pirates are drawn from Dow and Edmonds, *Pirates of the New England Coast* and Daniel Defoe's *A General History of the Pyrates.* Defoe's history is illustrative but is not used as a primary source for the remainder of the story told here. As Schonhorn notes in his introduction (pp. xxxv–xxxvi) to Defoe's *History of the Pyrates,* Defoe relied heavily on contemporary newspaper reports and other communications in compiling his history of pirates, but he also embellished these reports in many cases and some of the details in his book are simply wrong.

8. *Boston News Letter,* May 7, 1716.

9. Rediker, *Between the Devil and the Deep Blue Sea,* p. 231; Calendar of State Papers Colonial, America and West Indies, vol. 32 (1720–1721), pp. 388–402.

10. The signing of the Treaty of Utrecht, which ended the War of Spanish Succession, changed the political landscape of the Atlantic. England gained a number of new territories through the treaty, including the island of Saint Kitts (then known as Saint Christopher's), the major sugar-producing island in the West Indies, where the *Rebecca* had just stopped. Further to the north, where the conflict was known as Queen Anne's War, England also took possession of Nova Scotia and Newfoundland. This summary of the causes of the rise in piracy during the early 1700s is based largely on Marcus Rediker's *Villains of All Nations,* David Cordingly's *Pirate Hunter,* and Peter Earle's *Pirate Wars,* as well as Dow and Edmonds, *Pirates of the New England Coast.* The line that separated government-authorized privateering and illegal piracy was often a blurry one. Many men known today as pirates were initially privateers with official commissions. A generation before Low's time, Captain William Kidd launched a far-reaching campaign in search of pirates under an English privateering commission, but by 1699 he was arrested in Boston, accused of being a pirate himself, and shipped back to London, where he was tried and hanged in 1704. Even closer to home, the same thing

happened to a sea captain named John Quelch. Quelch set sail out of Marblehead harbor in 1703—also with a privateering commission—but upon his
return with a load of gold, sugar, and other goods taken from a Portuguese
ship, Quelch was arrested, tried, and hanged on the shore of Boston Harbor
in 1704. The fine line between privateering and piracy is illustrated in Zacks,
The Pirate Hunter, and Beal, *Quelch's Gold.*

11. Cordingly, *Pirate Hunter,* pp. 124–27; Earle, *Pirate Wars,* pp. 160–65.

12. Lydon, "Fish for Gold"; Shepherd and Walton, "Trade, Distribution,
and Economic Growth in Colonial America"; and Walton, "New Evidence
on Colonial Commerce."

13. Letter from Captain Peter Solgard, June 12, 1723, Admiralty Records
1/2452, National Archives, London; Earle, *Pirate Wars,* pp. 161, 179; Rediker,
Villains of All Nations, p. 8; Jarvis, *In the Eye of All Trade,* pp. 122–24.

14. *Boston News Letter,* June 18, 1722.

15. *New England Courant,* June 11, 1722; *American Weekly Mercury,* June
21, 1722; *Boston News Letter,* June 25, 1722; Records of the Colony of Rhode
Island and Providence Plantations, vol. 4 (1707 to 1740), p. 314. The adjutant of the militia regiment was aboard a sloop under the command of John
Hance, who had to get several residents from Block Island to help him bring
his disabled vessel back to a harbor there.

16. *New England Courant,* June 11, 1722. The news reports about Low's
attacks the first week of June 1722 also landed Benjamin Franklin's older
brother, James, in a Boston jail for three weeks. James Franklin was the
publisher of the *New England Courant,* which reported on June 11, 1722,
that in addition to the two ships setting out from Newport in search of
Low, a third ship was being prepared in Boston. The article in the *Courant*
stated, however, that "the Government of the Massachusetts are fitting
out a Ship to go after the Pirates . . . tis thought [the captain] will sail
sometime this Month, if Wind and Weather permit." Apparently colonial
officials in Boston interpreted the report as suggesting the government was
being lax in its attempts to hunt down Low, and the general court ordered
James Franklin jailed. This meant that sixteen-year-old Benjamin Franklin
was responsible for publishing the *Courant* over the next three weeks.
See Massachusetts Historical Society, "Benjamin Franklin—Newspaper
Publisher and Runaway," http://masshist.org/online/silence_dogood/essay.
php?entry_id=204. See also *Boston News Letter,* June 18, 1722; *New England
Courant,* June 18, 1722; "Trials of Thirty-Six Persons for Piracy," in Updike,
Memoirs of the Rhode Island Bar.

1. It is impossible to know precisely when Ashton and his crew left Marblehead or how long they had been fishing near southern Nova Scotia that month, but the men were almost certainly at the fishing grounds by the end of May, when Low captured the *Rebecca*. Ashton later said he had "been out for some time . . . upon the fishing grounds off Cape Sable shore." New England fishermen at the time would often head north to Nova Scotia and Newfoundland as early as March each year. Vickers, *Farmers and Fishermen*, p. 149.

2. When Richard Hanniford died in 1709, his daughter Sarah (Hanniford) Ashton was living in his house on Franklin Street. Sarah had married Ashton's father, also named Philip Ashton, in 1701, and the younger Philip Ashton was born in 1702. See "The Henley Families" in *The Magazine of History* 18 (January–June 1914): p. 42; and "Marblehead in the Year 1700" in The Essex Institute Historical Collections, vol. 47 (1911), p. 156. Ashton's perspective on the events at Port Roseway that June and in the years that followed are retold in the narrative by John Barnard, *Ashton's Memorial: An History of the Strange Adventures and Signal Deliverances of Mr. Philip Ashton*, published in 1725 by Samuel Gerrish in Boston. A second edition of *Ashton's Memorial* was published in London for R. Ford and S. Chandler in 1726, but except for slightly different wording on the title page and several lines of text (noted below), this second edition is essentially identical to the first edition. There are almost no surviving original copies of *Ashton's Memorial* today. The Massachusetts Historical Society in Boston has one copy of each edition. In *Ashton's Memorial*, Barnard spells Joseph Libbey's name as "Libbie," but trial records use "Libbey" and that is the spelling used here.

3. Kurlansky, *Cod: A Biography of the Fish that Changed the World*, p. 49; Vickers, *Farmers and Fishermen*.

4. Vickers, *Farmers and Fishermen*, p. 154. Most details regarding Ashton's livelihood and likely work experiences as a cod fisherman in colonial New England are drawn from Vickers, *Farmers and Fishermen;* see also Kurlansky, *Cod: A Biography of the Fish that Changed the World*, and Magra, "The New England Cod Fishing Industry and Maritime Dimensions of the American Revolution."

5. Bridenbaugh, *Cities in the Wilderness*, p. 230. "We would request one thing more of our fishermen—the conscience of holy Sabbatizing," Mather wrote in 1712. "'Tis that they would conscientiously avoid all needless encroachments on the Lord's Day; that they would conscientiously deny

themselves of all that may be forborne on the Lord's Day as religiously as men bound for heaven. Brethren, you would be no losers by the religion of the Sabbath. All things would go better for it, all the week ensuing." Cotton Mather, *The Fisher-man's Calling,* 1712.

6. Comptrollers of the Accounts of the Army to the King, America and West Indies: June 1717, Calendar of State Papers Colonial, America and West Indies, vol. 29: 1716–1717, pp. 322–36.

7. When Ashton was eleven years old, England took possession of Nova Scotia from France. The British had captured the French fort at Port Royal (now Annapolis) in 1710, near the end of Queen Anne's War, and had gained control of present-day Nova Scotia through the Treaty of Utrecht when the war ended three years later. The British built another fort at Canso, in the northern part of Nova Scotia, in 1720. But the communities of Mi'kmaq people who lived there, and had been there for more than a century before England and France began fighting over it, continued to resist the New Englanders' presence in the area. In 1715, just two years after the war ended, a Boston sea captain named Cyprian Southack, who had been part of several campaigns to take Nova Scotia from the French during the war, sailed into Port Roseway, the same harbor where Ashton was heading on June 15. Southack and his men built two shelters on the shore along Port Roseway and set up racks for drying codfish. They were soon joined by several other fishing vessels from New England, including one from Marblehead. But before long, the men were approached by two men, one Mi'kmaq and one Acadian, who told them that a hundred warriors were coming to destroy their camp. Southack and the other fishermen soon left, and Mi'kmaq warriors burned the fishing camp. Plank, *An Unsettled Conquest,* pp. 75–76.

8. Letter from David Jeffries and Charles Shepreve, merchants in Boston, to Capt. Robt. Mears, America and West Indies: August 1715, Calendar of State Papers Colonial, America and West Indies, vol. 28: 1714–1715, pp. 254–68. The Mi'kmaq made birchbark canoes and caught much of their food from the rivers and ocean that surrounded them. They caught fish and eels by setting weirs built with wooden stakes in rivers and streams, forcing the fish to swim into nets. The Mi'kmaq also caught eels by constructing stone dams in rivers, and they would sometimes fish at night by lighting a torch made of birch and then spearing the eels that were attracted by the light. The Mi'kmaq preserved some of their fish for the winter months by smoking it. In addition to fish, some villages also grew corn, beans, and peas, and they hunted moose, caribou, beaver, bear, and seal, particularly in the

winter months. The Mi'kmaq lived in cabins built by tying together several long poles that were then covered with large pieces of birchbark held together with strings made out of tree roots. In colder seasons, the cabin walls could also be covered with a layer of spruce boughs, adding more insulation. The huts had a hole at the top that allowed smoke from their fires to escape. Wicken, "Encounters With Tall Sails and Tall Tales"; Plank, *An Unsettled Conquest,* pp. 23–24.

9. *Boston News Letter,* August 20, 1722. Twenty of the fishermen captured that July would eventually be freed when a rescue party led by John Elliot of Boston spotted their vessels anchored just offshore. Elliot sent all but a handful of his men below deck and then sailed toward the captured vessels. There were at least twenty warriors on the vessels and they shouted for Elliot to surrender as he came closer. But Elliot kept on and prepared to attack. Seeing this, the natives cut their anchor line and tried to get onto land. Elliot's crew boarded the ships, and the two sides fought for about an hour. Some of the natives jumped into the water and swam for shore, and a number of others were killed. Elliot finally freed the captured fishermen and brought them back to Canso, Nova Scotia, with the scalps of several of his victims mounted on his ship.

10. *Boston News Letter,* July 23, 1722.

11. The popularity of Port Roseway as a protected anchorage for sailing ships of the period is drawn from Blunt, *The American Coast Pilot,* which describes Port Roseway, also known as Shelburne Harbor, as "justly esteemed the best in all Nova Scotia, from the ease of its access and perfect security of its anchorage. . . . Shelburne affords excellent shelter for ships in distress and is secure against any wind, except a violent storm at S.S.W. abreast of town." All distances reported in this book are in statute miles.

12. Throughout this book, Ashton's narrative is treated for the most part as if it were a journal, and for the sake of simplicity, quotations are generally attributed to Ashton using the words "Ashton wrote." As described in detail below, strictly speaking Ashton himself did not write the *Memorial.* It was written by his pastor, John Barnard. Ashton recounted his experiences over the course of several discussions with Barnard during his first few months after returning home to Marblehead, and the accuracy of the text is repeatedly supported by other sources. Barnard wrote that he met with Ashton on several occasions to record the narrative and subsequently verified its accuracy: "I have taken the minutes of all from his own mouth, and after I had put them together, I have improved the first vacant hour I could to read it over distinctly to him that he might correct the errors that might arise from my misunderstanding his report. Thus corrected, he has set his hand to it

as his own history." There are numerous examples of both major and minor events described in Ashton's narrative—the capture at Port Roseway, the ransacking of a Newfoundland town, the sinking of one of the pirates' vessels, attacks by British warships, and the pirates' activity in the Bay of Honduras—that are corroborated in detail by survivor accounts, ships' logbooks, and newspaper reports at the time.

13. The description of the brigantine *Rebecca,* based on the report of its capture on May 28, 1722, is from the *Boston News Letter,* June 18, 1722. The *Rebecca* is also described in a report of Low's earlier captures published in the *New England Courant,* June 11, 1722.

14. *Boston News Letter,* August 8, 1723.

15. *Boston News Letter,* May 6, 1717, and May 13, 1717.

16. Bellamy's ship, the *Whydah,* was located on the ocean floor near Marconi Beach on Cape Cod in 1984 by diver Barry Clifford. Many of the artifacts recovered by the divers are on display at the Pirate Museum in Provincetown, Massachusetts. Clifford, *Expedition Whydah.*

17. Cotton Mather, *Instructions to the Living from the Condition of the Dead,* 1717.

18. *Boston News Letter,* May 13, 1717; Deposition of Ralph Merry and Samuel Roberts, May 11 and 16, 1717, in Jameson, *Privateering and Piracy.*

19. The only possible hint of Low's stature is from the report of a ship captain who, in recounting Low's captures near Newfoundland, said Low was believed to be "a little man" and not a "lusty man." *American Weekly Mercury,* October 4, 1723.

20. *Boston News Letter,* July 2, 1722, and July 9, 1722.

21. Some young men, unlike Ashton, were enticed by the camaraderie and carefree lifestyle the pirates offered. A sailor named William White, who joined a pirate crew under the command of John Phillips in 1723, testified at his trial that "he is sorry he should commit such a sin, that he was in drink when he went away with" Phillips and the band of pirates. Trial of William White, John Rose Archer, and William Taylor, in Jameson, *Privateering and Piracy.*

22. The description of the *Rebecca* as a "dull sailer" is from *New England Courant,* June 11, 1722. The Marblehead schooner that Low took was relatively new—Ashton describes it as "new, clean, and a good sailer"—and was about fifty tons, according to the initial report of the capture in the *Boston News Letter,* July 2, 1722. A Marblehead schooner of fifty tons would have been just over fifty feet long with a breadth of about sixteen feet, based on the descriptions provided in MacGregor, *The Schooner,* p. 19. The schooner Low took had been owned by Joseph Dolliber of Marblehead, and its cap-

tain had been Thomas Trefry, who was freed that weekend and returned to Massachusetts with most of the other fishermen. See also Marquandt, *The Global Schooner.*

23. *Boston Gazette,* July 2, 1722; *Boston News Letter,* July 9, 1722. The capture by Low's crew did not deter Flucker from his career as a sea captain. Flucker set sail on another voyage for Saint Kitts within a month's time. *Boston News Letter,* August 6, 1722.

24. The sworn statements of the three ship captains appeared as follows: "The depositions of Thomas Trefry, late master of the schooner *Mary;* Robert Gilford, master of the shallop *Elizabeth;* and John Collyer, one of the crew belonging to the schooner *Samuel,* William Nichols master, all of Marblehead in the county of Essex, fishermen, testify and say that as they were upon their lawful employment nigh Cape Sables, on or about the 14th, 15th, and 16th days of June last past, they were taken prisoners by Capt. Edward Low, a pirate, then commander of the brigantine [*Rebecca*] but since removed himself into the before named schooner *Mary,* which they took from the deponent Trefry; and besides the deponents they took several other fishing vessels, viz. Nicholas Merritt, master of the shallop *Jane,* Philip Ashton, master of the schooner *Milton,* Joseph Libbey, one of said Ashton's crew, Lawrence Fabins, one of the crew belonging to the schooner *Rebeckah,* Thomas Salter commander, all these four men, to wit, Nicholas Merritt, Philip Ashton, Joseph Libbey, and Lawrence Fabins, being young nimble men of about twenty years of age, the pirates kept them by force and would not let them go though they pleaded as much as they dare to, yet nothing would avail, so as they wept like children; yet notwithstanding they forcibly carried them away to the great grief and sorrow of the afore named four young men, as well as these deponents; and when any of these deponents mentioned anything in favor of the said four young men, the quartermaster of the pirate publicly declared, they would carry them, and let them send to New England and publish it if they pleased. These deponents further say that the said pirates constrained four more fishermen belonging to Piscatequa and the Isle of Shoals to go with them against their wills also." *Boston News Letter,* July 9, 1722.

CHAPTER 3: TO THE AZORES

1. The arrival of the two British warships, the *Solebay* and the *Panther,* off of Newfoundland was reported in the *Boston News Letter,* June 18, 1722. Low's close encounter with the warship and the pirates' ransacking of the

town of Carbonear were confirmed by reports published in the *Boston News Letter*, August 26, 1722. From this report it seems likely that it was the *HMS Solebay* that Low saw.

2. Philbrick, *In the Heart of the Sea*, p. 37; Beal, *Quelch's Gold.*

3. Cordingly, *Pirate Hunter*, p. 50; Cordingly, *Under the Black Flag*, pp. 82–85; Volo and Volo, *Daily Life in the Age of Sail.*

4. Nordhoff, *Sailor Life on Man-of-War and Merchant Vessels*, pp. 174–75.

5. *Boston News Letter*, May 7, 1722; *London Post-Boy*, July 3, 1722.

6. "Trials of Thirty-Six Persons for Piracy," in Updike, *Memoirs of the Rhode Island Bar.*

7. Deposition of George Barrow, Master of the sloop *Content*, America and West Indies: November 1723, Calendar of State Papers Colonial, America and West Indies, vol. 33: 1722–1723, pp. 355–72; *American Weekly Mercury*, February 11, 1724.

8. Letter of Richard Hawkins, who was captured by Low's quartermaster, Francis Spriggs, in 1724, published in the *British Journal*, August 22, 1724. Hawkins' capture occurred after Spriggs separated from Low and is described in more detail in a later chapter.

9. "Trials of Thirty-Six Persons for Piracy," in Updike, *Memoirs of the Rhode Island Bar.*

10. Joseph Swetser had been aboard the *Rebecca* when it was captured (*Boston News Letter*, June 18, 1722). The details concerning the behavior and activities of Swetser and Thomas Mumford while aboard Low's ship are drawn from testimony provided in "Trials of Thirty-Six Persons for Piracy," in Updike, *Memoirs of the Rhode Island Bar.* One shipmate testified at the trial that Swetser "used often to get alone by himself, from amongst the rest of the crew, he was melancholy, and refused to go on board any vessels by them taken, and got out of their way."

11. *Boston News Letter*, August 22, 1720.

12. Low's articles specified that "if any gold, jewels, silver be found on board of any prize or prizes to the value of a piece of eight, and the finder do not deliver it to the quartermaster in the space of 24 hours shall suffer what punishment the captain and the majority of the company shall think fit." *Boston News Letter*, August 8, 1723.

13. *Boston News Letter*, June 25, 1722.

14. *Boston News Letter*, July 22, 1717.

15. *Boston News Letter*, August 22, 1720.

16. Ashton describes Merritt as "my townsman and kinsman," but most family genealogies indicate the two were cousins: Merritt was the son of

Elizabeth (Ashton) Merritt, the sister of Ashton's father. Merritt's experiences are described, as Ashton's are, based on his conversations with John Barnard after returning home to Marblehead. Merritt's story is recounted in a separate section of John Barnard's *Ashton's Memorial.*

17. *Boston News Letter,* October 18, 1723.

18. By the term *crusidore* Merritt may have meant a civil officer called a "corregidor." Describing his visit to the island of Saint Michael in the Azores nearly a century later, in 1817, John White Webster wrote, "Every foreigner landing in St. Michael is conducted, under a military guard, to the castle of St. Braz, that his views in visiting the island may be declared, and his passports examined. He is then required to appear before the corregidor, who repeats the examination, and, if satisfied that no danger will result, grants him leave to remain on shore. The slightest deviation from this routine would subject a stranger to many inconveniences, and even imprisonment." Webster, *A Description of the Island of St. Michael,* pp. 20–21.

CHAPTER 4: DANGEROUS WATERS

1. Chapelle, *The Search for Speed Under Sail,* p. 207.

2. Zacks, *The Pirate Hunter,* pp. 119–20; Cordingly, *Under the Black Flag,* pp. 95–96.

3. *Boston News Letter,* October 31, 1723; *American Weekly Mercury,* May 9, 1723; "Trials of Thirty-Six Persons for Piracy," in Updike, *Memoirs of the Rhode Island Bar.*

4. Nordhoff, *Sailor Life on Man-of-War and Merchant Vessels,* p. 751; Vickers, *Young Men and the Sea,* p. 91.

5. On riding out a storm at sea, see Philbrick, *In the Heart of the Sea,* pp. 39–40.

6. Description of Thomas Beale, who sailed aboard the *Kent* in the early 1800s, quoted in Druett, *Rough Medicine,* p. 97.

7. The pirates stopped to careen their ships at either Devil's Island (Île du Diable) or one of the other two islands that make up the Salvation Islands (Îles du Salut) off French Guiana. Ashton refers to these islands as "the three islands called the Triangles, lying off the main about 40 leagues to the eastward of Suriname." As noted in Raleigh, *The Discovery of the Large, Rich, and Beautiful Empire of Guiana* (p. 201), these islands were known at the time as the Triangle Islands.

8. Ashton's account, which is probably the most accurate, says that two members of the crew drowned when the pink sank, although a secondhand

report from several sea captains who had heard about the mishap during a voyage to the Caribbean claimed that a larger number of pirates were killed (*American Weekly Mercury,* March 14, 1723).

9. Druett, *Rough Medicine.*

10. Druett, *Rough Medicine.*

11. The poor quality of the medical supplies is based on the testimony of Archibald Fisher, the doctor serving aboard the HMS *Greyhound,* given at the trial of the pirates from Low's crew in Newport, Rhode Island. Fisher said that "he searched his medicaments, and the instruments, and found but very few medicants, and the instruments very mean and bad." "Trials of Thirty-Six Persons for Piracy," in Updike, *Memoirs of the Rhode Island Bar.* The hazards of life aboard a pirate ship could result in an urgent need for medicines and supplies. In a similar incident several years earlier, the pirate captain Edward Teach (Blackbeard) took a number of captives near Charleston, South Carolina, and threatened to kill them unless he was immediately sent a "chest of medicines" (Cordingly, *Pirate Hunter,* p. 168.)

12. *American Weekly Mercury,* December 18, 1722; *Boston Gazette,* December 10, 1722.

13. Logbook of HMS *Mermaid,* October 1722 to April 1723, Admiralty Records 52/440, National Archives, London.

14. Logbook of HMS *Mermaid,* October 1722 to April 1723, Admiralty Records 52/440, National Archives, London.

15. *American Weekly Mercury,* March 14, 1723; *American Weekly Mercury,* July 11, 1723; *American Weekly Mercury,* July 24, 1723.

16. Details of Low's close encounter with the HMS *Mermaid,* recounted by Ashton, were also brought back to the colonies by a ship captain returning from the Caribbean and reported in the *American Weekly Mercury,* May 2, 1723. Ashton describes the location where Spriggs came to rest after the chase as "about midway between" Cartagena, in Colombia, and Porto Bello, in Panama. Ashton says they sailed into "Pickeroon Bay, about 18 leagues" from Cartagena, Colombia.

17. Rediker, *Villains of All Nations,* p. 86; as Rediker (p. 85) notes, "pirates constructed their own social order in defiant contradistinction to the ways of the world they had left behind. They had special contempt for the merchant captain, the royal official, and the system of authority those figures represented and enforced."

18. It's almost certain that Low anchored his ships in the harbor off Port Royal on Roatan. Ashton says the pirates came into "Roatan Harbor" and came to rest near a cay called "Port Royal Key." Additional details concern-

ing the history of Roatan and Port Royal harbor are drawn from Davidson, *Historical Geography of the Bay Islands*, and from the 1742 map of Roatan, as surveyed by Lieut. Henry Barnsley.

19. Examinations of Captains John Morris, Jackman, and Morgan taken before Sir Thos. Modyford, Governor of Jamaica, 20 Sept. 1665, America and West Indies: March 1666, Calendar of State Papers Colonial, America and West Indies, vol. 5: 1661–1668, pp. 359–69; Talty, *Empire of Blue Waters*, pp. 61–67.

CHAPTER 5: ROATAN

1. Davidson, *Historical Geography of the Bay Islands;* Strong, *Archeological Investigations in the Bay Islands.*

2. Ashton's recollection about spreading turtle eggs on palm leaves to dry in the sun appears in the 1726 edition of *Ashton's Memorial* published in London, but not in the original edition printed in Boston in 1725. The 1726 edition includes the additional words, italicized here: "And in this way I sometimes got some eggs to eat, which *[I sometimes strung upon a strip of palmetto, and hung up in the sun, where, in a few days, they would become thickened, and somewhat hard, as if they had been boiled, and so be more palatable; but after all, they]* are not very good at the best, yet what is not good to him that has nothing to live upon but what falls from the trees?" This represents one of the few differences of any significance between the two early printings. The difference is most likely due to a typesetting error that resulted in the accidental omission of a few lines of text, rather than an editorial enhancement when the 1726 edition was printed in London.

3. Ashton's text describes the boa as an "owler," which is probably a reference to the local term for this snake, which is "wowla."

4. Strong, *Archeological Investigations in the Bay Islands.*

5. Ashton calls the shark a "shovel nosed shark." It seems likely it was a species of hammerhead shark. Humann and Deloach, *Reef Fish Identification*, pp. 450–51; Michael, *Reef Sharks and Rays of the World*, p. 68.

CHAPTER 6: THE BAYMEN

1. "Trials of Thirty-Six Persons for Piracy," in Updike, *Memoirs of the Rhode Island Bar; Boston News Letter*, May 16, 1723; *New England Courant*, May 20, 1723; *British Journal*, May 11, 1723. The *New England Courant* identifies the captain as Lyde rather than Loyd.

2. Andrews, "Anglo-American Trade in the Early Eighteenth Century"; Camara, "Logwood and Archaeology in Campeche"; Jarvis, *In the Eye of All Trade,* pp. 218–33; Finamore, "A Mariner's Utopia"; Camille, "Historical Geography of the Belizean Logwood Trade"; Craig, "Logwood as a Factor in the Settlement of British Honduras"; Rhind, *History of the Vegetable Kingdom,* pp. 494–98; Newton, "Good and Kind Benefactors." Based on correspondence between logwood traders in the Bay of Honduras and leaders of Christ Church in Boston, Newton suggests some Baymen may have had strong social ties to Boston and even attended church there when visiting, a perspective that stands in stark contrast to the more common picture of Baymen as rough, crude men who were barely a step removed from pirates.

3. Quoted in Jarvis, *In the Eye of All Trade,* p. 225.

4. As Michael Jarvis notes, "Rapacious Spanish captains were liberal in their views of what constituted damning evidence, deeming foreign vessels forfeit for possessing even a single piece of eight (a Spanish manufacture, they asserted, despite the near-universal circulation of this coin throughout the Americas) or a stick of dyewood (which they improbably claimed grew only on Spanish islands)." (*In the Eye of All Trade,* p. 203.)

5. *Boston News Letter,* May 7, 1716. The lagoon and Island of Trieste referenced in the article were popular logwood sites at the time, located near what is today Ciudad del Carmen, Mexico. Rhind, *A History of the Vegetable Kingdom,* p. 496; Jarvis, *In the Eye of All Trade,* pp. 219–21.

6. Uring, *History of the Voyages and Travels of Capt. Nathaniel Uring,* pp. 354–56. A recent archeological excavation of a Baymen's camp along coastal Belize from this period uncovered nails, hinges, spikes, gunshot, and other iron fragments, as well as hundreds of ceramic vessel fragments. The broken vessel fragments included pieces of high-quality, hand-painted Chinese porcelain, which the Baymen or pirates presumably had stolen or acquired from Spanish trading vessels coming from Asia. Finamore, "A Mariner's Utopia," pp. 74–75. Finamore also suggests that the tradition of drinking with ship captains before exchanging logwood was an important part of establishing a strong trading relationship. Finamore, "A Mariner's Utopia," p. 70. Logging would continue to bring a steady supply of men and ships into the region for another century until the advent of chemical dyes in the late 1800s.

7. Cordingly, *Under the Black Flag,* p. 13.

8. *Boston News Letter,* June 16, 1718.

9. *Boston News Letter,* June 16, 1718.

10. Ashton says of the small island where the Baymen set up camp, "They chose for their chief residence a small key about a quarter of a mile round,

lying near to Barbarat, which they called the Castle of Comfort, chiefly because it was low and clear of woods and bushes, where the wind had an open
passage, and drove away the pestering mosquitoes and gnats."

11. "Trials of Thirty-Six Persons for Piracy," in Updike, *Memoirs of the
Rhode Island Bar; Boston News Letter,* May 16, 1723; *New England Courant,*
May 20, 1723; *American Weekly Mercury,* June 13, 1723; *London Daily Cou-
rant,* August 26, 1723.

12. The captured vessel that told the *Greyhound* Low's crew was in the
area was a pink under the command of a captain named Pitman, which
had just left Virginia on a voyage to London. That ship was let go after the
pirates captured another ship, the sloop *Hopeful Betty,* taking most of the
sails and water aboard the vessel. Letter from Captain Peter Solgard, June
12, 1723, Admiralty Records 1/2452, National Archives, London; *American
Weekly Mercury,* June 13, 1723; *Boston Gazette,* June 24, 1723; *London Daily
Courant,* August 26, 1723.

13. Letter from Captain Peter Solgard, June 12, 1723, Admiralty Records
1/2452, National Archives, London; *Boston News Letter,* June 20, 1723;
American Weekly Mercury, June 27, 1723; "Trials of Thirty-Six Persons for
Piracy," in Updike, *Memoirs of the Rhode Island Bar.* On weaponry aboard a
pirate ship, see Little, *Sea Rovers' Practice;* and Volo and Volo, *Daily Life in
the Age of Sail.*

14. *British Journal,* August 22, 1724.

15. Volo and Volo, *Daily Life in the Age of Sail;* Little, *Sea Rovers' Practice.*

16. *Boston News Letter,* June 20, 1723.

17. Letter from Captain Peter Solgard, June 12, 1723, Admiralty Records
1/2452, National Archives, London; *Boston News Letter,* June 20, 1723.

18. *American Weekly Mercury,* August 8, 1723.

19. Hart to Council of Trade and Plantations, America and West Indies:
March 1724, 21–31, Calendar of State Papers Colonial, America and West
Indies, vol. 34: 1724–1725, pp. 71–76; *British Journal,* June 20, 1724; *Mist's
Weekly Journal,* August 10, 1723.

20. *Boston News Letter,* June 20, 1723, and June 27, 1723; *Mist's Weekly
Journal,* August 10, 1723; *American Weekly Mercury,* June 27, 1723.

21. *Boston News Letter,* June 27, 1723, September 19, 1723.

CHAPTER 7: THE BAY OF HONDURAS

1. The capture of the *Delight Galley* by Low's crew was almost certainly
on October 27, 1723, although the handwritten date in the deposition by the
Delight's captain, Henry Hunt, could read either October 24 or 27. Hunt's

deposition refers to Low's sloop at the time of the capture as the *Fortune,* although the narrative of one of the men taken from the *Delight Galley,* Jonathan Barlow, refers to Low's ship as the *Merry Christmas.* Deposition by Henry Hunt, late commander of the *Delight Galley,* Calendar of State Papers Colonial, America and West Indies, vol. 34, January 1724; Narratives of Barlow and Simmons, *The New England Quarterly* (vol. 2, no. 4), 1929; *Boston News Letter,* October 18, 1723.

2. Barlow was one of more than a dozen seamen taken captive from the *Delight Galley.* Jonathan Barlow and Nicholas Simmons both recorded short journals describing their experiences with the pirates; the journals are housed at the Massachusetts Archives. These narratives were reprinted in *The New England Quarterly* (vol. 2, no. 4) in October 1929. Their experiences were also described in several trial documents, including Trial of Matthew Perry and Others, High Court of Admiralty Records 1/99, National Archives, London; Statement concerning Matthew Parrey [*sic*] mate & ship John & Mary out of Boston, Feb. 1, 1724, Rhode Island Land & Public Notary Records, vol. 4, 1721–1741, pp. 76–78 (C#00481); and Deposition by Henry Hunt, late commander of the *Delight Galley,* Calendar of State Papers Colonial, America and West Indies, vol. 34, January 1724.

3. Richard Hawkins, letter published in *British Journal,* August 22, 1724; examination of John Brown, in Jameson, *Privateering and Privacy,* p. 294; Rediker, *Villains of All Nations,* pp. 65–70.

4. Trial of William White, John Rose Archer, and William Taylor, in Jameson, *Privateering and Privacy,* p. 340; Hawkins, letter published in *British Journal,* August 22, 1724; Rediker, *Villains of All Nations,* pp. 65–70; *Mist's Weekly Journal,* August 10, 1723.

5. *Boston Gazette,* April 20, 1724; Hawkins, letter published in *British Journal,* August 22, 1724; *American Weekly Mercury,* March 19, 1724; *British Journal,* June 20, 1724; Narratives of Barlow and Simmons, *The New England Quarterly;* Trial of Matthew Perry and Others, High Court of Admiralty Records 1/99, National Archives, London.

6. Fillmore's perspective on his captivity is presented in the *Narration of the Captivity of John Fillmore,* a monograph printed in 1790 by Haswell & Russell in Bennington, Vermont. The printer noted in the introduction to the narrative that the narrative was provided by Increase Mosely, who was "intimately acquainted with Mr. John Fillmore, the hero of the tale, both before and after his captivity." Many of the events described in Fillmore's narrative are corroborated by newspaper reports and trial records. Where there are discrepancies between Fillmore's narrative from 1790 and newspaper accounts and trial records from 1723 and 1724, details are generally taken

from the newspaper accounts and trial records since they were published almost immediately after the events. As with Ashton, quotations from Fillmore's narrative are attributed to Fillmore with the words "Fillmore wrote." Many of the details of Phillips' cruise as a pirate were reported in the *Boston Gazette,* May 4, 1724, and in the trial records, Cases of John Rose Archer and Others, in Jameson, *Privateering and Piracy.*

7. Ironically, Fillmore was selected as the only forced captive from the *Dolphin* because he was recognized by a boyhood friend, William White, who was one of the original members of Phillips' pirate crew. Years before, White had worked for a tailor who lived across the street from Fillmore and his mother. As boys, Fillmore and White had spent hours together when they weren't working. Fillmore hadn't seen White for years, until the moment White climbed aboard the *Dolphin* with several of the other pirates. Fillmore and White both recognized each other, but neither of them acknowledged the other as they stood on the deck of the schooner. White later told Phillips that he knew Fillmore and that the pirates should take him, since he was sure to be a "good stout resolute fellow," which resulted in Phillips' selection of Fillmore.

8. *Boston Gazette,* May 4, 1724; Cases of John Rose Archer and Others, in Jameson, *Privateering and Piracy.*

9. Details of Hawkins' capture are from two letters written by Hawkins and published in the *British Journal,* August 8, 1724, and August 28, 1724.

10. Earle, *Pirate Wars,* p. 179.

11. Hart to Council of Trade and Plantations, America and West Indies: March 1724, 21–31, Calendar of State Papers Colonial, America and West Indies, vol. 34: 1724–1725, pp. 71–76.

12. Cooper was taken from a ship under the command of Captain DeHawes. *Boston Gazette,* April 20, 1724; *British Journal,* July 18, 1724 and August 8, 1724.

13. *Boston News Letter,* August 13, 1724, January 28, 1725, and April 15, 1725; Narratives of Barlow and Simmons, *The New England Quarterly*; London *Weekly Journal,* August 29, 1724.

14. *American Weekly Mercury,* January 12, 1725.

15. Ketton-Cremer, *Felbrigg: The Story of a House,* pp. 84, 94–101.

16. According to one economic analysis, the rapid spike in South Sea stock in 1720 was more than double the rise in price of even the largest and most successful high-tech stocks that U.S. investors were frantically buying during the dot com bubble of the 1990s. See Temin and Voth, "Riding the South Sea Bubble"; Hoppit, "The Myths of the South Sea Bubble."

17. Ketton-Cremer, *Felbrigg: The Story of a House*, pp. 94–101.

18. *New England Courant*, June 11, 1722.

19. Logbook of HMS *Diamond*, Admiralty Records 51/4161, National Archives, London.

20. *American Weekly Mercury*, May 28, 1724; *British Journal*, July 18, 1724.

21. Logbook of HMS *Diamond*, Admiralty Records 51/4161, National Archives, London; *Boston News Letter*, December 10, 1724, *American Weekly Mercury*, January 12, 1725; *Mist's Weekly Journal*, January 16, 1725. This was one of the last battles fought by Captain Windham of the *Diamond*. Windham died about four months later, in the first week of January 1725, on another voyage between Jamaica and the bay (*New England Courant*, April 5, 1725 and *American Weekly Mercury*, April 15, 1725).

22. In addition to the Narratives of Barlow and Simmons, Matthew Perry's description of the events was recorded in a sworn statement he provided upon his return to Rhode Island. Statement concerning Matthew Parrey [*sic*] mate & ship John & Mary out of Boston, Feb. 1, 1724, Rhode Island Land & Public Notary Records, vol. 4, 1721–1741, pp. 76–78 (C#00481).

23. *Boston News Letter*, May 7, 1724; *Boston Gazette*, May 4, 1724; Cases of John Rose Archer and Others, in Jameson, *Privateering and Piracy*.

24. *Boston Gazette*, April 20, 1724; *Boston News Letter*, April 13, 1724; *New England Courant*, April 13, 1724; *Boston Gazette*, May 4, 1724; Cases of John Rose Archer and Others, in Jameson, *Privateering and Piracy*.

25. The *New England Courant*, May 4, 1724, reported that "they have brought the head of Phillips and that of a young man" back with them. *Boston News Letter*, May 7, 1724; *Boston Gazette*, May 4, 1724; Cases of John Rose Archer and Others, in Jameson, *Privateering and Piracy*.

CHAPTER 8: AS ONE COMING FROM THE DEAD

1. Statement concerning Matthew Parrey [*sic*] mate & ship John & Mary out of Boston, Feb. 1, 1724, Rhode Island Land & Public Notary Records, vol. 4, 1721–1741, pp. 76–78 (C#00481).

2. By the time of the trial, Barlow was so sick that he could not attend, and his testimony was provided in writing. Trial of Matthew Perry and Others, High Court of Admiralty Records 1/99, National Archives, London; "Petition of Nicholas Simmons. May 1725," in Jameson, *Privateering and Privacy*. Petition of William Nathaniel Brown, Small Lewis, and Francis

Mozley, Records of the Colony of Rhode Island and Providence Plantations, vol. 4 (1707 to 1740), p. 361.

3. Logbook of HMS *Diamond,* Admiralty Records 51/244, National Archives, London.

4. These dates are from the logbook of the HMS *Diamond.* The dates given in Ashton's narrative are slightly different, stating that "the latter end of March 1725 we came to sail, and kept company with the man-of-war, who was bound to Jamaica; the first of April we parted, and through the good hand of God upon us came safe through the Gulf of Florida, to Salem harbor, where we arrived upon Saturday evening, the first of May," whereas the logbook from the *Diamond* indicates that the fleet did not even leave Guanaja until April 3. It seems likely that the logbook, which was recorded each day, presents the most accurate timeline. Logbook of HMS *Diamond,* Admiralty Records 51/244, National Archives, London.

CHAPTER 9: *ASHTON'S MEMORIAL*

1. *Boston News Letter,* November 20, 1721; Silverman, *Life and Times of Cotton Mather,* pp. 350–51.

2. Silverman, *Life and Times of Cotton Mather.*

3. Silverman, *Life and Times of Cotton Mather,* p. 358; Williams, *The Pox and the Covenant.* Silverman identifies Mather as the person who accosted James Franklin in November 1721, although the report by Franklin in the *New England Courant* (December 4, 1721) does not name the person involved.

4. Rediker, *Between the Devil and the Deep Blue Sea,* p. 176.

5. Cotton Mather, "The Fisherman's Calling," 1712; Silverman, *Life and Times of Cotton Mather.*

6. Cotton Mather, *Faithful Warnings to Prevent Fearful Judgements,* 1704; Cotton Mather, *Instructions to the Living from the Condition of the Dead,* 1717; Cotton Mather's Diary, volume 2, p. 488, quoted in Jameson, *Privateering and Piracy,* p. 306; see also Williams, "Puritans and Pirates," and Zacks, *The Pirate Hunter,* p. 276.

7. Cotton Mather, *Useful Remarks: An Essay Upon Remarkables in the Way of Wicked Men,* 1723.

8. Cotton Mather, *The Converted Sinner,* 1724.

9. Silverman, *Life and Times of Cotton Mather,* pp. 148–49; Bridenbaugh, *Cities in the Wilderness;* Toulouse, "Syllabical Idolatry."

10. Silverman, *Life and Times of Cotton Mather,* p. 146. Details of Bar-

nard's life are largely drawn from his "Autobiography," in *Collections of the Massachusetts Historical Society;* and Smith, "Strange Adventures and Signal Deliverances."

11. Barnard, "Autobiography"; Vickers, *Farmers and Fishermen*, p. 172. Barnard's appointment to Marblehead's First Church followed a bitterly disputed contest between him and another candidate, Edward Holyoke, who went on to lead a second congregational church in the village. Heyrman, *Commerce and Culture,* pp. 276–77.

12. Barnard, Autobiography, in *Collections of the Massachusetts Historical Society;* Vickers, *Farmers and Fishermen.*

13. Bridenbaugh, *Cities in the Wilderness,* p. 330.

14. Heyrman, *Commerce and Culture,* pp. 247–51, 285–86; Barnard, "Autobiography"; Williams, "Of Providence and Pirates."

15. Williams, "Of Providence and Pirates." The historian Christine Heyrman interprets Barnard's sermon and *Ashton's Memorial* differently, suggesting it was an allegorical attack on the Anglican Church. *Commerce and Culture,* pp. 290–91.

16. The scholar Leanne Beukelman Smith notes, "If we look carefully at *Ashton's Memorial* we will discover it to be a singularly vital expression of a conventionalized American form worthy the recognition already accorded Barnard's sermons and autobiography, for in shaping Philip Ashton's history, Barnard skillfully stretched the traditions of providential shipwreck narrative and spiritual autobiography to fill the interstices between the certainties and anxieties of identity so widely experienced in a period of shifting religious and cultural references." Smith, "Strange Adventures and Signal Deliverances," p. 61.

17. As Daniel Williams has noted, "Published during a period of cultural, intellectual, and theological flux in New England, *Ashton's Memorial* was part of a large body of religious writing that sought to revitalize Christianity and respiritualize life." Williams, "Of Providence and Pirates," p. 171.

18. *New England Courant,* May 10, 1725.

19. Williams, "Of Providence and Pirates"; Smith, "Strange Adventures and Signal Deliverances."

20. *Boston Gazette,* October 23, 1727; *Weekly Journal / British Gazetteer,* March 5, 1726.

21. Smith, "Strange Adventures and Signal Deliverances."

22. Rediker, *Villains of All Nations,* p. 119; Cordingly, *Pirate Hunter,* pp. 239–48.

23. Schonhorn, "Defoe's Four Years Voyages." It is impossible to know for

certain if Daniel Defoe wrote *The Four Years Voyages of Capt. George Roberts.* Many students of Defoe's writings believe he did (see Schonhorn, "Defoe's Four Years Voyages," note 1). But scholars have debated for years about which books and tracts Defoe wrote and which he did not. Some researchers have concluded that Defoe did not write *Four Years Voyages* (Furbank and Owens, *Defoe De-Attributions*, pp. 142–43) and have even argued that Defoe did not write *A General History of the Pyrates,* which has been widely attributed to Defoe. Whether or not Defoe wrote or contributed to *Four Years Voyages,* there is no question that *Ashton's Memorial* was being read in London by 1726 and its impact was felt there, as well as in Boston. Whoever wrote *Four Years Voyages* almost certainly took new details about Low's crew of pirates, revealed in *Ashton's Memorial,* and incorporated them into the storyline of the new book.

24. Writing in 1975, Schonhorn noted that the reprint of *Ashton's Memorial* was published in London a month *after* the printing of Defoe's *The Four Years Voyages* (Schonhorn, "Defoe's Four Years Voyages," p. 94). Schonhorn went on to argue, however, that "Sailing time from Boston to London was about six to eight weeks. *Ashton's Memorial* could have been in London before the end of 1725. . . . Defoe could have had access to the Boston publication months before it was printed by Ford [the London printer]; that is, if he did not receive a copy through private parties in Boston or London." In fact, there is no question that the story of Ashton's voyage reached London by early 1726. A detailed summary of *Ashton's Memorial* was published there in the *Weekly Journal* on March 5, 1726.

CHAPTER 10: PIRATE EXECUTIONS AND PIRATE TREASURE

1. Correspondence from the *Diamond,* Admiralty Records 1/2882, National Archives, London.

2. Deposition of Walter Moor, America and West Indies: March 1724, 21–31, Calendar of State Papers Colonial, America and West Indies, vol. 34: 1724–1725; Rediker, *Villains of All Nations,* p. 163; Earle, *Pirate Wars.*

3. The letters by Richard Hawkins, published in the *British Journal* August 8 and August 22, 1724, mention a Joseph Cooper who then served on Spriggs' crew. The link between Spriggs and Cooper is also drawn by Rediker, *Villains of All Nations,* pp. 80–81.

4. *British Journal,* August 22, 1724.

5. Correspondence from the *Diamond,* Admiralty Records 1/2882, National Archives, London; *American Weekly Mercury,* June 23, 1726; Logbook of HMS *Diamond,* Admiralty Records 51/244, National Archives, London.

6. Deposition of Roger Stevens, America and West Indies: June 1725, Calendar of State Papers Colonial, America and West Indies, vol. 34: 1724–1725, pp. 381–401; *Boston News Letter,* August 5, 1725.

7. *Boston Gazette,* December 6, 1725.

8. *Boston Gazette,* September 13, 1725; *Boston News Letter,* September 16, 1725.

9. *American Weekly Mercury,* February 22, 1726; *Boston Gazette,* March 28, 1726; *New England Courant,* January 8, 1726.

10. Mitchell-Hedges, *Danger My Ally,* pp. 221, 228. Some critics have questioned Mitchell-Hedges' approach as an archeologist and the legitimacy of his finds. Davidson, for example, says that Mitchell-Hedges would have been a "good subject" for an "exposé of pseudo-archeologists in Middle America" (*Historical Geography of the Bay Islands,* pp. 143–44). And some islanders on Roatan claim that Mitchell-Hedges did not discover a gold statue he purportedly brought back to America; instead he bought it from an islander for $100 and a bag of flour. Jane MacLaren Walsh, an anthropologist at the Smithsonian Institution's National Museum of Natural History, has dismissed another of Mitchell-Hedges' well-known finds, a crystal skull purported to have been discovered on the Central American mainland. In addition to reviewing newspaper stories and correspondence, Walsh analyzed the Mitchell-Hedges crystal skull under high-power light and scanning-electron microscopes. She concluded, based on the microscopic evidence, that the skull was carved with high-speed, modern, diamond-coated lapidary tools and was not a pre-Columbian artifact. Jane MacLaren Walsh, "The Skull of Doom," Archaeological Institute of America Online, http://www.archaeology.org/online/features/mitchell_hedges, accessed March 28, 2011.

11. Moore and Jennings, *Treasure Hunter,* pp. 51–52, 57; Brown, *Roatan Odyssey,* pp. 32–33. Moore and Jennings (p. 57) date the Mitchell-Hedges treasure discovery on Roatan in 1935, but since Strong, in *Archeological Investigations in the Bay Islands,* was already familiar with the Mitchell-Hedges artifacts in February 1935, it seems likely that the discovery was in 1934.

12. Moore and Jennings, *Treasure Hunter,* pp. 59, 82–90. The truth of these stories of Jennings' discovered pirate treasure has been called into question as well. Another perspective on Howard Jennings is presented by his former wife, Anne Jennings Brown, in her own book, *Roatan Odyssey.*

13. Snow, *True Tales of Pirates and Their Gold,* chapter 8. In addition to the names "E. Low" and "Victoria," the notes on the map read "23758 P/8" and "1355 G" which Snow interpreted as indicating 23,758 pieces of eight and 1,355 pieces of gold ("Red Taped Gold," *Life Magazine,* July 21, 1952, pp. 37–38).

14. *American Weekly Mercury,* June 27, 1723; "Red Taped Gold," *Life Magazine,* July 21, 1952, pp. 37–38; *Boston Globe,* June 30, 1952; Snow, *True Tales of Pirates and Their Gold,* ch. 8.

15. Sidney Perley, ed., *The Essex Antiquarian,* Volume V (1901), p. 185; *Magazine of History With Notes and Queries,* Volume XVIII (1914), p. 42.

16. Barnard, "Autobiography."

17. *Boston News Letter,* July 25, 1723; Mather, *Useful Remarks: An Essay Upon Remarkables in the Way of Wicked Men,* 1723.

18. "Trials of Thirty-Six Persons for Piracy," in Updike, *Memoirs of the Rhode Island Bar.*

19. "Trials of Thirty-Six Persons for Piracy," in Updike, *Memoirs of the Rhode Island Bar; New England Courant,* July 22, 1723; Notice of pardon to Lieutenant Governor Dummer, America and West Indies: March 1724, 11–20, Calendar of State Papers Colonial, America and West Indies, vol. 34: 1724–1725 (1936), pp. 56–71. The older John Brown, who was about twenty-seven years old, was executed.

20. Cases of John Rose Archer and Others, in Jameson, *Privateering and Piracy.*

21. Cases of John Rose Archer and Others, in Jameson, *Privateering and Piracy;* Address of Lt. Governor Dummer to the King, America and West Indies: May 1724, Calendar of State Papers Colonial, America and West Indies, vol. 34: 1724–1725, pp. 86–105; Duke of Newcastle to Lt. Governor Dummer, America and West Indies: February 1725, Calendar of State Papers Colonial, America and West Indies, vol. 34: 1724–1725, pp. 320–35; *Boston News Letter,* June 4, 1724.

22. *Boston News Letter,* July 25, 1723 and August 1, 1723; *New England Courant,* July 22, 1723.

23. "An Account of the Pirates With Divers of their Speeches and Letters," in Cotton Mather, *Useful Remarks: An Essay Upon Remarkables in the Way of Wicked Men,* 1723; "Trials of Thirty-Six Persons for Piracy," in Updike, *Memoirs of the Rhode Island Bar.*

24. Cotton Mather, *Useful Remarks: An Essay Upon Remarkables in the Way of Wicked Men,* 1723.

25. Calendar of State Papers Colonial, America and West Indies, vol. 33: 1722–1723, pp. 282–301; *American Weekly Mercury,* September 26, 1723; *New England Courant,* August 12, 1723.

26. Petition of Nicholas Simmons, May 1725, printed in Jameson, *Privateering and Piracy.*

27. The New England Historical and Genealogical Register, vol. XI (1857), pp. 141–45; Scarry, *Millard Fillmore,* p. 348.

28. *Boston Gazette,* February 2, 1726.

29. *The Tryals of Sixteen Persons for Piracy.* Boston: Joseph Edwards, 1726; Cotton Mather, *The Vial Poured Out Upon the Sea; Boston News Letter,* July 7, 1726; Williams, "Puritans and Pirates."

30. Calendar of State Papers Colonial, America and West Indies, vol. 35: 1726–1727, pp. 129–39.

31. Cotton Mather, *The Vial Poured Out Upon the Sea;* Benjamin Colman, *It Is A Fearful Thing to Fall into the Hands of the Living God;* Williams, "Puritans and Pirates."

32. Williams, "Puritans and Pirates."

33. *Boston News Letter,* July 14, 1726.

Bibliography

Andrews, John H. "Anglo-American Trade in the Early Eighteenth Century." *Geographical Review* 45 (1955): pp. 95–110.

Banner, Stuart. *The Death Penalty: An American History.* Cambridge, Mass.: Harvard University Press, 2002.

Barnard, John. "The Autobiography of the Reverend John Barnard." *Collections of the Massachusetts Historical Society* 5 (1836).

Beal, Clifford. *Quelch's Gold: Piracy, Greed, and Betrayal in Colonial New England.* Westport, Conn.: Praeger, 2007.

Blackman, Paul H., and Vance McLaughlin. "Mass Legal Executions in America Up to 1865." *Crime, History & Societies* 8 (2004).

Blunt, Edmund M. *The American Coast Pilot.* New York: E. & G. W. Blunt, 1847.

Bridenbaugh, Carl. *Cities in the Wilderness: The First Century of Urban Life in America, 1625–1742.* New York: Knopf, 1964.

Brown, Anne Jennings. *Roatan Odyssey.* Wiltshire: Patricia J Mills, 2007.

Camara, Luis Millet. "Logwood and Archaeology in Campeche." *Journal of Anthropological Research* 40 (1984): pp. 324–28.

Camille, Michael A. "Historical Geography of the Belizean Logwood Trade," Department of Geosciences, Northeast Louisiana University http://sites.maxwell.syr.edu/clag/yearbook1996/camille.htm.

Chapelle, Howard I. *The Search for Speed Under Sail 1700–1855.* New York: Bonanza Books, 1967.

Clifford, Barry, with Paul Berry. *Expedition Whydah: The Story of the World's First Excavation of a Pirate Treasure Ship and the Man Who Found Her.* New York: Cliff Street Books, 1999.

Colman, Benjamin. *It Is a Fearful Thing to Fall into the Hands of the Living God. A Sermon Preached to Some Miserable Pirates July 10 1726.* Boston: John Phillips and Thomas Hancock, 1726.

Cordingly, David. *Pirate Hunter of the Caribbean: The Adventurous Life of Captain Woodes Rogers.* New York: Random House, 2011.

———. *Under the Black Flag: The Romance and Reality of Life Among the Pirates.* New York: Random House, 1996.

Craig, Alan K. "Logwood as a Factor in the Settlement of British Honduras." *Caribbean Studies* 9 (1969): pp. 53–62.

Davidson, William. *Historical Geography of the Bay Islands, Honduras.* Birmingham, Ala.: Southern University Press, 1974.

Defoe, Daniel. *A General History of the Pyrates.* Edited by Manuel Schonhorn. Mineola, N.Y.: Dover Publications, 1999.

Drake, Francis. *Life and Correspondence of Henry Knox.* Boston: Samuel G. Drake, 1873.

Druett, Joan. *Rough Medicine: Surgeons at Sea in the Age of Sail.* New York: Routledge, 2000.

Dow, George Francis, and John Henry Edmonds. *The Pirates of the New England Coast, 1630–1730.* New York: Dover Publications, 1996.

Earle, Peter. *The Pirate Wars.* New York: Thomas Dunne Books, 2005.

Fillmore, John. *Narration of the Captivity of John Fillmore and His Escape from the Pirates.* Bennington, Vt.: Haswell & Russell, 1790.

Finamore, Daniel. "A Mariner's Utopia: Pirates and Logwood in the Bay of Honduras." In *X Marks the Spot: The Archaeology of Piracy,* ed. Russell K. Skowronek and Charles R. Ewen. Gainesville: University Press of Florida, 2006.

Furbank, P. N., and W. R. Owens. *Defoe De-Attributions: A Critique of J. R. Moore's Checklist.* London: The Hambledon Press, 1994.

Heyrman, Christine Leigh. *Commerce and Culture: The Maritime Communities of Colonial Massachusetts, 1690–1750.* New York: Norton, 1984.

Hoppit, Julian. "The Myths of the South Sea Bubble." *Transactions of the Royal Historical Society,* Sixth Series 12 (2002): pp. 141–65.

Humann, Paul, and Ned Deloach. *Reef Fish Identification, Florida, Caribbean, Bahamas.* Jacksonville, Fla.: New World Publications, 2002.

Jameson, John F. *Privateering and Piracy in the Colonial Period: Illustrative Documents.* New York: MacMillan, 1923.

Jarvis, Michael J. *In the Eye of All Trade: Bermuda, Bermudians, and the Maritime Atlantic World, 1680–1783.* Chapel Hill: University of North Carolina Press, 2010.

Ketton-Cremer, R. W. *Felbrigg: The Story of a House.* London: Century/Random House, 1976.

Kurlansky, Mark. *Cod: A Biography of the Fish that Changed the World.* New York: Penguin Books, 1998.

Little, Benerson. *The Sea Rover's Practice: Pirate Tactics and Techniques,
1630–1730.* Washington D.C.: Potomac Books, 2005.

Lydon, James. "Fish for Gold: The Massachusetts Fish Trade with Iberia,
1700–1773." *The New England Quarterly* 54 (1981): pp. 539–82.

Magra, Christopher. "The New England Cod Fishing Industry and Maritime Dimensions of the American Revolution." PhD dissertation, University of Pittsburgh, 2006.

MacGregor, David Roy. *The Schooner: Its Design and Development From
1600 to the Present.* London: Chatham Publishing, 1997.

Marquandt, Karl Heinz. *The Global Schooner: Origins, Development, Design,
and Construction.* London: Conway Maritime Press, 2003.

Massachusetts Historical Society. "Benjamin Franklin—Newspaper Publisher and Runaway." http://masshist.org/online/silence_dogood/essay
.php?entry_id=204.

Mather, Cotton. *The Converted Sinner: The Nature of a Conversion to Real
and Vital Piety.* Boston: Nathaniel Belknap, 1724.

———. *The Fisher-man's Calling. A Brief Essay to Serve the Great Interests of
Religion Among Our Fisher-men.* Boston: T. Green, 1712.

———. *Instructions to the Living from the Condition of the Dead.* Boston:
John Allen, 1717.

———. *Useful Remarks: An Essay Upon Remarkables in the Way of Wicked
Men.* New London, Conn.: T Green, 1723.

———. *The Vial Poured Out Upon the Sea: A Remarkable Relation of Certain Pirates Brought Unto a Tragical and Untimely End.* Boston: T. Fleet,
1726.

Michael, Scott W. *Reef Sharks and Rays of the World: A Guide to Their Identification, Behavior, and Ecology.* Annapolis, Md.: Lighthouse Press, 1993.

Mitchell-Hedges, F. A. *Danger My Ally.* Boston: Little, Brown & Co., 1954.

Moore, Robin, and Howard Jennings. *The Treasure Hunter.* Englewood
Cliffs, N.J.: Prentice-Hall, 1974.

Neal, Daniel. *The History of New England, Containing an Impartial Account
of the Civil and Ecclesiastical Affairs of the Country.* Vol. II, 2nd ed., London: A. Ward, 1747.

Newton, Ross A. "'Good and Kind Benefactors': British Logwood Merchants and Boston's Christ Church." *Early American Studies* 11 (2013):
pp. 15–36.

Nordhoff, Charles. *Sailor Life on Man-of-War and Merchant Vessels.* New
York: Dodd, Mead, and Company, 1884.

Philbrick, Nathaniel. *In the Heart of the Sea: The Tragedy of the Whaleship
Essex.* New York: Penguin, 2001.

Plank, Geoffrey. *An Unsettled Conquest: The British Campaign Against the Peoples of Acadia*. Philadelphia: University of Pennsylvania Press, 2001.

Raleigh, Sir Walter. *The Discovery of the Large, Rich, and Beautiful Empire of Guiana*. London: Hakluyt Society, 1848.

Rediker, Marcus. *Between the Devil and the Deep Blue Sea: Merchant Seamen, Pirates, and the Anglo-American Maritime World, 1700–1750*. New York: Cambridge University Press, 1987.

———. *Villains of All Nations: Atlantic Pirates in the Golden Age*. Boston: Beacon Press, 2004.

Rhind, William. *A History of the Vegetable Kingdom*. Glasgow: Blackie and Son, 1857.

Scarry, Robert. *Millard Fillmore*. Jefferson, N.C.: McFarland & Company, 2001.

Schonhorn, Manuel. "Defoe's Four Years Voyages of Capt. George Roberts and Ashton's Memorial." *Texas Studies in Literature and Language* 17 (1975): pp. 93–102.

Shepherd, James, and Gary Walton. "Trade, Distribution, and Economic Growth in Colonial America." *The Journal of Economic History* 32 (1972): pp. 128–45.

Silverman, Kenneth. *The Life and Times of Cotton Mather*. New York: Harper & Row, 1984.

Smith, Leanne Beukelman. "'Strange Adventures and Signal Deliverances': Narrative Masks in John Barnard's Ashton's Memorial." *The New England Quarterly* 63 (1990): pp. 60–79.

Snow, Edward Rowe. *True Tales of Pirates and Their Gold*. New York: Dodd, Mead, and Company, 1966.

Strong, William D. *Archaeological Investigations in the Bay Islands, Spanish Honduras*. Washington, D.C.: Smithsonian Institution, 1935.

Talty, Stephan. *Empire of Blue Water: Captain Morgan's Great Pirate Army, The Epic Battle for the Americas, and the Catastrophe that Ended the Outlaws' Bloody Reign*. New York: Three Rivers Press/Crown, 2007.

Temin, Peter, and Hans-Joachim Voth. "Riding the South Sea Bubble." *The American Economic Review* 94 (2004): pp. 1654–68.

Toulouse, Teresa. "'Syllabical Idolatry': Benjamin Colman and the Rhetoric of Balance." *Early American Literature* 18 (1983/1984): pp. 257–74.

The Tryals of Sixteen Persons for Piracy. Boston: Joseph Edwards, 1726.

Updike, Wilkins. *Memoirs of the Rhode Island Bar*. Boston: Thomas H. Webb & Company, 1842.

Uring, Nathaniel. *A History of the Voyages and Travels of Capt. Nathaniel Uring*. London: Printed by W. Wilkins for J. Peele, 1726.

Vickers, Daniel. *Farmers and Fishermen: Two Centuries of Work in Essex County, Massachusetts, 1630–1850*. Chapel Hill: University of North Carolina Press, 1994.

——. *Young Men and the Sea: Yankee Seafarers in the Age of Sail*. New Haven, Conn.: Yale University Press, 2007.

Volo, Dorothy Denneen, and James Volo. *Daily Life in the Age of Sail*. Westport, Conn.: Greenwood Press, 2002.

Walsh, Jane MacLaren. "The Skull of Doom." Archaeological Institute of America Online. http://www.archaeology.org/online/features /mitchell_hedges. Accessed May 27, 2010.

Walton, Gary. "New Evidence on Colonial Commerce." *The Journal of Economic History* 28 (1968): pp. 363–89.

Webster, John D. *A Description of the Island of St. Michael*. Boston: R. P. & C. Williams, 1821.

Wicken, William. "Encounters With Tall Sails and Tall Tales: Mi'kmaq Society, 1500–1760." PhD dissertation, McGill University, 1994.

Williams, Daniel E. "Of Providence and Pirates: Philip Ashton's Narrative Struggle for Salvation." *Early American Literature* 24 (1989): pp. 169–95.

——. "Puritans and Pirates: A Confrontation Between Cotton Mather and William Fly in 1726." *Early American Literature* 22 (1987): pp. 233–51.

Williams, Tony. *The Pox and the Covenant: Mather, Franklin, and the Epidemic That Changed America's Destiny*. Naperville, Ill.: Sourcebooks, 2010.

Zacks, Richard. *The Pirate Hunter: The True Story of Captain Kidd*. New York: Hyperion, 2002.

Index

Ashton, Sarah Bartlett (Ashton's wife), 183
Ashton, Sarah Hanniford (Ashton's mother), 204n2
Ashton's Memorial (Barnard), 150–72; advertisements, 168; author, 206n12; comparisons of Ashton with Robinson Crusoe, 169; editions, 168–69, 204n2, 212n2; influence on Defoe, 169–72, 220nn23–24; interpretations of, 219nn15–16; Merritt's escape, 210n16; purpose, 219nn15–17; veracity, 206n12; writing of, 166–67
Atkinson, William, 193–94
Azores, 35–51; escape of Low's captives, 47–51; Low's attack, 43–46; Low's cruise, 35–43; Portuguese-English relations, 48

Bachelor's Delight (pirate vessel), 127, 130–31
Bahamas: as pirate base, 12
Barbareta (island), 101
Barlow, Jonathan: capture by Low, 112–13, 215nn1–2; capture of *John and Mary*, 133–34, 139–41; shipwreck, 131–33; trial, 141, 217n2
Barnard, John: Ashton and, 164, 182–83; *Ashton's Memorial*, 166–67, 169, 204n2, 206n12, 210n16; attachment to Marblehead, 183–84; background, 156–57; Brattle Street Church, Boston, 157–58; church appointments, 161–62; Colman and, 157–58, 161; divine intervention (signal deliverances), 158, 160–61, 166; First Church, Marblehead, 162–64,

219n11; Mathers and, 157–58, 161, 162; Queen Anne's War, 158–61; "A Serious Address to Those Who Unnecessarily Frequent the Tavern," 154; travel, 162; use of Ashton's story for religious purposes, 150–51, 156, 164–68, 219n15
Barnes, Henry, 104
Bartlett, Sarah, 183
Bay Islands: geography, 68; islands near Roatan, 83–86; Low's cruise, 68–69
Baymen, 91–111; archaeological evidence, 213n6; with Ashton, 4, 100–103, 142–45, 213n10; association with pirates, 93, 103; attack by pirates on Guanaja, 142–44; attack on Campeche Town, 94; definition, 93; drinking with ship captains, 95, 213n6; location of operations, 94; Spanish campaign against, 13, 94, 101; ties to Boston, 213n2. *See also* logwood trade
Bay of Honduras. *See* Honduras, Bay of
Bellamy, Samuel ("Black Sam"), 27–28, 113, 155–56, 207n16
Bird Island, Boston Harbor, 138
Blackbeard (Edward Teach), 67, 95–96, 211n11
Black River, Honduras, 176
Blades, William, 186
Block Island, Rhode Island, 15–16, 203n15
Blunt, Edmund M., 206n11
Boa Vista, Cape Verde Islands, 52–53

Fly, William, 192–95
Flying Horse (vessel), 32
Ford, John, 101
Fortune (sloop), 103, 105–10, 215n1
*The Four Years Voyages of Capt.
George Roberts* (Defoe), 170–72,
220nn23–24
Franklin, Benjamin, 203n16
Franklin, James, 153, 203n16, 218n3
French Guiana, 210n7

Gallison, Jane, 183
A General History of the Pyrates (Defoe), 170, 171, 172, 202n7, 220n23
Gerrish, Samuel, 168–69
Gilford, Robert, 208n24
Goat Island, Rhode Island, 189
Granada, Nicaragua, 70
Grand Banks: pirate attacks, 37, 46
Gravelly Point, Newport, Rhode
Island, 1–2, 188–89
Green, John, 192–93
Greenville, Henry, 194, 195
Grenada: Low's cruise, 58–59
Greyhound (Boston logging ship),
39
Greyhound, HMS: battle with
pirates, 105–10, 156, 182, 184,
189–90; doctor, 211n11
Guanaja (island): Ashton and Baymen on, 142–46; Ashton's exploration, 97–99; Ashton's rescue,
148–49, 166; geography, 68, 98;
indigenous people, 79; pirates,
95, 129, 139–40, 142–44, 174–75,
179; released pirate captives, 125
guarda costas, 94. *See also* Spanish
ships
Guiana: Low's cruise, 56–58

hammerhead sharks, 86
Hance, John, 203n15
Hanniford, Richard, 204n2
Harradine, Andrew, 136–38
Harris, Charles: battle with *Greyhound,* 105–10; as quartermaster,
39, 103, 113, 171; signing on as pirate, 39, 104; trial and execution,
39, 110, 185, 186
Hart, John, 4, 121–22
Hawkins, Richard, 118–25, 175,
209n8
health and medicine, 50, 59–61,
152–53, 211n11
Heyrman, Christine, 219n15
Holman, John, 33
Holyoke, Edward, 219n11
Honduras, Bay of, 112–38; islands,
101–2; logwood conflicts, 10, 92–
93; logwood industry, 10, 94–95;
pirates, 65, 95–97
Hope, John (governor of Bermuda),
93
Hope, John (leader of Baymen), 101,
144–45
Hopeful Betty (sloop), 214n12
Hornigold, Benjamin, 113
hull maintenance, 52–53, 56–57,
62–63, 146
Hunt, Henry, 214n1
hurricanes, 54–56, 61

Ipswich, Massachusetts, 115
Isle Haute, Nova Scotia, 181–82

Jacob (pirate), 46, 47
Jamaica: as British naval base, 61,
129, 146–47; as pirate base, 69;
pirate trials, 64, 176, 178

Newfoundland attack, 36–37; securing drinking water, 58–59, 72–75; treasure map, 181–82, 221n13; vessel maintenance, 52–53
Low, Eliza Marble, 10
Lowther, George: background, 202n7; capture of vessels, 14, 39, 60, 92; crew's trials and executions, 174; cruelty, 122; as mutineer, 11; sailing with Low, 9, 11, 13–14; suicide, 174
Loyd (Lyde), Edward, 91
Lyne, Philip, 176–78

Marble, Eliza, 10
Marblehead, Massachusetts: Ashton's return, 149, 150, 164, 182–83, 218n4; economic conditions, 163; fishermen, 17–19, 204n1; as fishing village, 162–63; sinfulness, perceptions about, 163–64
Mary (schooner), 31–32, 207n22. See also *Fancy* (schooner)
Massachusetts Bay Colony: fishing industry, 18; Sabbath-day prohibitions, 19, 204n5
Massey, John, 11
Mather, Cotton: background, 151–52; Barnard and, 157–58, 161, 162; intensity of faith, 153; "News from Robinson Cruso's Island," 169; North Church, Boston, 157; outrage over Brattle Street Church, 157; Puritan traditions, 153–55, 161; Sabbath-day prohibitions, 19, 204n5; "A Serious Address to Those Who Unnecessarily Frequent the Tavern," 154; sermons on pirates, 28, 155–56,

165–66, 189, 194; on sinfulness of seafarers, 155; smallpox inoculations, 152–53, 218n3
Mather, Increase, 157–58, 162, 168
McNutt's Island, Nova Scotia, 22
medicine and health, 50, 59–61, 152–53, 211n11
Mermaid, HMS, 62–65, 211n16
Merritt, Nicholas: abuse by pirates, 46, 47; in *Ashton's Memorial,* 167; escape from pirates, 47–51, 210n16; family background, 209n16; fictional accounts, 171–72; as fisherman, 22; imprisonment, 49–51; as pirate captive, 26–27, 32, 33–34, 208n24; smallpox, 50–51, 152
Merry Christmas (sloop), 215n1
Mexico: pirate attacks, 69–70
Mi'kmaq: conflicts with fishermen, 19–22, 205n7, 206n9; fishing techniques, 205n8
Milton (schooner), 17–18, 22–24
Miskito Indians, 176
Mitchell-Hedges, Frederick, 180–81, 221nn10–11
Moll Flanders (Defoe), 170
Moore, Robin, 181, 221n11
Morgan, Henry, 69–70
Mosely, Increase, 215n6
Mower, Ebenezer, 177
Mumford, Thomas, 42, 43, 185, 186

Nantucket (island), Massachusetts: pirate attacks, 16, 19, 29, 42, 110, 186
navigation, 38, 137
New England Courant, 138, 153, 168